WITHDRAWN

The Color of Representation

The Color of Representation

Congressional Behavior
and Black Interests

KENNY J. WHITBY

Ann Arbor

THE UNIVERSITY OF MICHIGAN PRESS

2000   1999   1998   4   3   2

A CIP catalog record for this book is available from the British Library.

Library of Congress Cataloging-in-Publication Data

Whitby, Kenny J., 1953–
    The color of representation : congressional behavior and Black
interests / Kenny J. Whitby.
        p.   cm.
    Includes bibliographical references and index.
    ISBN 0-472-10805-0 (cloth : acid-free paper)
    1. Afro-Americans—Suffrage—History.   2. Afro-Americans—Civil
rights—History.   3. Afro-Americans—Politics and government.
4. United States. Congress. House—Voting—History.   5. United
States. Congress. House—Election districts—History.
6. Representative government and representation—United States—
History.   I. Title.
JK1924.W48   1997
324.6'2'08996073—dc21   96-51291
                                                                  CIP

Acknowledgments

This book was begun while I was a visiting professor in the Department of Political Science at Wayne State University. There I found an environment conducive to research and writing. I am especially grateful for the comments and suggestions that I received from Timothy Bledsoe, Ronald Brown, and Mary Herring, a group of fine scholars on minority politics who made hard work a joy. In addition, I had the good fortune to present my research to the faculty and graduate student body in the Department of Political Science at the University of California, Los Angeles. I benefited enormously from their thoughtful criticisms of my research. In particular, Franklin D. Gilliam Jr., a close friend and colleague, gave me valuable advice throughout the project.

Debts of gratitude are due to several of my colleagues at the University of South Carolina. William Jacoby, George Krause, David Lublin, and David Whiteman all provided sound scholarly advice to me. I would like to acknowledge a special debt to William Mishler at the University of Arizona, who read my manuscript and who incisively critiqued the work. His scholarly advice and counsel contributed enormously to this book. I am also indebted to Lakisha Fields, an exceptional undergraduate student, who gave me much needed research assistance during various phases of the project.

Dianne Pinderhughes and an anonymous reviewer gave generously of their time in reading my manuscript. Their comments and suggestions greatly improved the work, and they cannot be faulted for any of its shortcomings. I was very fortunate that the University of Michigan Press provided me with the assistance of an excellent editor, Charles T. Myers, who, with Kevin M. Rennells, Elizabeth Gratch, Jillian Downey, and Michael Landauer, contributed greatly to making sense of what I had to say.

Finally, I am indebted to my family and many friends for helping me to bring this project to fruition. This book is dedicated to my late father, Ulysses Whitby Sr., who inspired me to try to do my best. I would not be what I am today if it weren't for his many sacrifices.

Contents

Chapter 1. Introduction: The Quality of
Representation for African-Americans   1

Chapter 2. Federal Protection of Voting Rights: The
Role of Congress in the Black Struggle for the Franchise   17

Chapter 3. The Quest for Equal Opportunity   49

Chapter 4. The Color of Congress: The Impact of
Race and the Role of Issues in Congressional Roll
Call Votes   81

Chapter 5. Racial Redistricting and the
Representation of Black Interests   113

Chapter 6. Epilogue: Black Policy Preferences,
Congressional Behavior, and the Future of
Representation for African-Americans   135

Appendixes

Appendix A. Description of Voting Rights Measures
during Amending Phase   147

Appendix B. Description of Amendments   151

Appendix C. Description of Bills as They Appear in
Table 14   153

Notes   157

References   173

Court Cases   183

Index   185

CHAPTER 1

Introduction: The Quality of Representation for African-Americans

The problem of the 20th Century is the problem of the color line.
—W. E. B. Du Bois, *The Souls of Black Folks*

The authors of the United States Constitution viewed Congress as the chief repository of governmental powers. Article 1 provides that "All legislative power herein granted shall be invested in a Congress of the United States." As the nation's chief policy-making institution, Congress' actions or inactions have a profound impact on the quality of life for individuals and groups throughout American society. As the people's branch of the government, Congress claims a central position in writing laws that will provide protection for all U.S. citizens. Over the course of America's history no issue has been more difficult for Congress to deal with than that of race. In his influential book *An American Dilemma* Gunnar Myrdal argues that the issue of race is one of America's biggest paradoxes and dilemmas. On one hand, most Americans recognize the evils of racial inequality and believe that it has no place in American society; on the other hand, while Americans harbor ill feelings toward the evils of racial inequality, they have been reluctant to take steps to eliminate it.[1]

From an institutional standpoint Congress captures the essence of the American racial dilemma. Despite those precious few words in the Declaration of Independence that "all men are created equal," for most of the nation's history the issue of racial equality was not the business of Congress. The ambivalence of Congress toward the plight of black America can be seen as early as 1776, when the Second Continental Congress convened to draft the Declaration of Independence. Thomas Jefferson's original draft of the document called for the condemnation of slavery and the slave trade, but this section was deleted from the final draft by the Second Continental Congress.[2] Thus, the same Congress that issued the proclamation that all men are created equal simultaneously sanctioned the practice of human bondage. The refusal of the earliest congresses in America to resolve the discrepancy between noble ideals and the practice of slavery was to cost millions of Americans, both black and white, dearly in decades following the signing of the Declaration of Independence.

For a decade after the Civil War Congress concerned itself with civil rights by passing three far-reaching constitutional amendments—the Thirteenth, Fourteenth, and Fifteenth Amendments—to protect the rights of blacks. Not only did Congress pass the Civil War Amendments that guaranteed blacks full equality and citizenship, but it took seriously the section included in each that gave Congress the "power to enforce the article by appropriate legislation." As a means of ensuring the civil and voting rights of newly freed blacks, Congress passed the Civil Rights Acts of 1866, 1870, 1871, and 1875. The Civil Rights Act of 1875, for example, declared that all persons were entitled to the full and equal enjoyment of all public accommodations. The resulting Civil Rights Acts provided some evidence that Congress could implement provisions within the constitutional amendments. As a consequence of congressional action, the political, social, and economic status of African-Americans improved dramatically during the Reconstruction period.

After 1875, however, effective civil rights legislation ceased to be implemented by Congress. In effect, congressional inertia, coupled with the United States Supreme Court's defense of racial inequality for decades after Reconstruction, meant a slowdown in black progress toward full equality.

All things being equal, congressional responsiveness to black interests is a relatively recent occurrence. The foundation for congressional action had been laid during Reconstruction, but it was not until the enactments of the Civil Rights Act of 1964 and the Voting Rights Act of 1965 that Congress made a concerted effort to combat racial discrimination. Since the mid-1960s civil rights policy has sustained a place on the national political agenda. But it would be misleading to assert that Congress has been highly responsive to the policy wishes of African-American citizens. As shall be demonstrated later, there is sufficient evidence to show that continuing discrimination against African-Americans still exists in America despite constitutional protection and the enactments of civil rights laws.

The brief historical account provides the backdrop against which *The Color of Representation* is written. It provides the context for understanding the crucial role of Congress in racial politics. The historical overview implies that the quality of life for blacks is very much tied to the actions or inactions of Congress.

This book provides a comprehensive examination of congressional responsiveness to black interests. The title seems appropriate given the fact that the central domestic issue in the United States over the long history of the nation has been the inclusionary rules for people of color, most notably blacks, in American society. The opening quote by the eminent black scholar W. E. B. Du Bois nearly a century ago prophetically sums up the tremendous strain that race has on a multiracial society. In contemporary America many civil rights advocates believe that a great deal more progress could be made toward fulfillment of the American creed of equality if Congress would commit itself to the passage of civil rights legislation of the type enacted in the mid-1960s.

What is the current status of Congress' response to issues of primary interest to black constituents in modern society? To answer that question this book critically assesses the voting behavior of members of the U.S. House of Representatives on a variety of important topics directly relevant to the black community. Why the House? The House has a unique status as a representative body. Under the original Constitution the House was the only national institution whose members were chosen by popular election. Biennial elections were designed to ensure that House members would remain as close as possible to the people. More important, frequent elections were meant to ensure that citizens' interests would be converted into public policy. Thus, there is no better governmental institution to choose than the House of Representatives for an examination of responsiveness to the policy wishes of black citizens.

To accomplish the objectives of this book different topics have been selected for analysis. Each chapter begins with a brief overview of the selected topic. The overview provides the background necessary for a full appreciation of the analysis that follows in each chapter. It is also designed to afford the reader a thorough understanding of the crucial role that Congress plays in helping to resolve continuing race relations problems in the United States.

Chapter 2 looks at congressional responsiveness to black voting rights protection. After a brief overview of the history of the black struggle to gain access to the voting booth, the discussion then turns to an examination of congressional behavior on federal voting rights bills. The issue of civil rights is taken up in chapter 3, which begins with a brief historical summary followed by some of the main events during the civil rights movement leading to the passage of the landmark Civil Rights Act of 1964. The next section of the chapter provides evidence that continuing discrimination against blacks persist in America. The empirical analysis in the final section assesses the response of House members to black interests on a broad scale other than through their federal voting rights legislation.

Chapter 4 addresses the following questions: Does race matter in congressional voting decisions? What is the relationship between descriptive and substantive representation on policies related to race? In other words, is the racial identity of the member a factor in legislative voting on black policy preferences? Chapter 5 examines the racial redistricting debate in the context of policy responsiveness. Has the creation of black majority districts adversely affected the voting behavior of House members? What are the policy implications of racial redistricting? Chapter 6 concludes this study with an overall assessment of the quality of representation for blacks and offers some observations for the future.

Congress is not, of course, the only governmental institution involved in policy-making, nor are its actions alone sufficient to breach existing barriers of discrimination. But Congress does claim a central position. Its role is crucial because there is no executive order, court decision, or bureaucratic action that can match what can be achieved through the formal decree of legislation.

The remainder of the present chapter is devoted to defining some key concepts and developing a framework for analysis. The discussion that follows provides the theoretical parameters for an analysis of the level of policy responsiveness to black interests.

Representation and Policy Responsiveness

Congressional action is considered to be the ultimate expression of the representative principle. What is representation, and how does it apply to black policy preferences? The concept is a difficult one to define, as Gerhard Lowenberg points out in the following statement:

> Representation . . . is an ill-defined concept that has acquired conflicting meanings through long use. It may be employed to denote any relationship between rulers and ruled or it may connote responsiveness, authorization, legitimation, or accountability.[3]

Representation is essentially a normative concept that conveys a variety of meanings about what should be the proper linkage between legislators and citizens. While the concept is a peculiar and elusive one to define, Hanna Pitkin, in her book *The Concept of Representation,* provides some useful ways of understanding its meaning. The author distinguishes four different dimensions of representation: "formal," the authority to act in another's behalf gained through an institutional arrangement such as elections; "descriptive," the extent to which a representative mirrors the social characteristics of the people he or she formally represents; "symbolic," the extent to which a representative is accepted as believable, that is, as "one of their own" by constituents; and "substantive," a legislator's responsiveness to the political expectations of constituents.[4]

The principal definition applied to the investigation in this book is *substantive representation.* The term, according to Pitkin, is the essence of political representation. More precisely, Pitkin defines *substantive representation* in terms of a representative "acting in the interest of the represented, in a manner responsive to them."[5] But, as Heinz Eulau and Paul Karps astutely point out, different activities may be included in the category of substantive representation. Members of Congress may respond to constituents' expectations on matters of *policy,* of *service,* of *allocation,* and of *symbolism.* That is, representatives may respond to the policy wishes of constituents on roll calls (policy); they may respond to individual inquiries and problems (service); they may respond in a way that would obtain more public funds or projects for citizens in the district or state (allocation); or they may respond in a manner that would secure constituents' political support (symbolic).[6]

While substantive representation encompasses the various tasks that legislators perform for their constituents, the main component of the concept is policy responsiveness. The policy-making process lies at the heart of substantive representation and is crucial to an understanding of how well Congress and its members are responding to black interests. The term requires that legislators be aware of and sensitive to the policy preferences and wishes of the represented and implement policies that reflect their interests.[7] The major emphasis placed in this research is on the match between black policy preferences and legislative roll call voting behavior. That is, the major focus of this research is on examining the link between the policy wishes of black constituents and the representative's official behavior. By examining this connection (*policy congruence*), we can provide some answers to the following questions: To what extent do representatives reflect black policy preferences in their congressional voting behavior? Moreover, what factors are related to this Congress-black constituency correspondence?

The dyadic relationship is in itself important, but Congress' performance as an institution is also crucial to an understanding of the quality of substantive representation for blacks. In other words, for black policy preferences to find their way into the statute books, members of Congress must act in a collective fashion.[8] Clearly, the movement toward racial equality for the brief period after the Civil War was largely due to the collective actions of lawmakers serving during the Reconstruction congresses. Has collective policy representation on civil rights–related issues declined in recent times? If so, why?

Though the primary focus of this investigation is on substantive representation, other dimensions of representation are a matter of some interest in this research. For instance, the interaction of descriptive and substantive representation may be crucial because of the possible connection between black constituents' desires and the racial composition of the legislature. During the era of the American Revolution and the framing of the Constitution, John Adams understood the connection between the two kinds of representation. His words illustrate how they can be mutually reinforcing in the makeup of legislatures:

> The principle difficulty lies, and the greatest care should be employed in constituting this representative assembly. It should be in miniature an exact portrait of the people at large. It should think, feel, reason and act like them. That it may be the interest of this assembly to do strict justice at all times, it should be an equal representation, or, in other words, equal interests among the people should have equal interests in it.[9]

Implicit in Adams's words is the notion that a legislator will act in terms of his or her own social and economic background. The rationale here is that the legislator who mirrors his or her constituents' social characteristics will likely provide a spontaneous form of representation. One legislator described this predisposition tendency in the following manner:

> Basically you represent the thinking of the people who have gone through what you have gone through and who are what you are. You vote according to that. In other words, if you come from a suburb you reflect the thinking of people in the suburbs; if you are of depressed people, you reflect that. You represent the sum total of your background.[10]

The four different dimensions of representation provide a useful conceptual framework for determining how responsive Congress really is to black policy concerns. Expressed in the form of a model (fig. 1), the four types of representation can be viewed in the following manner:

That is, if elections are properly structured then the composition of Congress should mirror the composition of society. Having members of Congress who share the sociological attributes of the electorate is a powerful symbol of representation. And, presumably, if the legislature is properly constructed, it will be better able to respond effectively to policy concerns of different groups in society. Therefore, in order to determine the level of policy responsiveness to black interests, this research will address other aspects of representation when appropriate.

It is important to emphasize that the representation of black interests

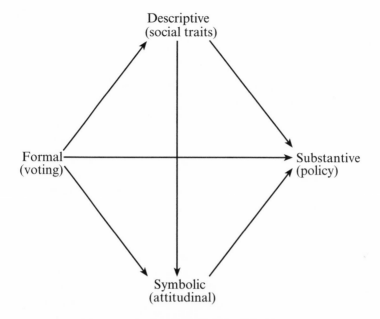

Fig. 1. **Causal model of representation**

does not occur in a vacuum. Members of Congress must weigh their decision to vote for black policy preferences against other competing forces, some of which appear to be party and regional pressure, a representative's own belief system, and white constituency pressure. Notwithstanding these forces, there should be a meaningful connection between the representative and the represented. As a representative body, it is incumbent upon Congress to respond to the differing interests and demands of individuals and groups throughout American society. If Congress does not, then its own authority and indeed the legitimacy of the entire government may be reduced. One writer on Congress describes the potential problem in the following way:

> Failure of Congress to represent may, in systemic terms, lead to a loss of support for the legislature. An institution, Congress or any other, that does not respond to the expectations people hold about it soon ceases to have the respect of the populace and finds that its pronouncements no longer are regarded as legitimate. In such circumstances, the system must adapt—that is, redefine its mission and readjust its procedures—to produce acceptable outputs, or it cannot survive.[11]

The Use of the Terms *Black* and *African-American*

There is no consensus among blacks about how they would like to identify themselves or how they would like to be identified by others. Recent survey data reveal that three in ten prefer the term *African-American,* and four in ten prefer to be called *black.* [12] To a large degree the choice of terms is a subjective one. As a result, scholars conducting research on the issue of race have used the terms interchangeably. [13]

In this book the term *black* is preferred over *African-American* because it more accurately conveys the meaning of the title of this book and its contents. Throughout the course of American history the issue of political equality has been defined mainly in terms of color, not ethnicity. Though white ethnics have faced discrimination in America (e.g., Irish Americans, Polish Americans), after a generation or so they have been able to shed their ethnicity and assimilate into the mainstream of U.S. society with relative ease. The United States has not been a melting pot for people of color, ceteris paribus; African-Americans, in particular, have been stigmatized for generations because of their skin color. Clear examples of the emphasis that American society has placed on skin color are the institutions of slavery and segregation.

The previous discussion merely highlights and calls attention to why one term is preferred over the other in this book. On occasion the term *African-American* will be used in a given sentence because it conveys a meaning beyond the color of skin. Simply put, the term implies that black people have an ancestry that should not be underappreciated by other individuals and social groups in America.

Black Policy Preferences

Like any other racial or ethnic group in the United States, the opinions of individual African-Americans vary widely, especially on racial, economic, and social welfare issues. [14] In the main, however, blacks favor liberal policies. That is, black policy preferences, as expressed in public opinion polls, are skewed in the direction of affirmative action policies and programs that would assist the economically disadvantaged. As table 1 shows, there are sizable racial differences between the attitudes and preferences of blacks and whites on questions of affirmative action and the role of the government in aiding the economically disadvantaged. Blacks are nearly three times more likely than whites to favor educational quota programs for minority applicants, four times more likely to support policies that would give preferences in the hiring of minority employees, and twice as likely to believe that the government should implement policies guaranteeing everyone a decent standard of living.

Preferences among most blacks for a stronger federal role in the area of civil rights stem from the belief that subtle forms of racial discrimination still exist in the United States. This discrimination is often considered a primary explanation for the relatively poor standard of living confronting disproportionately more blacks than whites. While it is true that there is a growing conservative black middle class in the United States, as a group African-Americans remain economically deprived. For example, in 1994, 26.3 percent of all African-American families earned under $10,000 per year, compared to only 11.7 percent of all white families. In 1994 the poverty level among blacks in the United States was 30.6 percent; among whites it was 11.7 percent. In 1995 the unemployment rate among blacks in the United States was 10.4 percent, compared to 4.9 percent for whites.[15] Whether or not discrimination is to blame for the worse condition of blacks is, of course, a debatable issue.[16] Nonetheless, the fact remains that disproportionately more blacks than whites are poor and unemployed in the United States. And it is the belief among many blacks that the federal government is and should be a key player in equalizing opportunities between the races.[17]

Evaluating Congressional Responsiveness to the Policy Interests of Black Constituents

Roll call votes are used to examine legislator behavior. Why roll call votes? First, they constitute one of the most important types of sources for systematic inquiry in political science. Roll call votes can reveal important information about what Congress has done and what it might do on select

TABLE 1. Race and Opinion on Selected Affirmative Action and Social Services

Issues	White (%)	Black (%)	Difference (%)
Favor education quota	24	70	+46
Favor preferences for blacks in hiring and promotion	13	53	+40
Government should provide more services and increase spending	50	81	+31
Government should see that people have jobs and a good standard of living	34	68	+34

Source: 1992 National Election Studies, Center for Political Studies, University of Michigan.

important issues of a given time. The issue of race has been a persistent source of political cleavage throughout this nation's history, and the dilemma over what to do about racial inequality continues to be a lingering problem for policymakers in American society. The positions taken by legislators on civil rights issues can provide important information on the status of policy responsiveness to blacks.

Second, roll call votes can be used to learn more about the policy-making behavior of House members without the researcher having to go through the painstaking, expensive, and time-consuming task of interviewing 435 representatives. This is not to suggest that interviews, surveys, and other techniques of gauging legislative behavior should be ignored but only illustrates that roll call analysis can reveal valuable information when properly conducted. For instance, roll call votes can be used to draw comparisons about a legislator's voting behavior with all other legislators on the same votes. Thus, we can compare legislators' votes on federal voting rights legislation and be able to draw safe conclusions about who are the supporters and nonsupporters of black voting rights in Congress.

Third, roll call votes are important for examining the roles played by political parties, coalitions, and individuals in a legislative chamber. For example, the following kinds of questions can be answered: What is the effect of political parties on black policy preferences, and how has their impact changed over time? What role does region play in assessing the quality of substantive representation? What impact does the racial identity of the House member have on (his or her) roll call voting behavior? An analysis of roll call votes can reveal a great deal about what policies might emerge based on the role of party and other factors.

Fourth, recorded congressional roll call votes can be used to determine if change has occurred within the political system. For example, an analysis of roll call votes can tell us whether behavioral change has taken place as a consequence of racial redistricting. It is often asserted that Congress can be used as a yardstick for evaluating the actions of governmental institutions. If this be the case, then roll call votes in the House can reveal much about what political trends have developed since Congress renewed its concern with civil rights policy in the late 1950s.

Finally, and most important, an extensive examination of the way members vote can increase our understanding about the nature of representation. That is, an analysis of legislative voting behavior can tell us more about who is being represented and who is not. Congress is the chief repository of governmental power, and its policy decisions can have a profound impact on the citizenry. For those individuals and groups who seek to influence legislative outcomes so that they can receive better representation, they would be well advised to learn more about how lawmakers reach their policy decisions.

Key votes are used as the approach to analyzing the roll call voting behavior of House members. In chapters 2 and 3 selected federal voting rights and civil rights measures are used to examine congressional responsiveness to black interests. In chapters 4 and 5 the key vote index compiled by the Leadership Conference on Civil Rights (LCCR) is used to determine whether the race of the member matters in Congress and to examine the policy consequences of racial redistricting. The LCCR is a coalition of over 180 national organizations seeking to advance the interests of African-Americans and other racial minorities, elderly citizens, women, and the economically disadvantaged. The biennial report card issued by the organization was first computed for the 91st Congress (1969–70) and reflects the coalition's concerns for issues ranging from civil rights legislation to government spending for social programs.

LCCR scores measure the proportion of roll calls in which legislators have supported positions endorsed by the conference.[18] Although some of the bills included in the scale are tangential to civil rights, research has shown that the index is an appropriate measure of support for black interests and is a reliable, though imperfect, indicator of congressional voting behavior.[19] Through the use of the LCCR index, along with the employment of statistical analysis, the investigation in this research should produce safe findings about the behavior of legislators on policies of primary concern to the African-American community.

Of course, there are limits to what roll call data can tell us about the voting behavior of legislators. As Malcolm Jewell and Samuel Patterson state: "Roll call statistics can tell us *how* legislators vote. . . . The roll calls cannot tell us *why* legislators vote that way."[20] The strategy used in this book is to take into account the limitations of roll call analysis in interpreting the observed voting patterns.

Amendment and Final Passage Roll Calls

A host of strategies and tactics may influence a legislator's voting decisions.[21] The policy decisions that a legislator prefers may reflect a variety of factors—constituents, interest groups, party and committee leaders, the president, his or her own views, and so forth. While it is difficult to determine specifically why members of Congress vote the way they do on any single vote, it is possible to draw reasonable inferences about broader patterns of voting behavior. In order to understand the behavior of House members, much of the investigation in this research makes a distinction between voting on amendments and voting on final action roll call bills. A major argument in this book is that a different pattern of voting behavior is likely to emerge on black interest legislation during the amending process than on final roll calls. The theoretical reasoning here is in part based on the "strategic voting" literature—that is, strategies that might be employed when some members cast roll call votes. One such tactic, according to Jerrold Schneider, involves "voting for a bill on final passage in order to appear favorable to the legislation to constituents after having voted to "gut" the bill with weakening amendments."[22]

In the same vein James Enelow and David Koehler state, "congressmen do not always vote sincerely."[23] What can be inferred from these remarks is that a pattern of deviant voting behavior may be taking place on black interest legislation. The underlying assumption is that the nature and strength of civil rights–related bills not only vary from Congress to Congress but also among the different stages of the legislative voting process. Merle Black, for example, has argued that a legislator's vote on final passage tends to be a decision on the "desirability" or "principle" of a bill, while a vote on amendments indicates a decision to "strengthen or weaken" the legislation.[24]

The amending process can be critical to policy formulation, yet it has been largely ignored by researchers on this topic. It is during the amending stage that the language of a bill can be altered, revised, or deleted. As John Kingdon notes, members of Congress are keenly aware that civil rights legislation is one of the few policy issues that can invoke intense feelings among voters, especially black voters.[25] Consequently, legislators who may oppose black interest legislation might try to dilute the bill with amendments or kill it on procedural grounds. Having failed to do so, they might vote for the bill on final passage in order not to offend their black constituents and run the risk of losing votes on election day. Beyond the electoral motives of some members, others might be attempting to water down the bill so that it will reflect their sincere position on civil rights. By distinguishing between the way members vote on amendments and final passage, this research should enrich our understanding about the level of the quality of policy responsiveness to blacks.

The belief that a systematic pattern of voting variability exists across the two stages of legislative voting contradicts the conventional view of voting behavior in Congress. This view of voting behavior instructs us that there is a "drive toward consistency" in legislative voting.[26] According to this body of research, members of Congress tend to establish a pattern of voting behavior early in their tenure that serves as a guide for voting in a specific policy area.[27] Once a legislator develops a framework for categorizing political issues, it then becomes "kind of a conditional reflex" for that lawmaker, who will not deviate from that stance on the issue in any measurable way.[28]

The contention in this book is that some members of Congress do alter their voting behavior on civil rights–related issues from amendment to the bill. Because voting variability is a testable proposition, we should be able to obtain a complete and accurate empirical representation of voting behavior across different stages of the legislative voting process.

A Model of Policy Responsiveness

In order to describe and explain congressional roll call behavior on black policy preferences, it would be useful to develop a framework, or model, for analysis. The purpose here is to present one such model, which will then be used as the basis for investigation in this book.

As figure 2 shows, the model embraces four possible combinations of roll call voting behavior. The categories are arranged in the way that the data would appear on a scatter plot. In cell 1 (low amendment/low final passage) are those members who give low levels of support on both amendments and final decision bills. They are the legislators who are the least responsive to black policy preferences. The pattern of voting behavior for these members is stable and in the low range of conservative voting. In most instances they represent districts in which the black population is low. They can be expected to vote against civil rights legislation regardless of the stage of the roll call voting process.

Members of Congress who fall in cell 2 (low amendment/high final passage category) exhibit low levels of support on amendments but are likely to increase their support for black interest legislation on final roll calls. They are the ones most likely to engage in what is sometimes referred to as "deceptive voting." The example described earlier by Schneider might be considered a form of deceptive voting. In a similar vein Steven Smith describes the strategy as "a member who holds a strong policy preference and works hard behind the scenes to push his point of view, and yet votes the other way on the floor to make folks back home happy."[29]

The assumption here is that the amending process allows legislators more discretion in deciding how to cast their roll call votes. On average final roll call votes tend to be more publicized than amendment votes. As a consequence, members have to be cognizant of the fact that they might be called upon to explain their votes to some constituents, especially if black voters constitute a sizable proportion of the district's population.

Cell 2:	Cell 3:
high final passage	high final passage
low amendment	high amendment
Cell 1:	Cell 4:
low amendment	high amendment
low final passage	low final passage

Fig. 2. Model embracing four combinations of voting behavior

Therefore, it is during the amending stage that some members might oppose black interest legislation outright or attempt to amend the bill so as to make it innocuous.

In cell 3 (high final passage/high amendment category) are those members who give relatively high levels of support on civil rights legislation from its introduction through final passage. Their voting behavior is diametrical to lawmakers in cell 1. The pattern of voting behavior for these members is one of stable and high-range liberal voting. Legislators who fall in quadrant 3 are more apt to support strengthening civil rights laws that would help remedy the effects of past and continuing discrimination against blacks. These are the representatives who display the kind of voting behavior that civil rights advocates would like to see more of in the chambers of Congress.

Finally, in cell 4 (high amendment/low final passage category) is another form of deviant voting behavior. This scenario is likely to come forth when a legislator votes for civil rights legislation during the amending process but later decides to vote against final passage. Two types might behave in this fashion: (1) liberals who support strong civil rights language during the amending stage but view the compromises as too weak to support on final passage; and (2) conservatives who support strong civil rights amendments in hopes of making the final bill too liberal for moderates to vote for on final roll call. While voting in this manner is theoretically plausible, the tactic discussed in cell 2 is more likely to occur in the real world of voting behavior on legislation of primary interest to blacks. That is, it is safe to say that virtually all members would state that they support the principle of civil rights and equal justice for all American citizens. But the proof is in the way they vote, and the contention of this book is that it is during the amending process that a more stringent test is provided of the commitment of legislators to civil rights.

The model is intended to provide an analytic framework within which congressional policy responsiveness to black interests can be analyzed. It should prove useful in detecting systematic patterns of voting behavior and thus give a better picture of the overall quality of substantive representation for African-Americans in Congress.

CHAPTER 2

Federal Protection of Voting Rights: The Role of Congress in the Black Struggle for the Franchise

The vote is the most powerful instrument ever devised by men for breaking down injustices and destroying the terrible walls that imprison men because they are different from other men.
—President Lyndon B. Johnson, upon signing of the Voting Rights Act of 1965

There is no better place to begin the search for an understanding of the quality of representation for blacks than in the area of voting rights. The right to vote is a sacred feature of American democracy and is fundamental to formal representation. According to democratic theory, elections serve as the means through which citizens can affect governmental decisions so that they can better safeguard and promote their interests (see Fig. 1). If representation is defined in this manner—that is, in terms of policy congruence—then citizens must be given the opportunity to participate fully in the political process; otherwise, there can be no meaningful correspondence between the representative and the represented.

One can also argue that there are symbolic benefits attached to voting. As some academicians have argued, voting itself is a major source of satisfaction for individuals in a political system.[1] A system of government that deprives citizens of their right to participate fully in the decisions that affect their lives is likely to lower their self-esteem. The inability to vote implies that an individual does not have full citizenship status within society. From the perspectives of policy congruence and symbolism, a system of government that restricts the franchise because of a person's skin color or sex would be considered less representative than others. Indeed, the franchise tells us much about how representative a system of government is.

Americans place enormous emphasis on the ideas of political equality. Yet, despite discourse on egalitarianism in documents such as the Declaration of Independence and the U.S. Constitution, the struggle for the

17

most basic of human political rights, the right to vote, has been a long, arduous, and oftentimes violent process for blacks. It has taken over two centuries of laws, court decisions, constitutional amendments, and protest actions by civil rights activists to grant the franchise to blacks in America.

The first part of this chapter gives a brief discussion of the legislative history of federal voting rights. The objective here is to provide the background necessary for a full appreciation of the two hundred–year black struggle for the franchise and to do it in such a way as to highlight the importance of congressional protection of minority voting rights. The second section is devoted to a discussion of the major provisions in federal voting rights laws enacted by Congress since the late 1950s. This section details why the Voting Rights Act of 1965 was a revolutionary measure that went far beyond the previous two federal voting rights bills of 1957 and 1960 in accelerating black voter participation. The third part analyzes the roll call voting behavior of members of the House on voting rights legislation. The fourth section examines the nexus between congressional decision making and black constituents while controlling for other explanatory variables. The analyses in the third and fourth sections will enable us to draw some safe conclusions about the quality of substantive representation to black interests in both dyadic and collective terms. The chapter concludes with some comments about the current and future status of federal regulation of voter qualifications in the United States.

The Black Struggle for the Franchise

When the U.S. Constitution went into effect in 1789, neither slaves nor free blacks could vote in the South. Black men residing in the North could vote in a few states. Even though blacks could not vote in the South, the Constitutional Convention of 1787 specified that a slaveholding state should count them to determine the number of representatives the state would be entitled to in the House of Representatives. In the "Three-fifths Compromise" the delegates to the Constitutional Convention agreed that slaves would count as three-fifths of a person for the purposes of apportioning representation and taxes among the states. Thus, while blacks were not considered persons when it came to the franchise, slaveholding states could simultaneously count them to increase their representation in Congress.[2] One can certainly argue that the compromise over slavery greatly influenced the South to give its support to the establishment of a new government. It is equally important, however, to point out the fact that, by acknowledging slavery and rewarding slave owners, the Constitution, in its original form, gave positive recognition to a representative form of government that was clearly not color-blind.

From the founding of this nation until the passage of the Thirteenth Amendment (1865) forbidding involuntary servitude, public policy was aimed at perpetuating slavery. Slavery and the slave trade had been sanctioned by the Constitutional Convention, and Congress was given no authority to interfere with the institution. Article I, Section 9, of the Constitution specifically denied Congress the power to stop the slave trade before 1808. The provision states: "The Migration or Importation of Such persons as any of the States now existing shall think proper to admit, shall not be prohibited by the Congress prior to the Year one eight hundred and eight." The term *such persons* was obviously a euphemism for slaves, whom the framers of the Constitution eschewed mentioning in the document out of moral consciousness. After 1808 Congress possessed the requisite power to act on the slavery question, but it failed to bring the issue to a satisfactory resolution before the Civil War.

The infamous Dred Scott court decision of 1857 summed up the central theme of interracial social relationships before the Civil War. In this decision Chief Justice Roger Taney of the U.S. Supreme Court bluntly announced that blacks, free or slave, "had no rights which the white man was bound to respect." Moreover, according to Taney, Congress had no authority to ban slavery in the territories. The coexistence of slavery and the principles of liberty and equality created a dilemma in American politics, which resulted in a civil war that threatened the existence of the Union.

The horrors of the Civil War made it clear that, once slaves were emancipated, the federal government would have to play a more active role to prevent retrogression of black Americans' newly acquired civil liberties and civil rights. Though the new constitutions of the southern states had bestowed the franchise to blacks after the Civil War, there was nothing to prevent revocation of that guarantee if conservative whites were to regain control of decision making in state governments. Thus, between 1865 and 1870 a trilogy of post–Civil War constitutional amendments (Thirteenth, Fourteenth, and Fifteenth) intended to grant full citizenship to blacks was passed. One, the Fifteenth Amendment, ratified in 1870, specifically prohibits denying the right to vote on the basis of "race, color, or previous condition of servitude." Section 2 of the amendment grants to Congress the power to enforce the provisions of the constitutional law by "appropriate legislation."

Following ratification of the Fifteenth Amendment, Congress passed a series of civil rights laws designed to provide additional protection for black suffrage. Known as the Enforcement Acts, they provided for criminal penalties to anyone interfering with the right to vote. The Enforcement Act of 1870 prohibited state election officials from applying local election laws in a racially biased manner. The second Enforcement Act (1871) placed federal elections in the South under direct federal supervision. In addition, the Ku Klux Act of 1871 dispatched federal troops to the South to stem the rising tide of violence by white terrorist groups against blacks who wanted to exercise their right to vote.[3]

At first the Civil War Amendments, civil rights laws, and the presence of a northern military in the South provided adequate protection for blacks desiring to vote (at that time approximately 90 percent of the U.S. black population lived in the South). As a consequence, blacks not only voted during this period but also were elected to office in some areas of the South. To illustrate, between 1869 and 1877 two blacks from the South were elected to the Senate, and fourteen were elected to the House (see chap. 4, table 11).

Reconstruction policy had been effectively shaped by Congress through constitutional amendments and civil rights laws, but it was the federal judiciary that had the final say as it began to interpret the words emanating from the amendments and laws. When the U.S. Supreme Court began to interpret the meaning of federal legislation, it did so favorable to proponents of states' rights. It is noteworthy that the Supreme Court relied heavily on the ambiguous wording of the Fifteenth Amendment to hasten the end of Reconstruction. In *United States v. Reese* (1876) the Supreme Court pointed out the important fact that the Fifteenth Amendment did not confer the suffrage on anyone but merely stipulated that citizens could not be discriminated against in voting by the states on the basis of race, color, or previous condition of servitude.[4] By interpreting the Fifteenth Amendment in this manner, the Court gave southern states the freedom to devise ingenious discriminatory devices to prevent newly enfranchised blacks from exercising their right to vote, so long as southern lawmakers did not blatantly violate the voting rights of blacks.

The federal judiciary also dealt a severe blow to the protection of black voting rights by limiting the effectiveness of the Enforcement Acts. In *United States v. Cruikshank* (1876) the Supreme Court made it clear that, in order for federal attorneys to convict scores of Louisiana whites for conspiring to deprive blacks of their right to vote under the Enforcement Acts, they had to prove that the offenders intended to discriminate for reasons of race.[5] As civil rights laws were invalidated by the high Court, Congress refused to intervene on behalf of blacks to provide effective federal voting rights protection.

The reestablishment of white supremacy became evident when, in 1877, southern Democrats agreed to support the presidential candidacy of Rutherford B. Hayes in exchange for the termination of a northern military presence and a policy of noninterference toward activities in the South.

"The Compromise of 1877," as it is commonly called, marked the end of Reconstruction and the beginning of repression of black voting rights.

To ensure the continuation of white hegemony in the South, a variety of methods including legal stratagems, physical violence, economic sanctions, and psychological coercion were used to bar blacks from the voting booth. Some of the most effective legal devices, or "Jim Crow" laws, used included: the poll tax (designed to impose an economic burden to voting for blacks); literacy tests (a reading, or "understanding," test intended to deny blacks without educational opportunities the right to vote); and the white primary (exclusion of blacks from the primary elections of the dominant Democratic Party in the region).

Moreover, state and local election registrars exercised a great deal of discretion in deciding who would be eligible to vote. For example, since various qualifying devices (literacy tests) could reduce the white potential electorate, clauses were included in many state constitutions to make it easier for whites to exercise the franchise. The most often used clauses were the "Grandfather clause" and the "Good moral character" clause. Under the first any citizen whose grandfather had been eligible to vote before 1867—that is, before blacks could legally vote in the South—was excused from meeting the other voter qualifications. Good moral character clauses were intended to exempt whites who purportedly had such character.[6] V. O. Key Jr., one of the earliest progenitors on southern politics, summed up the ethical and legal use of the literacy test in the following way: "no matter from what direction one looks at it, the Southern literacy test is a fraud and nothing more."[7]

Beyond legal maneuvers often blacks who sought to vote were physically threatened, beaten, or even murdered by white vigilante groups.[8] In some instances blacks attempting to vote would lose their jobs or be denied credit in stores. In addition, the psychological effect felt by blacks of a caste system that reversed earlier trends toward black equality constituted a major obstacle to voting.[9]

Through revisions in their state constitutions and laws southern lawmakers by the early part of the twentieth century had effectively disenfranchised most of the eligible black voting population throughout the South. To illustrate, historian C. Vann Woodward reported that there were 130,000 registered black voters in Louisiana in 1896; by 1904 that number had dwindled to 1300.[10]

It took over a half-century after Reconstruction for the federal government, and especially Congress, to abandon its laissez-faire position toward protecting civil rights for blacks. In the case of *Guinn v. United States* (1915) the Court invalidated the Grandfather clause, and in *Smith v. Allwright* (1944) the white primary was nullified. The Twenty-Fourth

Amendment passed by Congress in 1964 abolished the poll tax as a prerequisite for voting in federal elections, and in *Harper v. Virginia State Board of Elections* (1966) the Court invalidated the tax for state elections. Finally, evidence of discriminatory use of literacy tests led to the passage of the Voting Rights Act of 1965 and the suspension of the tests in federal elections. The suspension of all literacy tests was included as part of the provisions in the Voting Rights Act of 1970 and was upheld by the U.S. Supreme Court in *Oregon v. Mitchell* (1970).

Congressional Responsiveness to Black Voting Rights: 1950s to the Present

It is important to note that between 1883 and 1957 Congress passed no civil rights statute. Congressional inaction proved to be a serious impediment to black suffrage. To illustrate, in 1940 just 5 percent of the eligible black adult population was registered to vote; in 1952, 21 percent; and only 29 percent in 1960.[11] Needless to say, with such limited voting strength blacks had little chance of influencing their representatives to support black policy preferences, nor did they have much success in electing members of their choice to Congress.

One of the major goals of the civil rights movement of the 1950s was to regain black suffrage rights. The movement's goal was partially realized when the Civil Rights Act of 1957 was enacted into law. The act was a modest attempt to address concerns over the exclusion of blacks from the voting booth. Much of the focus of the act was devoted to strengthening judicial enforcement of voting rights in the South. The law established a temporary six-man U.S. Commission on Civil Rights to investigate civil rights complaints and violations. It empowered the Department of Justice to seek court injunctions against any practices that deprived blacks of their voting rights and so authorized criminal prosecutions for violations. The act also created the Civil Rights Division in the Department of Justice. In reality, however, the law had little effect, primarily because the Eisenhower presidential administration refused to enforce many of its key provisions.[12] But the act was significant because it signaled a renewed federal legislative concern with the protection of black voting rights.

The second installment of federal voting rights legislation came three years later, when the Civil Rights Act of 1960 was enacted. After the Civil Rights Commission reported almost no progress in registering black voters, the 1960 act gave authority to the federal courts to appoint referees to help blacks register to vote after a "pattern or practice" of discrimination was found. It also required state and local officials to preserve voting records for twenty-two months for federal inspection of possible discriminatory practices. Other provisions made racially motivated bombings and burnings federal crimes when the offenders crossed state lines to carry out these horrible acts, provided for the desegregated education of children of the armed forces when local and state facilities were not made available for such individuals, and imposed a one thousand dollar fine and a year's imprisonment for noncompliance with federal court mandates. The Civil Rights Act of 1964 further strengthened provisions in voter registration laws. While the 1964 act did include provisions designed to erase racial discrimination in voting, the major focus of the legislation was concerned with barring discrimination in public accommodations, a topic for discussion in the next chapter.

The effectiveness of the earliest two civil rights acts was limited as evidenced by the fact that by the early 1960s more than three-fifths of the eligible black population still was not registered to vote. The ineffectiveness of these acts stems from a variety of factors, including a shortage of manpower in the Department of Justice, apathy or reluctance of presidential administrations to enforce voting rights policies, and hostile state and local officials continuing to find ways to keep blacks off voter registration rolls. The major defect of the two civil rights acts was their reliance on litigation to remedy discriminatory practices. In other words, seeking remedies through the courts proved to be too time-consuming a process to eradicate discriminatory voting practices prior to an election. In order to obtain relief in the courts black voters who felt they were discriminated against had the burden of proving their case on an individual basis, a process that was expensive, time-consuming, and ineffective, especially in view of the fact that federal district courts in the South tended to be presided over by local judges who were sympathetic to the views of southern white supremacists.[13] The House Judiciary Committee in the spring of 1965 summed up the problems of litigation when it stated: "Judiciary relief has had to be gauged not in terms of months—but in terms of years" (U.S. House of Representatives [1965], 2440–41).

It should be noted that there was some success in registering more blacks to vote prior to the passage of the Voting Rights Act of 1965. The Voter Education Project (VEP) of the Southern Regional Council played an important role in this endeavor.[14] The first VEP (1962–64) coordinated registration drives as well as provided funds for many of the voter registration drives conducted by civil rights organizations such as the National Association for the Advancement of Colored People, Southern Christian Leadership Conference, Student Nonviolent Coordinating Committee, Congress of Racial Equality, and the National Urban League. Furthermore, the presidential campaign of 1964 may have caused some blacks to register and vote. The presidential campaign, pitting liberal Democrat

Lyndon Johnson against conservative Republican Barry Goldwater, saw shifting racial party coalitions emerge when the two candidates opposed each other on the sensitive issue of civil rights. The possibility of a Goldwater presidency and a less active role of the federal government in the area of civil rights may have motivated previously unregistered blacks to exercise their right to vote.[15]

As a consequence of the cumulative efforts of the VEP, civil rights groups, the Justice Department, and the fear of a Goldwater presidency, black voter registration in the South jumped from 35 percent in February 1964 to 45 percent by the time of the November 1964 elections.[16] Yet, despite these gains, the majority of blacks in the region remained unregistered to vote before the passage of the Voting Rights Act of 1965.

The elections of 1964 made it clear that black suffrage was still not a reality in the South. In early 1965, stimulated by black protest activity and supremacist violence shown by the national news media, the federal government once again intervened on behalf of blacks in their quest for equal access to the voting ballot.[17] On March 15, 1965, President Lyndon Johnson, in defense of a stronger voting rights bill, addressed Congress to deliver his famous "We Shall Overcome" speech. On August 6 members of Congress signed into law the Voting Rights Act of 1965. With civil rights leader Dr. Martin Luther King Jr. beside him when he signed the bill, President Johnson stated, "the vote is the most powerful instrument ever devised."

The Voting Rights Act of 1965 is widely regarded as the most significant and successful piece of voting rights legislation ever enacted by Congress.[18] It offers several noteworthy improvements over previous voting rights laws. A major provision of the act is the section 4 "triggering" formula, which provides for automatic coverage of jurisdictions in which less than 50 percent of the voting-age population had been registered in 1964 or had voted in the 1964 presidential election. Originally, the provision was drafted specifically to apply to those southern states in which flagrant discrimination against blacks existed. The states originally targeted to "trigger" federal government involvement were Alabama, Georgia, Louisiana, Mississippi, South Carolina, Virginia, twenty-six counties in North Carolina, and parts of Arizona. Another key provision suspended for five years the use of literacy and understanding tests as a requirement for voting. The act also authorized voter registration by federal examiners in areas in which such tests are used. Section 5 of the act requires preclearance of state and local voting law changes with the attorney general or the Federal District Court of Washington, D.C. The major objective of the preclearance provision is to prevent states and their localities from implementing new voting laws discriminating against racial minorities.

Other sections authorize the assignment of federal examiners to enforce the right to vote, provide for fines of not more than five thousand dollars or imprisonment for depriving or conspiring to deprive any person of their voting rights, and permit federal observers to monitor elections. The legality of the Voting Rights Act was upheld by the U.S. Supreme Court in the decision of *South Carolina v. Katzenbach* (1966). The effect of this legislation was significant. Between 1964 and 1969 black voter registration in the eleven southern states increased from 35 percent to 65 percent. In comparison, white voter registration increased from 73 percent to 84 percent.[19]

Since 1965 the Voting Rights Act has been renewed and amended in 1970, 1975, and 1982. The 1970 extension continued the preclearance provision of section 5 and also expanded the section 4 trigger mechanism by making the bill applicable to all jurisdictions using a literacy test in which less than 50 percent of the voting age population participated in the 1968 presidential election. In 1975 the Voting Rights Act was extended to 1982, with several additional provisions: making permanent the previously temporary ban on literacy tests; a bilingual ballot requirement in areas in which over 5 percent of the voting-age population were of a single-language minority and less than 50 percent were registered or had voted in the 1972 presidential election; and election law changes in states and localities covered by the act are required to be approved by either a United States attorney or a federal court. In 1982 the Voting Rights Act was again extended for another twenty-five years.

Two of the more important features in the 1982 act are the controversial "bail-out" provision, which allows those covered states showing a clean voting rights record for ten years to escape from close federal scrutiny, and the provision (sec. 2) that states that "intent" to discriminate need not be proved if the "results" of a voting law is discriminatory. The section 2 results test overturns the controversial 1980 U.S. Supreme Court decision in *City of Mobile v. Bolden.*[20] In that decision the Court ruled that an aggrieving party had to show that the voting practice or procedure had been intentionally designed for the purpose of racial discrimination.

To summarize, this historical overview conveys two significant pieces of information. First, from an institutional standpoint congressional support for black voting rights has vacillated widely over time. Between the end of Reconstruction and 1957 congressional responsiveness to blacks in the area of voting rights was nonexistent. Since the late 1950s Congress has assumed a more active role in protecting the voting rights of racial minorities by enacting six major federal voting rights laws.

Second, it is important to note that voting rights complaints have not remained constant over the past forty years. The early battles waged by blacks for equal access to the voting ballot were against literacy tests, poll taxes, and voter registration barriers that served as the political armor of Jim Crow to reduce black voter strength. The three civil rights acts, passed in 1957, 1960, and especially in 1965, were designed to enfranchise more blacks. When blacks began to exercise their right to vote, more subtle methods of voting discrimination emerged aimed at diluting black voting strength. Consequently, voting rights complaints have shifted from disenfranchising strategies to subtle forms of voter discrimination in the form of designing electoral systems that would deprive blacks and other minorities of an opportunity to elect candidates of their choice to Congress (e.g., negative racial gerrymandering). The extensions of the Voting Rights Act of 1965 are efforts by Congress to address this "second generation" of voter discrimination.[21] Acknowledgment of the changing nature of voting rights complaints will be taken into account when the data in the empirical sections of this chapter are examined.

Before turning to an examination of congressional support for federal voting rights, it is useful to review the extant literature on the relationship between the racial composition of congressional districts and congressional protection of black voting rights.

The African-American Connection

Implicit in this discussion of congressional voting on federal voting rights legislation is the notion that there is a relationship between the racial composition of congressional districts and congressional patterns of voting behavior. Previous research has paid special attention to this relationship in the South because it has been the region of the country in which white legislators were the most conservative and the area in which blacks met the most resistance to their political participation. The basic assumption is that legislator responsiveness is associated with the size of the black population in a district; that is, as the black population increases across districts, representatives should become increasingly more supportive of federal voting rights protection.

Of course, the positive relationship between the proportion of blacks in a district and legislator responsiveness depends on the level of black voter participation. Consequently, previous research has demonstrated that different patterns of legislative voting behavior have emerged based on the time frame in which federal voting rights measures were voted on by southern members of the House. Merle Black offers the most thorough analysis of House members' voting behavior on federal voting rights legislation.[22] Examining the connection between the southern black electorate and the voting behavior of southern white representatives on final roll call federal voting rights bills passed in 1957, 1960, 1965, 1970, and 1975, the author found three distinct patterns of voting behavior.[23] With black population in districts coded into five categories, the author observed a pattern of conservative voting across all black categories in 1957 and 1960. In other words, the size of the black population had no impact on legislator behavior. Southern representatives, especially Democrats, since there were very few Republicans in the delegation, were clearly united against any policies that would enfranchise more black citizens. The fact that many blacks were kept from the polls through legal devices and intimidation meant that they were unable to organize and mobilize effectively to influence their representatives' roll call voting behavior in a positive direction.

An inverse pattern emerged on final roll calls in 1965 and 1970. That is, southern congressional districts containing large numbers of blacks tended to have the most conservative representatives.[24] The most commonly accepted explanation for this finding is that the preoccupation with the maintenance of the racial status quo was greater in areas in which whites lived in close proximity to a large black population. The higher the proportion of blacks in the area, the greater the fear of whites that they would lose control to blacks.[25] Consequently, influential whites in districts in which a relatively large percentage of blacks resided were able to impress upon their representatives that they should oppose any policies that would elevate the social and political status of blacks.

The third pattern of voting behavior emerged on roll call votes in 1975. For the first time in the century a majority of southern representatives supported a federal voting rights bill. The increase in legislator support of federal voting rights is mainly attributed to growing black voter registration and voter participation. Moreover, the pattern of less conservative voting on final roll calls in 1975 was found to be associated with increasing levels of black populations across congressional districts. Black found the greatest level of support came in the 20 to 29 percent black category.[26]

As stated earlier, Black's research did not address the roll call voting behavior of nonsouthern representatives, nor did it cover the 1982 Voting Rights extension because of the date of its publication. One of the major objectives of the empirical analysis in the following sections is to learn more about the relationship between black constituency influence and congressional voting on federal voting rights in both regions of the country. The investigation is designed to be comprehensive in coverage so that we can provide some answers to the central topic of congressional responsiveness to black voting rights.

An Analysis of Congressional Support for Federal Voting Rights Legislation

Who supports black voting rights on Capitol Hill? How has legislator support changed over time? What influences tend to increase or decrease congressional responsiveness to black policy preferences? One way to gain a thorough understanding of the intricacies of legislative voting on federal voting rights is through a longitudinal analysis. A time series approach can be used to detect trends and patterns of responsiveness as well as to determine the impact of factors influencing the roll call voting behavior of House members. The analysis covers the Civil Rights Act of 1957 through the 1982 extension of the Voting Rights Act and includes both amendment and final passage roll call votes (see app. A, for a list and description of roll calls selected during the amending phase).

The examination of congressional support for federal voting rights begins by revealing patterns and levels of mean support. In order to accomplish this objective, on both amendment and final passage roll calls, a value of one (1) was assigned to each House member who voted for the bill, a value of zero (0) for those who opposed it. Favorable votes on final roll call for each of the six bills were aggregated and then divided by the sum of yes and no votes. The same method was used for operationalizing amendments. The higher the value of the mean score, the greater the level of congressional support for federal voting protection.[27]

It is expected that the level of congressional support will be higher on the more publicized and highly visible final passage bills than on amendments. The logic here is that the amendment stage of legislative voting allows members of Congress more discretion in deciding how to cast their roll call votes. Even though amendments are now subjected to recorded roll calls, citizens and groups pay less attention to them than they do votes on final roll call. Consequently, legislators who oppose black voting rights may attempt to water down the bill before a final vote is taken. Simply put, the amendment stage provides a stronger test of the commitment of lawmakers to federal voting rights protection.

It is widely agreed that party is the major source of voting cleavage in Congress, all things being equal. Thus, the analysis that follows uses party as the principal guide for detecting patterns of voting behavior.[28] The findings are reported in figures 3 and 4. The figures present overall mean federal voting rights support scores as well as a breakdown of those scores by party affiliation. As figure 3 shows, the overall pattern for amendment voting varies in the low-to-moderate range with mean support scores reaching their peak in 1975 at 66 percent. In contrast, the overall pattern for final passage votes (fig. 4) fluctuates in the moderate-to-high range over

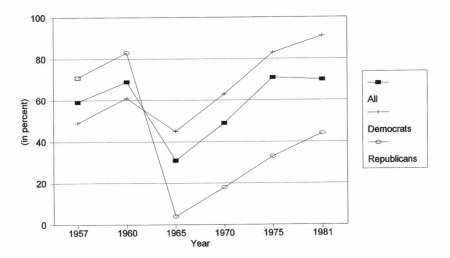

Fig. 3.   Mean voting rights support scores (amendment votes of representatives). (Note: 1957 = 85th Congress; 1960 = 86th Congress; 1965 =
89th Congress; 1970 = 91st Congress; 1975 = 94th Congress; 1981 = 97th
Congress. Computed by the author from data collected by the LCCR and
Congressional Quarterly Almanac.)

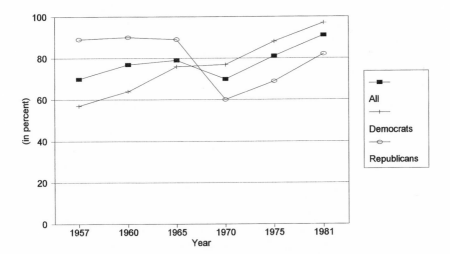

Fig. 4.   Mean voting rights support scores (final passage votes of representatives). (Note: 1957 = 85th Congress; 1960 = 86th Congress; 1965 =
89th Congress; 1970 = 91st Congress; 1975 = 94th Congress; 1981 = 97th
Congress. Computed by the author from data collected by the LCCR and
Congressional Quarterly Almanac.)

time. The highest level of support came on House passage of the 1982 extension, at 90 percent. As expected, a comparison of the data in the two figures shows that in each Congress the support level is indeed higher on final roll call votes than on amendment votes. The disparity between the two stages of roll call voting is also evident when one examines the mean scores by party affiliation. In each instance party support is greater on final roll calls than on amendments.

The findings show that Democratic support has steadily increased over time on both final passage and amendment roll calls. House Republican support on final roll call has varied in the moderate-to-high range across the four decade period. Interestingly, Republican support on amendment roll calls has actually declined from highs of 71 percent in 1957 and 83 percent in 1960 to levels of only 4 percent in 1965, 18 percent in 1970, 33 percent in 1975, and 44 percent in 1981. Furthermore, an inspection of the mean support scores between the two parties reveals that, in the earliest two congresses, House Republicans were more supportive of black voting rights than were House Democrats. The finding is somewhat of a surprise when one considers that federal voting rights legislation is usually sponsored and advocated by the Democratic Party.

An explanation for this unexpected finding can be best understood when we examine the influence of region—that is, the differences in party support between nonsouthern and southern members of the House. Mean support scores of regional party members are displayed in figure 5 (amendments) and figure 6 (final roll calls). As the data in the figures show, region remains an important cleavage in American political life. The patterns across time show that nonsouthern Democrats, on average, are more likely to support legislation of this nature than any other regional party group in the analysis. The patterns, especially on final passage votes, are in the high range and are relatively constant over time.

A finding of significance is the patterns of support for nonsouthern Republicans. Though they have not abandoned their support for final suffrage bills, their commitment to strong federal voting rights protection has waned since 1960. As the figures illustrate, their mean support scores on the two types of roll calls begin to diverge significantly after 1960. Votes on amendments are significantly lower than votes on final roll calls. What explanations can be given for these findings? Edward Carmines and James Stimson note that House Republicans were decidedly more liberal on racial issues before the mid-1960s and more conservative after the congressional elections of 1964.[29] In the two earliest congresses House Republicans and nonsouthern House Democrats were able to proffer bipartisan support in order to pass two moderate civil rights bills pertaining to voting. The elections of 1964 brought about some significant changes in the

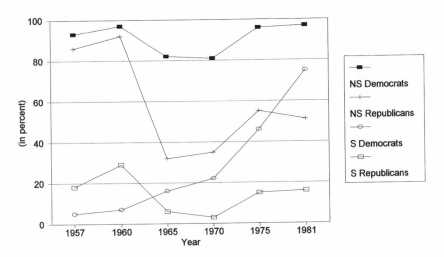

Fig. 5.   Mean voting rights support scores (amendment votes of representatives). (Note: Comparison of regional party members federal voting
rights support scores. Computed by the author from data collected by
the LCCR and *Congressional Quarterly Almanac*.)

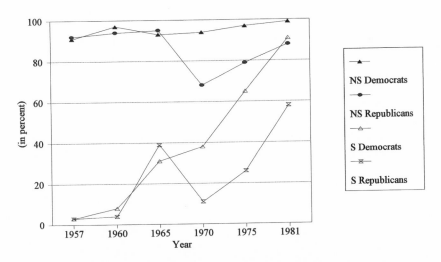

Fig. 6.   Mean voting rights support scores (final passage votes of representatives). (Note: Comparison of regional party members federal voting
rights support scores. Computed by the author from data collected by
the LCCR and *Congressional Quarterly Almanac*.)

American political landscape, including the replacement of many racially moderate-to-liberal House Republicans with liberal House Democrats from the non-South. The results reported in the figures support the contention of a growing trend toward greater Republican conservatism on racial issues after 1964. The conservative roll call voting behavior displayed by House Republicans on amendments in the more recent congresses does not appear to be an aberration; instead, it appears to be a systematic effort by House Republicans, and the Republican presidential administrations of Richard Nixon and Ronald Reagan, to subterfuge federal voting rights legislation by attaching amendments that would dilute the strength of voting rights bills.[30]

Southern Democrats have undergone the greatest transformation in their voting behavior, from virulent opponents of federal voting rights in 1957 and 1960 to supporters by 1981. On House final passage (fig. 6) of the 1982 extension, on average, southern Democrats were nine times more likely to support the bill than they were on votes for the 1957 Civil Rights Act. Also, by 1981 their support scores of 75 percent on amendments (fig. 5) placed them second to nonsouthern Democrats in the rankings among regional party groups.

Finally, whereas southern Democrats once occupied the position as the most recalcitrant party members toward federal regulation of voter qualification, they now have been replaced by southern Republicans. Relative to other regional party members in the analysis, they are the strongest opponents of federal voting rights legislation. Their support scores are especially low on amendments. It should be noted that the number of southern Republicans in the House grew steadily over time, from seven in 1957 to thirty-eight by 1981.[31] Since the early 1980s the number of House seats held by the Republican Party has continued to grow in the region. After the 1994 congressional elections (104th Congress) southern Republicans, for the first time in American history, held a majority of the House seats in the region. Southern Republicans again won a majority of House seats in the South after the 1996 congressional elections (105th Congress). The growth in their numbers is undoubtedly due to the growing dissatisfaction among conservative southern whites with the liberalization of the Democratic Party.[32] Whether or not the region is experiencing a permanent swing toward the Republican Party at the congressional level is a moot issue; one fact is clear from the findings: the impact of southern Republicans' voting behavior cannot be ignored, since they have become a critical mass in the House.

In the context of the changing nature of voting rights complaints it is interesting to note the patterns of behavior manifested by party members. As stated earlier, voting rights complaints have shifted from deprivation of fundamental rights of voting to dilutive electoral devices such as racial ger-rymandering. While the nature of voting rights complaints may have changed in recent decades, Republican opposition to federal voting rights protection has remained relatively constant. Democrats, on average, have been generally supportive of black voting rights, despite the shift from one generation of voting discrimination to another. Some of them, however, support diluting amendments as well. Consider, for example, the amend-ment (see app. A) offered by Republican Caldwell Butler in 1981 that would have transferred jurisdiction for bail-outs from the District of Columbia to local federal district courts. Civil rights advocates were opposed to the transfer of authority from Washington for fear that liti-gants would experience greater difficulty getting fair hearings in their states and that local federal judges would more easily approve bail-outs for covered jurisdictions that had not complied with the letter and spirit of the law. The amendment was rejected by a vote of 132 to 277. Signs of party unity did emerge on roll call, with 58 percent (102–75) of voting Republi-cans supporting the Butler proposal and 87 percent of voting Democrats (30–202) opposing the measure. Although Democrats were generally sup-ported, 13 percent of the party delegation did support the Butler amend-ment, which was opposed by civil rights organizations. And, as shall be demonstrated later in the chapter, many who voted for diluting voting rights amendments later decided to support final passage of the bill.

A More Systematic Investigation of Legislator Support for Federal Voting Rights Legislation

The analysis presented in the previous section provides some important information about the relationship between party, region, and congres-sional voting behavior. But what about the influence of black constituents? Previous research has attributed many of the changes that have occurred in the voting behavior of House members to the acceleration of black voter participation.[33] But there are important questions that still remain unan-swered about the impact of black constituency influence. For example, does the relationship differ between the two types of roll calls? To show the impact of black political participation along with the other explanatory variables, the data were subjected to a more stringent statistical test. Two separate regression models were constructed for votes on amendments and votes on final roll calls. A multiple item scale was devised, ranging from zero (0) to the total number of voting rights amendments (four for 1957–58 and 1965–66 and three for 1959–60, 1969–70, 1975–76, and 1981–82) in the congressional session in which the amendments were voted on by House members.[34] Each representative's score was computed by dividing his or her support for federal voting rights by the total number of roll calls votes used in that congressional session. On final roll call the categorical nature of the bills suggests the use of logit models. For those who are unfamiliar with this statistical technique, typically, logit models use dichotomous choice variables.[35]

Ordinary least squares regression tests and evaluates the impact of the independent variables on amendment voting, and logistic regression is used to show the effect of the explanatory factors on final passage voting. Four independent variables are included in the model. They are: party, region, percentage black, and percentage urban. Beyond the potential impact of the proportion of black citizens in a district, other constituency variables might influence the roll call voting behavior of representatives. The constituency variable found to be more consistently related to congressional roll call voting on the topic is urbanization.[36] The proportion of urban constituents measures the relative liberalism of urban versus rural legislators. Urban representatives may be more liberal than rural lawmakers because they represent constituents (e.g., residents of housing projects) who believe they will benefit from liberal economic programs. The basic model takes the following form:

$$Y = a + b_1X_1 + b_2X_2 + b_3X_3 + b_4X_4 + e \tag{1}$$

where:

Y is the House member's support for amendments, ranging from 0 (opposition to all amendments) to 100 (support for all amendments); and in the final passage model Y is the House member's support for each final roll call bill during the six congresses, coded 1 if the representative supported the bill, 0 if he or she opposed it.

a is the constant.

X_1 is coded as a dichotomous variable: 1 if the member is a Democrat, 0 if a Republican.

X_2 is also dichotomized, taking on the value of 1 if the member is from the non-South, 0 if a southern representative.

X_3 is the percentage of a district's population in urban areas.

X_4 is the percentage of population that is black in each district.

e is the error term.

This research predicts that House Democratic support will increase over time and House Republican support will decrease. It is expected that nonsouthern House members will be more supportive than their southern colleagues. Based on previous research, this study expects to find a negative relationship between an increase in the percentage of blacks across districts and the voting behavior of members in the earliest congresses and a positive relationship in the more recent congresses. This research also predicts that support for federal voting rights will increase as the proportion of urbanization rises from district to district.

Tables 2 and 3 show the results of the regression analysis. Unstandardized regression coefficients are used to compare the strength of a particular variable across the four-decade period. *T*-ratios are reported in the tables to show levels of statistical significance. Other relevant statistics are reported at the bottom of each table. Overall the models performs well in confirming theories about relationships. The explanatory power of the regression model ranges from .72 in 1957–58 to .38 in 1981–82. The overall fit of the logistic model, represented by the model chi-square statistics, is significant for each of the six congresses under study. The model correctly predicts at least 77 percent of legislators' votes on federal voting rights legislation in a given Congress.

As hypothesized, the estimated regression coefficients in both tables reveal that the impact of party has grown over time. The party variable was statistically insignificant in the earliest congresses, which supports the patterns observed earlier—that is, after controlling for the impact of region, both major parties were highly supportive of the passages of the earliest two civil rights acts. It is statistically significant in four of the six congresses in the amendment model and in the three most recent congresses in the final roll call model. The finding suggests that distinct partisan differences have evolved across time, especially on amendments with House Democrats emerging as the strongest supporters of federal voting rights protection.

A second finding of note is that, although region is highly statistically significant at the .000 level and its sign is in the expected direction for each of the six congresses under investigation, its impact has declined from levels of 78.973 in 1957 to levels of 23.268 on amendment votes in 1981 and has dropped from 5.563 in 1957 to 1.730 in 1981 on final passage votes. The declining influence of region is primarily a function of the confluence of regional Democrats voting in support of federal voting rights. In other words, southern Democrats are voting less conservatively and more like their party colleagues from the non-South.

As predicted, urbanization influences representatives' voting decisions on federal voting rights. The impact of urbanization is greater on amendment votes than on final passage votes. While urbanization is a factor that helps to explain legislator behavior, its probability of affecting the outcome of voting rights legislation is much less than that of party and region.

TABLE 2. Effects of Party, Region, Race, and Urbanization on House Members' Support for Federal Voting Rights Amendments Preferred by Blacks: Regression Estimates

Variables	Unstandardized	t-ratio
Members' Political Party		
1957–58 (85th Congress)	–3.359	1.012
1959–60 (86th Congress)	–.571	.186
1965–66 (89th Congress)	41.851	18.042***
1969–70 (91st Congress)	39.751	11.301***
1975–76 (94th Congress)	37.899	11.894***
1981–82 (97th Congress)	37.800	13.329***
Region		
1957–58 (85th Congress)	78.973	24.309***
1959–60 (86th Congress)	49.080	15.991***
1965–66 (89th Congress)	45.000	17.125***
1969–70 (91st Congress)	51.830	12.554***
1975–76 (94th Congress)	42.072	10.978***
1981–82 (97th Congress)	23.268	5.636***
Percent Urban		
1957–58 (85th Congress)	.231	4.841***
1959–60 (86th Congress)	.160	4.432***
1965–66 (89th Congress)	.378	8.402**
1969–70 (91st Congress)	.099	2.790***
1975–76 (94th Congress)	.231	3.695***
1981–82 (97th Congress)	.257	3.571***
Percent Black		
1957–58 (85th Congress)	–.099	–1.012
1959–60 (86th Congress)	–.809	–6.921***
1965–66 (89th Congress)	.019	.775
1969–70 (91st Congress)	.069	.894
1975–76 (94th Congress)	–.059	–.485
1981–82 (97th Congress)	.087	.486

1957–58 (R^2 = .72), 1959–60 (R^2 = .57), 1965–66 (R^2 = .65), 1969–70 (R^2 = .41), 1975–76 (R^2 = .44), 1981–82 (R^2 = .38).

Source: Data for federal voting rights legislation compiled from various editions of *Congressional Quarterly Almanac* (Washington D.C.: Government Printing Office).

Note: N of cases for 1957–58 = 407, 1959–60 = 410, 1965–66 = 407, 1969–70 = 380, 1975–76 = 395, and 1981–82 = 400.

***$p \leq .001$ **$p \leq .01$ (one-tailed tests)

TABLE 3. Effects of Party, Region, Race, and Urbanization on House Members' Support for Federal Voting Rights on Final Passage: Logit Estimates

Variables		Unstandardized	*t*-ratio
Members' Political Party			
1957–58	(85th Congress)	−.436	1.011
1959–60	(86th Congress)	−.697	1.446
1965–66	(89th Congress)	−.405	1.055
1969–70	(91st Congress)	1.769	8.069***
1975–76	(94th Congress)	1.911	5.851***
1981–82	(97th Congress)	2.134	4.805***
Region			
1957–58	(85th Congress)	5.563	7.947***
1959–60	(86th Congress)	4.353	9.940***
1965–66	(89th Congress)	3.415	8.777***
1969–70	(91st Congress)	2.760	5.630***
1975–76	(94th Congress)	2.150	5.709***
1981–82	(97th Congress)	1.730	3.709***
Percent Urban			
1957–58	(85th Congress)	.032	3.632***
1959–60	(86th Congress)	.006	1.950*
1965–66	(89th Congress)	.018	2.575**
1969–70	(91st Congress)	.003	.712
1975–76	(94th Congress)	.009	1.900*
1981–82	(97th Congress)	.008	1.087
Percent Black			
1957–58	(85th Congress)	.009	.331
1959–60	(86th Congress)	−.046	3.443***
1965–66	(89th Congress)	.003	.240
1969–70	(91st Congress)	−.006	.482
1975–76	(94th Congress)	−.007	.623
1981–82	(97th Congress)	−.001	.036

Source: Data for federal voting rights legislation comes from various editions of *Congressional Quarterly Almanac* (Washington, D.C.: Government Printing Office).

Note: 2 × log-likelihood: 1957–58 = 197.62, 1959–60 = 213.50, 1965–66 = 264.32, 1969–70 = 407.40, 1975–76 = 321.42, 1981–82 = 215.88.

Model chi-square: 1957–58 = 326.0, $p < .0001$; 1959–60 = 272.0, $p < .0001$; 1965–66 = 174.2, $p < .0001$; 1969–70 = 123.0, $p < .0001$; 1975–76 = 90.2, $p < .0001$; 1981–82 = 51.0, $p < .0001$.

Percent correctly predicted: 1957–58 = 93.0, 1959–60 = 94.15, 1965–66 = 88.1, 1969–70 = 77.5, 1975–76 = 83.4, 1981–82 = 94.0.

Percent reduction in error: 1957–58 = 76.0, 1959–60 = 76.8, 1965–66 = 42.8, 1969–70 = 25.0, 1975–76 = 24.0, 1981–82 = 0.

N of cases for 1959–60 = 395, 1965–66 = 402, 1969–70 = 404, 1975–76 = 411, 1981–82 = 413.

***$p \leq .001$ **$p \leq .01$ *$p \leq .05$ (all one-tailed tests)

As expected, the negative relationship between proportion black in districts and black voting rights shows up in both models in 1960. The relationship is also significant in the amendment model in 1957–58. The finding can be explained by the fact that during this period the vast majority of districts with a relatively large black population were located in the South. And in these districts, as Black observed in his research, congressmen were the most resistant to federal protection of black voting rights.

It was hypothesized that on extensions of the 1965 act there would be a positive linear relationship between the percentage of blacks in districts and congressional support for federal voting rights. The parameter estimates show, however, that the proportion black variable is statistically insignificant once party, region, and urbanization are controlled for. Several factors may help to account for this finding. One explanation may be the perception that representatives have of their constituencies. As Richard Fenno points out in his book *Home Style,* there are different constituencies to represent in a district.[37] Fenno notes that representatives may perceive their constituencies in terms of a nest of concentric circles of which the largest is the geographical constituency (the district), followed by the reelection constituency (voting supporters), then the primary constituency (strongest supporters), and, finally, the personal constituency (closest supporters). A member, for example, may decide to vote in accordance with the wishes of the primary constituency, instead of the geographical one. If this is the case, then a group of white conservative financial supporters in a district with a high proportion of black citizens may be able to influence the member to vote against strong federal voting rights legislation. This may be especially true in those districts in which black voter participation is low, which in turn may cause a legislator to look to his or her personal and primary constituency for guidance in roll call voting.

In addition, members have white constituency opinion to consider when deciding to vote. During the period under investigation there were very few black majority-minority districts nationwide. For example, when the Voting Rights Act came up for renewal in 1981 only 15 of the 435 congressional districts included a majority-black population. Only two (5th District in Georgia, 9th District in Tennessee) of the 15 districts were located in the South. Consequently, if the district is majority-white, and if white opinion in the district is conservative on the issue of federal regulation of voter qualification, then the representative may decide to go with majority sentiments.

But before we dismiss the positive impact of black constituency size on levels of support for federal voting rights, one should consider the possible indirect effect of race. For instance, the impact of the proportion of blacks in districts may be working through partisan channels. It is important to note that black constituency size is a factor in determining whether Democrats or Republicans are initially elected to office. To illustrate, table 4 shows the number of nonsouthern Democrats to nonsouthern Republicans and the number of southern Democrats to southern Republicans in five categories of the percentage of the district population that is black. The data are based on the Congress that voted on the 1982 extension of the Voting Rights Act. As the table reveals, on average Democrats are more likely to be elected to office as the proportion of blacks increases across congressional districts. For instance, nonsouthern Republicans outnumbered nonsouthern Democrats by a ratio of .8 in districts that were less than 10 percent black, and southern Democrats held only a slight edge (ratio = 1.2) over southern Republicans in the smallest-percentage black category. In contrast, virtually all representatives were Democrats in the highest-percentage black category. When blacks make up a sizable proportion of the population in a district, they may join with moderate to liberal whites to elect more Democrats to office. In turn, they reap policy rewards because Democrats are more likely to support policies preferred by blacks than Republicans. Consequently, the percentage of blacks in districts may help explain why party has become so crucial in terms of distinguishing levels of support for federal voting rights legislation.

Furthermore, there may be more prudent ways of examining the relationship between the racial composition of districts and legislator voting behavior on black policy preferences. Research has shown that race in conjunction with urbanization is crucial in explaining legislator responsiveness to black constituents. Previous research has demonstrated that the joint effect of race and urbanization has a powerful effect on support for black-favored legislation. Urban areas provide a setting by which African-Americans can elect to office candidates they prefer. Moreover,

TABLE 4. Number of Nonsouthern Democrats to Nonsouthern Republicans and Number of Southern Democrats to Southern Republicans in the 97th Congress

	Percent Black in District				
	0–9	10–19	20–29	30–39	40+
Nonsouthern Democrats	117	23 (2.1)	9 (9.0)	3	16
Nonsouthern Republicans	140 (0.8)	11	1	—	—
Southern Democrats	13 (1.2)	23 (2.3)	13 (2.2)	15 (1.5)	6 (6.0)
Southern Republicans	11	10	6	10	1

Note: House passage of the 1982 extension of the Voting Rights Act took place in the 97th Congress (1981–82).

Figures in parentheses represent the ratio of Nonsouthern Democrats to Nonsouthern Republicans and the ratio of Southern Democrats to Southern Republicans.

blacks are more likely to feel a greater sense of political empowerment in urban settings than in rural areas.[38] Also, mobilization and organizational efforts are less difficult to develop in urban areas than in rural districts. Finally, the close proximity of blacks in urban areas leads to more effective communication than in rural districts, where there is greater distance between black residents. The cumulative effect of these factors is to give blacks in highly urbanized districts the political leverage needed to induce their representatives to better respond to black interests.[39]

These explanations suggest that the relationship between black district size and legislators' roll call voting behavior cannot be thought of in simplified terms. Many factors must be taken into account before drawing conclusions about the impact of the racial composition of the congressional district. Its effect may be indirect or better measured in other ways.

The Extent of Support for Federal Voting Rights

One of the major objectives of the research in this book is to determine the quality of substantive representation to blacks by evaluating the myriad of ways that House members cast their roll call votes. This concluding section uses the model of voting behavior described in chapter 1 as a guide for investigating differences in voting patterns.

The central question to be addressed is: Do members of the House vary in their commitment to black voting rights during the two stages of the legislative voting process? This is an important question because the quality of substantive representation for blacks may be affected by the way members vote across the various stages of the legislative process. By distinguishing between the way legislators cast their roll call votes on amendments and the final bill, we can learn more about who among representatives supports federal voting rights overall.

The findings in table 5 provide some answers to the question of variation in voting behavior. The table shows a scale that is used to document differences in voting behavior among House members. The scale has been standardized to show the proportion of regional party members who opposed some or all of the amendments then voted for the final bill and those legislators who voted for some or all of the amendments then voted against final passage. Essentially, these patterns of voting behavior are described in cell 2 (low amendment/high final passage) and cell 4 (high amendment/low final passage) of chapter 1. The middle range value of 0.0 represents those lawmakers who display the highest level of consistency in voting behavior. They are the ones who either supported all of the amendments and the final bill or who opposed all of the amendments and the

TABLE 5. Degree of House Members' Support for Federal Voting Rights Legislation from the Amendment to the Final Bill (in percent)

	Oppose Amendments (Support Final Bill)				Support Amendments (Oppose Final Bill)				

1957–58

	−1.0[a]	−.75	−.50	−.25	0.0	+.25	+.50	+.75	+1.00
NSD[b]	—[c]	—	—	5 (6)[d]	87 (109)	—	5 (6)	—	—
NSR	—	—	—	14 (27)	76 (150)	3 (6)	—	—	—
SD	—	—	—	—	87 (84)	—	9 (9)	—	—
SR	—	—	—	—	88 (7)	—	—	—	—

1959–60

	−1.0	−.67	−.33	0.0	+.33	+.67	+1.00
NSD	—	—	5 (9)	94 (163)	—	—	—
NSR	—	—	6 (8)	88 (127)	4 (6)	—	—
SD	—	—	—	94 (91)	—	—	—
SR	—	—	—	100 (7)	—	—	—

1965–66

	−1.0	−.75	−.50	−.25	0.0	+.25	+.50	+.75	+1.00
NSD	—	3 (6)	9 (17)	33 (65)	48 (94)	—	—	—	4 (7)
NSR	—	70 (86)	19 (23)	4 (5)	4 (5)	—	—	—	—
SD	5 (4)	9 (8)	11 (9)	—	54 (46)	17 (15)	—	—	—
SR	—	31 (5)	—	44 (7)	—	—	—	—	—

1969–70

	−1.0	−.67	−.33	0.0	+.33	+.67	+1.00
NSD	3 (5)	10 (17)	13 (21)	72 (118)	—	—	—
NSR	21 (32)	11 (17)	12 (18)	48 (74)	3 (5)	—	—
SD	9 (7)	16 (12)	8 (6)	51 (39)	16 (12)	—	—
SR	15 (4)	—	—	78 (21)	—	—	—

1975–76

	−1.0	−.67	−.33	0.0	+.33	+.67	+1.00
NSD	—	—	6 (11)	91 (172)	—	2 (4)	—
NSR	10 (11)	11 (12)	18 (20)	56 (64)	5 (6)	—	—
SD	5 (4)	—	16 (12)	58 (45)	—	—	—
SR	15 (4)	—	—	62 (16)	—	—	—

1981–82

	−1.0	−.67	−.33	0.0	+.33	+.67	+1.00
NSD	—	—	—	96 (149)	—	—	—
NR	22 (34)	16 (24)	18 (27)	42 (64)	—	—	—
SD	—	13 (9)	16 (11)	66 (45)	—	—	—
SR	26 (10)	21 (8)	—	42 (16)	—	—	—

Note: Support for federal voting rights on amendments is based on the position endorsed by the Leadership Conference on Civil Rights (LCCR) and black members of the House.

[a]Number of amendments used in the analysis for 1957–58 = 4, 1959–60 = 3, 1965–66 = 4, 1969–70 = 3, 1975–76 = 3, 1981–82 = 3 (see app. A for description of amendments).

[b]NSD = nonsouthern Democrats, NSR = nonsouthern Republicans, SD = southern Democrats, SR = southern Republicans.

[c]Dash indicates three cases or less in cell.

[d]Number of cases in parentheses.

final decision bill in the congressional session in which federal voting rights legislation was considered. These representatives would fall in cell 1 (low amendment/low final passage) or cell 3 (high amendment/high final passage) of the model. The scale ranges from -1 (oppose all amendments/support final passage) to +1 (support all amendments/oppose final passage).

There are several findings of significance. One noteworthy finding concerns consistency in voting from amendment to final bill. The highest levels of consistency among the four regional party groups came on votes in 1957–58 and 1959–60. Consistency in support of federal voting rights legislation in those years was relatively high among nonsouthern members and low among southern members. Since 1960 nonsouthern Democrats have maintained a relatively high level of consistency, while consistency levels for other regional party members have declined or have become less stable.

The findings in the table reveal that few members of the House voted to support voting rights amendments then decided to oppose final passage of the bill (plus columns). All things being equal, the voting pattern of voting liberal on amendments and then deciding to oppose the final bill is not a major factor in the real world of congressional voting on federal voting rights.

The pattern of changing voting behavior used most often by legislators is the one described in cell 2. A fair share of voting members opposed one or more of the amendments then decided to vote for the final version of the federal voting rights bill (minus columns). Moreover, this pattern of roll call voting becomes more pronounced across time. For instance, in 1957 less than 5 percent of voting nonsouthern Republicans voted against one or more of the amendments then decided to vote for the final bill. In contrast, on House roll calls in 1981 well over a majority of them voted against some or all of the amendments then decided to vote for the extension of the Voting Rights Act. It is also interesting to note that the *degree* of variation in voting behavior has increased among House Republicans over time. In other words, since 1960 more Republicans have voted against all of the amendments used in this analysis then decided to vote for the final bill. For example, in 1981 nearly one-quarter (23 percent) of voting House Republicans cast their votes against all of the voting rights amendments in the study then later decided to vote for the extension of the act. No Republicans voted in this manner in 1957 or 1960, and less than 5 percent did so in 1965.

An interesting pattern of changing behavior from amendment to final bill is the one displayed by southern Democrats since 1965. It is a well-known fact that blacks vote overwhelmingly for Democratic Party candidates. And yet, on the three extensions of the Voting Rights Act, about one-third of voting southern Democrats chose to give low levels of support for voting rights amendments endorsed by the LCCR. It is interesting to find such a pattern of behavior because blacks are a major part of the "supporting coalition" of southern Democrats. Consequently, support for voting rights legislation can be a means by which southern Democrats can enhance their electoral fortunes. But, as noted earlier, representatives have different perceptions about who is part of his or her supporting coalition. Or some southern Democrats may be attempting to maximize white support by distancing themselves from voting rights on the amendments. Another explanation is provided by Kenny Whitby and Franklin Gilliam Jr., who argue that in the early 1980s some southern Democrats were slow to respond to black constituency interests because their perceptions of the political world continued to be colored by a period during which blacks were not major political actors.[40] Thus, it is conceivable that the pattern of roll call voting may reflect some southern Democrats' conservative beliefs on racial politics, despite the fact that they tend to receive electoral benefits from greater black voter participation.

But do differences in voting behavior relate to the percentage of blacks in districts? That is, do members undergo behavioral change from the amendment to the bill based on the proportion of blacks in their constituencies? To answer that question House members' roll call votes were regressed on the explanatory variables of party, region, and the percentage of blacks in congressional districts.[41] The model takes on the following form:

$$Y = a + b_1 X_1 + b_2 X_2 + b_3 X_3 + e \tag{2}$$

where:

Y is a dichotomous variable coded as 1 if the representative opposed a majority of the amendments in the analysis then voted for the final bill, 0 if not. The analysis is conducted for each of the six congresses in which voting rights legislation was considered and passed.

   a is the constant.

   X_1 is coded as a dichotomous variable: 1 if the member is a
      Republican, 0 if a Democrat.

   X_2 is a dummy variable: 1 if the representative is from the South,
      0 if from the non-South.

   X_3 is the proportion of African-Americans in the congressional
      district.

   e is the error term.

It is expected that b_1, b_2, and $b_3 \geq 0$; that is, House Republicans will be more likely to oppose voting rights amendments then later decide to vote for final passage than House Democrats. Likewise, it is predicted that a similar pattern of voting behavior will more likely occur among southern representatives than among nonsouthern legislators. The nature of the relationship between changing voting behavior and the proportion of blacks in districts is less certain. If behavioral change occurs, however, on the basis of the district's black population size, then one would expect that it might take place in districts in which a higher percentage of black constituents reside. The rationale here is that few representatives will risk voting against a final passage voting rights bill for fear of electoral reprisal from their black constituents. Instead, they might try to water down a bill by voting for diluting amendments then voting for the bill claiming that they are supporters of federal voting rights. If this relationship exists, it should occur on extensions of the Voting Rights Act in which black political influence and participation is likely to weigh more in the decision calculation of House members. The signs of the coefficients should be positive, which would support the contention that representatives who are more likely to oppose amendments then later decide to vote for final passage will be from the Republican Party, from the South, and from districts containing a relatively high proportion of black constituents.

Logistic regression results are reported in table 6. The model is statistically significant in each of the four most recent congresses. In general, the findings on party and region are consistent with the patterns observed in table 5. The explanatory variable that has the biggest impact on the probability of legislators changing their behavior on federal voting rights is partisanship. The party variable is statistically significant at the .001 level for the four most recent congresses.

Table 6 suggests that Republicans quite often engage in the practice of voting for diluting amendments before supporting the final passage of a federal voting rights bill. Region also significantly affects the extent of voting rights support. On House roll calls in 1975 and 1981 southern members were more likely to vote against the preferred position on federal voting rights amendments then vote for passage of the final bill. It is worth noting that most of the southern representatives who supported diluting amendments were Democrats, not Republicans, because the latter were generally opposed to federal voting rights legislation regardless of the stage of the legislative voting process. It is also interesting to note that this pattern of voting behavior occurred in the more recent extensions of the act. The results indicate that there is still a blend of conservatism and progressivism in the voting behavior of many southern Democrats on issues of race.

As for the proportion black variable, the findings run contrary to expectations. A systematic pattern of voting variability does emerge from the data, but it comes from legislators who represent districts with a small proportion of black citizens. Though the statistical significance of the percent black variable is underwhelming, nonetheless, it does exist and cannot be dismissed as simply a random occurrence.

TABLE 6. Effects of Party, Region, Race on Behavioral Change among House Members from the Amendment to the Final Bill: Logit Estimates

Variables		Unstandardized	t-ratio
Members' Political Party			
1957–58	(85th Congress)	1.962	1.611
1959–60	(86th Congress)	.818	.817
1965–66	(89th Congress)	3.132	9.690***
1969–70	(91st Congress)	.771	3.154***
1975–76	(94th Congress)	1.524	4.358***
1981–82	(97th Congress)	1.997	3.352***
Region			
1957–58	(85th Congress)	1.022	.932
1959–60	(86th Congress)	.463	.505
1965–66	(89th Congress)	−.424	.940
1969–70	(91st Congress)	.573	1.813*
1975–76	(94th Congress)	1.949	4.627***
1981–82	(97th Congress)	1.219	3.216***
Percent Black			
1957–58	(85th Congress)	.022	.629
1959–60	(86th Congress)	−.043	.661
1965–66	(89th Congress)	−.063	2.093**
1969–70	(91st Congress)	−.027	2.142**
1975–76	(94th Congress)	−.031	1.700*
1981–82	(97th Congress)	−.033	2.000**

Note: 2 × log-likelihood: 1957–58 = .68, 1959–60 = 52.6, 1965–66 = 292.8, 1969–70 = 449.2, 1975–76 = 254.2, 1981–82 = 368.0.

Model chi-square: 1957–58 = 3.3, $p < .3439$ (statistically insignificant); 1959–60 = 2.0, $p < .6107$ (statistically insignificant); 1965–66 = 176.0, $p < .0001$; 1969–70 = 21.2, $p < .0001$; 1975–76 = 41.6, $p < .0001$; 1981–82 = 76.8, $p < .0001$.

Percent correctly predicted: 1957–58 = 98.0, 1959–60 = 98.0, 1965–66 = 86.0, 1969–70 = 77.0, 1975–76 = 89.0, 1981–82 = 78.0.

Percent reduction in error: 1957–558 = 0, 1959–60 = 0, 1965–66 = 39.0, 1969–70 = 10.0, 1975–76 = 4.0, 1981–82 = 8.0.

Federal Voting Rights legislation: behavioral change is defined as roll calls on which a member opposed a majority of the amendments and supported final passage of the bill in a given Congress.

***$p \le .01$ **$p \le .05$ *$p \le .10$ (one-tailed tests for party and region, two-tailed test for percent black)

Discussion

The essence of representation is that those who are selected through a formal institutional arrangement (e.g., elections) will serve as the faithful agents of their constituents. For decades after the end of Reconstruction, however, some states, especially in the South, employed a variety of practices designed systematically to exclude blacks from the electorate. As a consequence of low black voter registration and participation, blacks were unable positively to affect the roll call voting decision of their representatives. It was not until the black protest activities began in the mid-1950s that a concerted effort was again made by Congress to provide some protection for blacks' rights to vote. Although two civil rights bills were passed in 1957 and 1960, it was the Voting Rights Act of 1965 that had a significant impact on successfully dismantling what has been termed the "first generation" of overt barriers to black voter registration and participation.

This chapter examined the extent to which there is a relationship between representatives' behavior and support for federal voting rights. The results reveal that the congruence between members' roll call voting behavior and federal voting rights is based largely upon party, region, and, to a lesser extent, the proportion of urban citizens residing in the district. Party affiliation now appears to be the major source of voting cleavage in Congress on the issue of federal voting rights. This finding is noteworthy because of recent Republican gains in Congress especially after the 1994 and 1996 elections in which the party held a majority of the seats in both chambers of Congress. The Voting Rights Act is once again up for congressional consideration in the year 2007. The renewal of the act may well depend on the party composition of Congress in that year.

The findings do not reveal that the proportion of black residents in a district directly relates to support for black voting rights. Some caution should be used, however, in interpreting the results. The impact of race may be more indirect than direct. For example, as the proportion of blacks in a district rises, the greater is the likelihood that a Democrat will be elected to office. And, as the analysis clearly illustrates, Democrats are more likely to support federal protection of minority voting rights than are Republicans. Consequently, it is critical to understand the impact of black constituency influence in more general terms.

The results of the analysis also reveal that the extent of support for federal voting rights varies between the two stages of the legislative voting process. Patterns of voting variability are related to party, region, and, to a lesser extent, the size of the black population in a district. It must be underlined that a causal argument cannot be made unequivocally for a practice of deceptive voting. That is, while it is true that some representatives might deliberately attempt to subterfuge voting rights legislation before a final vote is taken on the bill, others may be engaging in sincere behavior; the final version of the bill may reflect their sincere position on the issue. The most relevant point to be made here is that the quality of representation for African-Americans can be affected by the way legislators cast their roll call votes throughout the legislative process, regardless of the lawmaker's intent.

In collective terms congressional protection of black voting rights has grown since the mid-1950s. But extensions of the 1965 act have not been entirely free from controversy. As illustrated in the analysis, a sizable contingency of the House delegation (Republicans and some southern Democrats) has attempted to weaken the bill with diluting amendments. Even the 1982 law, which enjoyed widespread and bipartisan support on final roll call, saw raucous debates over some key provisions. The debates were not specifically directed at the premise of the law but were efforts designed to water the law down with amendments or kill the law on procedural grounds. For example, southern Republicans attempted to dispose of the provision for federal preclearance of all voting law changes because they felt that it singled out southern states for federal violations. They argued that there was no need for the provision because discriminatory voting practices no longer existed. But there is considerable evidence to suggest otherwise. It now appears that a "second generation" of voter discrimination is becoming more prevalent in the United States. This kind of electoral discrimination exists when state and local public officials design electoral systems to dilute the voting strength of racial minorities. From 1965 through 1980 the Justice Department vetoed over eight hundred proposed changes in election laws and redistricting.[42] In some cases local governments were still attempting to dilute black voting strength by altering election districts' boundaries. The controversy over provisions within voting rights laws appears to have an endless future, as complaints and lawsuits continue to be heard by the federal government concerning attempts by local governmental bodies to dilute black voting power or to limit the opportunities for blacks to choose black public officials by such changes as shifts to at-large local elections and legislative redistricting to divide black voters among a number of districts.[43] Thus, the major battles now appear to be directed more at enforcement of the law to preserve hard-earned fundamental rights of citizenship.

This chapter instructs us that there are some lessons that can be learned from the first Reconstruction. It is important to keep in mind that the end of the first Reconstruction was not due simply to the fact that some whites hated blacks. Instead, as J. Morgan Kousser, a leading authority on Reconstruction policy, reminds us, "black voting rights and even legalized segregation were more matters of racial *power* than of unthinking racial *animosity*."[44] Kousser goes on to point out that "a decline in the overall level of white racism, which has obviously occurred since 1960, does not guarantee the fair treatment of racial minorities if, as in the nineteenth century, national legal and judicial safeguards were to be removed."[45] Until there is sufficient evidence to show that the United States is moving toward a color-blind society, then it would seem unwise for Congress to retreat from protecting minority voting rights. A society in which race-conscious voting is prevalent needs race-conscious remedies to bring about some fairness.

Of course, Congress is not the only key actor in the process of guaranteeing effective voting power for blacks and other minority groups. The effectiveness of voting rights legislation requires the forceful personal involvement of many governmental officials—most notably, the president, the courts, and the Department of Justice. While passage of voting rights bills does not guarantee implementation of their provisions, they are a crucial step in the direction of providing simple justice to all American citizens.

CHAPTER 3

The Quest for Equal Opportunity

In view of the Constitution, in the eyes of the law, there is in this country no superior, dominant, ruling class of citizens. There is no caste here. Our Constitution is color-blind, and neither knows nor tolerates classes among citizens. . . . The law regards man as man, and takes no account of his surroundings or of his color when his civil rights as guaranteed by the supreme law of the land are involved.
—Justice John Harlan, sole dissenting opinion in *Plessy v. Ferguson*

There was widespread hope among civil rights activists that the legislative enactments of the 1960s would create a more equitable world for all U.S. citizens. To some degree progress has been made toward fulfilling the American creed of full equality. But, as we shall see, old habits die slowly. There is sufficient evidence to show that the racial dilemma still persists in contemporary America. It is therefore important to examine congressional responsiveness, as a key facet of policy-making, beyond the realm of voting into the broader field of civil rights policy.

This chapter begins with a brief overview of the troubling history surrounding the black struggle for equality in the United States. Though the overview is brief, it is important, because the sound piece of civil rights legislation drafted and passed in 1964 owes some of its appeal to the accomplishments of the Reconstruction congresses of the 1860s and 1870s. It was during this period that the Thirteenth, Fourteenth, and Fifteenth Amendments were passed, which introduced equal rights principles into U.S. constitutional law. It was also during the Reconstruction era that important civil rights laws were written that would later serve as the foundation for incorporating important provisions within the 1964 law. The next section discusses major civil rights laws enacted over the past four decades, followed by a discussion of the continuing problems of discrimination against blacks in the areas of education, employment, housing, and public accommodations. The final part of this chapter is devoted to a systematic investigation of congressional responsiveness to black policy preferences. The analysis is similar to the one conducted in the previous chapter.

Again, the goal is to determine with greater accuracy patterns of congressional voting as they pertain to the four different combinations of voting behavior in the model presented in chapter 1.

The Evolution of Civil Rights Policy

The constitutional amendments passed immediately after the Civil War were designed to integrate the freed slaves into the political and social order on the basis of legal equality. In 1865 Congress passed the Thirteenth Amendment to the U.S. Constitution, which prohibited slavery and involuntary servitude (except as a punishment of crime) in the United States or its territories. In addition to the Thirteenth Amendment, one year later Congress passed the Civil Rights Act of 1866. It was specifically designed to provide a permanent guarantee of rights for freed blacks. Most notably, the law gave the national government some authority over the treatment of blacks by state officials. The act was a response to the "Black Codes," laws passed by the southern state governments after the Civil War that bore a disturbing resemblance to the antebellum slave codes. The Black Codes were primarily aimed at blacks, preventing them from testifying in court against whites, limiting their opportunities to find work, and containing harsh vagrancy and apprenticeship laws that forced many blacks into a state of peonage. In essence they were designed to relegate blacks to the position of second-class citizenship in the United States.

By far the Fourteenth Amendment was the most comprehensive of the three Civil War constitutional amendments. It states:

> No State shall make or enforce any law which shall abridge the privileges or immunities of citizens of the United States; nor shall any State deprive any person of life, liberty, or property, without due process of law; nor deny to any person within its jurisdiction the equal protection of the laws.

To enforce provisions within the Fourteenth Amendment Congress passed the Civil Rights Act of 1875. The act guaranteed that all persons were entitled to the full and equal enjoyment of public accommodations in inns, transportation facilities, and places of amusement. Furthermore, the law punished any person who denied others equal access in these places.

It would be difficult to compose legislation that would confer full equality to each U.S. citizen than that of the Civil War Amendments and the Civil Rights Acts of 1866 and 1875. But, from the perspective of the U.S. Supreme Court, civil rights policy meant something different from what the Reconstruction Congresses had envisioned. In a series of decisions over a two-decade period the Supreme Court vindicated federal power to protect civil rights for blacks and thus helped to effectuate the end of Reconstruction and the beginning of racial segregation in the South. The most notable U.S. Supreme Court decisions included: (1) the *Slaughterhouse Cases* [1873]; (2) the *Civil Rights Cases* [1883]; (3) *Hurtado v. California* [1884]; and (4) *Plessy v. Ferguson* [1896].[1]

It is interesting to note that neither the plaintiffs nor the defendants were black in the *Slaughterhouse Cases* of 1873. Nonetheless, the Court's decision in this case was one of the major reasons for the rapid deterioration of black social and political gains. The case involved the privileges and immunities clause of the Fourteenth Amendment. At issue was a law in the state of Louisiana that conferred a butchering monopoly of livestock to one slaughterhouse in the city of New Orleans and surrounding parishes. A group of independent butchering businesses adversely affected by the law brought suit in the Louisiana courts asserting, among other things, that the law was unconstitutional on the grounds that it violated the privileges and immunities clause of the Fourteenth Amendment by depriving them of their livelihood. The Supreme Court of Louisiana upheld the constitutionality of the state law. The court reasoned that the law constituted a legitimate exercise of the police power of the state. The plaintiffs in the dispute appealed the Louisiana court decision to the U.S. Supreme Court. In its decision the U.S. Supreme Court drew a sharp distinction between national citizenship and state citizenship. In making the distinction, the Court dismissed the claims of the excluded butchers on the grounds that the Fourteenth Amendment did not prohibit a state from abridging the privileges and immunities of "citizens of the states." Instead, according the Court, the amendment meant that the states could not violate the civil liberties and civil rights of "citizens of the United States." The Court's narrow interpretation of the privileges and immunities clause meant that the Fourteenth Amendment did nothing to alter the fact that the protection of life, liberty, and property that citizens were entitled to remained within the jurisdiction of the states. In effect, if blacks felt discriminated against within a state, they could not claim protection under the Fourteenth Amendment because it applied only to national citizenship and not state citizenship. This meant that southern states were free to legislate on civil rights matters without interference from the federal government.

In the *Civil Rights Cases* (1883) the Court again acted adversely to black interests when it declared the Civil Rights Act of 1875 unconstitutional. The Court held that Congress did not possess the requisite power to pass a law prohibiting discrimination practiced by private individuals— that is, owners and managers of public accommodations and facilities. The logic behind the Court's ruling was that the Fourteenth Amendment did not give Congress the power to prevent discrimination in privately owned accommodations because the amendment referred only to state action ("No *State* shall . . . nor shall any *State* . . ."). According to the Court's interpretation of the Fourteenth Amendment, the provisions within the Civil Rights Act of 1875 that imposed a penalty for discrimination in privately owned accommodations applied only to discrimination practiced by the states, not individuals.

The U.S. Supreme Court continued its assault on federal protection of civil rights in *Hurtado v. California* (1884). In its decision the Court made it clear that the due process clause of the Fourteenth Amendment did not make the Bill of Rights binding upon state governments. The Reconstruction Congress that wrote and adopted the Fourteenth Amendment clearly intended for it to guarantee all individuals in America all of the freedoms of the Bill of Rights against infringement by the states. But the Supreme Court decided that the amendment did not incorporate the Bill of Rights so as to make it a limitation on state power. In ruling that the states did not have to honor the Fifth Amendment's requirement that individuals be indicted by a grand jury before being tried for a capital offense, the Court in effect was saying that the states did not have to observe Bill of Rights freedoms under the due process clause of the Fourteenth Amendment. This court ruling meant that there would be no nationalization of the Bill of Rights during this period. It would take a number of court rulings over the next several decades to reverse the Court's decision and nationalize the Bill of Rights under the due process clause of the Fourteenth Amendment.[2]

The ultimate abandonment of federal civil rights protection came in 1896, with the legal sanctioning of the "separate but equal" doctrine. By the 1890s most of the former Confederate states had enacted Jim Crow laws requiring separate but equal facilities for blacks and whites on passenger trains. Louisiana was one of the states to enact such a law. When Homer Plessy, who was one-eighth black, refused to leave a section of a railway passenger car compartment reserved for whites only, he was arrested and convicted for his actions. Plessy appealed his conviction to the U.S. Supreme Court. The Court rejected Plessy's arguments, finding no constitutional objection to the Louisiana law requiring separate railway coaches, provided that blacks were furnished accommodations equal to those of whites.[3] Separation of the races on a legal basis was thus legitimized by the high court and was rapidly extended to schools and most other social institutions.

By the turn of the twentieth century the states of the Old Confederacy had erected a system that replaced slavery with segregation. Before 1900 the only segregated law adopted by the majority of southern states was that applying to railway passenger cars. Afterward segregation between blacks and whites came to include public schools, theaters, restaurants, hotels, public parks, recreation facilities, streetcars, restrooms, and homes for the indigent and the aged. Legally sanctioned segregation in the South was now firmly entrenched, and the dreams and hopes of first-class citizenship for blacks had sunk to a cruel nadir. Segregation became a way of life for blacks and shadowed them throughout their lives—from birth in segregated hospitals to burial in segregated graveyards.

As the Court defended and gave constitutional legitimacy to racial segregation during the late nineteenth century, Congress remained unwilling to act on behalf of black citizens. Control over race relations was once again under the complete jurisdiction of the states. As noted previously, Congress passed no civil rights statute during this time period and would not do so until 1957. To be sure, the federal judiciary's legal sanctioning of segregation was, to a large degree, responsible for the worsening political and social conditions of blacks; equally to blame was Congress' refusal to enforce its own reconstruction policy mandate.

Though the flame of equality by law had been reduced to a mere flicker at the turn of the twentieth century, forces were slowly at work to begin bringing about a few legal victories and positive political changes for blacks. Two events helped to improve black political prospects: (1) the founding of the National Association for the Advancement of Colored People (NAACP) in 1909; (2) the heavy migration of blacks out of the South to northern cities. The foundation of the NAACP was important because it gave blacks the organizational strength needed to campaign for black equality through legal action. The NAACP's first major victory came in 1915, when the U.S. Supreme Court struck down laws aimed at denying blacks their right to vote.[4] The general exodus of over 700,000 blacks from the South to northern cities between 1900 and 1920 was important because it gave them some political power.[5] As one writer on the political significance of the migration noted, "the move was more than a simple migration and change in folkways; for blacks, it was a move, almost literally, from no voting to voting."[6] Bargaining with urban political machines meant that blacks could trade votes in return for jobs in the city bureaucracy. The practice of logrolling between blacks and urban machine politicians was beneficial for blacks during World War I because of the demand for workers to fill the labor shortage caused by the war effort. This is not to say that the social and economic conditions for blacks improved significantly when they migrated from the South. To be sure, black poverty levels were high, and residential segregation between blacks and whites was widespread. But, as one political scientist has stated, "at least blacks could vote and attend better schools, and were not obliged to step off the sidewalk into the gutter when a white man approached."[7]

The political implications of the black migration to northern cities became more apparent when, in 1928, the black residents of Chicago elected the first black representative since 1900, Oscar DePriest, to the U.S. House of Representatives. The election sent a signal to white politicians in urban areas that the black vote could not to be taken for granted. This was especially true in presidential contests because of the method for selecting the chief executive. In other words, when most blacks moved to the North and West, they settled in the key states of New York, New Jersey, Pennsylvania, Ohio, California, Illinois, and Michigan. These states were important to the black struggle for equality because of the winner-take-all provision in the electoral college. The fact that blacks now resided in these states meant that they constituted an important voting bloc that could not be ignored by most candidates who aspired to become president of the United States. When blacks broke their historic allegiance to the Republican Party and joined Franklin Roosevelt's New Deal coalition in 1932, they were able to obtain some positions in the lower federal bureaucracy for helping Roosevelt to become president of the United States. While Roosevelt was no strong supporter of civil rights, blacks benefited to some degree from the social and economic programs of the New Deal (provisions for social security, old-age pensions and relief programs, public housing projects, and minimum wage laws) under his presidential administration.

Between 1940 and 1950 there was once again a significant migration of blacks from the South to the North. More than 1,500,000 blacks migrated north, mainly because of the expansion of the defense industry during World War II.[8] When blacks saw few signs that the rigid antiblack policy in the defense industry was undergoing any change, they developed a plan for drastic action. Under the leadership of A. Phillip Randolph, the president of the Brotherhood of Sleeping Car Porters, blacks demanded that their government do something to ensure the employment of blacks in defense industries. Specifically, Randolph requested that Roosevelt issue a proclamation barring discrimination against blacks in defense industries with government contracts. When Roosevelt was slow to issue such a decree, Randolph threatened to lead a massive march of blacks on Washington. In June 1941 Roosevelt acquiesced and issued an executive order establishing a Fair Employment Practices Commission and prohibiting discrimination by race in defense industries and the government.[9]

World War II aided the black struggle for equality in another important way. The war gave blacks the irrefutable moral claim to equality in the United States. It was difficult for the nation to ignore the stark contrast between the condemnation of Nazi racism in American wartime propaganda and the reality of the black experience in the States. The nation's profession of democratic ideals during the war simply did not coincide with the reality of racial inequality in the United States.

Harry Truman's commitment to civil rights equality was stronger than any president before him in the twentieth century. When President Truman submitted legislation to Congress proposing to enforce civil rights, Congress was unwilling to act. In 1948 Truman issued an executive order creating a fair employment board in the Civil Service Commission and mandated equal treatment "without regard to race, color, religion or national origin" in the military.[10] As a consequence of Truman's actions, blacks and whites were immediately integrated at military installations throughout the country. Desegregation of the armed services meant that blacks and whites for the first time were forced to live and work together under federal mandate. Truman's push for racial equality did not end with desegregating the military. During the 1948 Democratic Party convention Truman urged his party's members to adopt a civil rights plank in their platform. His request for civil rights legislation to promote racial equality got nowhere and even led many southern Democrats to leave the party and form the conservative states' rights Dixiecrat Party, with then Democrat Strom Thurmond as its presidential candidate.[11]

Ironically, of the three national branches of the government it was the Supreme Court, not Congress or the president, that took the lead in attempting to protect the civil rights of blacks in the twentieth century. The governmental institution that once defended and gave constitutional legitimacy to racial segregation gradually began to declare laws such as the Grandfather clause and the "White Primary" unconstitutional. The executive branch was next to join the fight against racial inequality in the United States. President Roosevelt's Executive Order 8802 created a Committee on Fair Employment Practices with authority over businesses working for the federal government. The actions of Roosevelt's successor, Harry Truman, were more assertive and significant. In 1948 he boldly ordered an end to racial segregation in the military, and he outlawed racial discrimination in the federal government.

Thus, the stage was set for major public policy changes in the area of civil rights. A variety of forces during the century had been at work to undermine the old regime of segregation. The founding of the NAACP, the migration of massive numbers of blacks from the South to the North, and the strategic location of black voters in key states outside the South had far-reaching political implications. Furthermore, the end of the South's total dependence on cotton was an important factor in improving black political conditions. So long as "King Cotton" flourished as it had between 1876 and 1892, there would be a need for a large force of menial laborers (namely, blacks). Yet its demise—as a consequence of such factors as black out-migration, the Great Depression, and mechanization of southern agriculture—meant greater freedom for blacks to organize and generate the political leverage necessary to begin breaking the racial stalemate in the South.[12] Finally, the nation's profession of democratic ideals had always been inconsistent with the status accorded to blacks since their coming to America. Moreover, as the nation became more involved in international affairs after World War II, with its profession of respect for human rights to the rest of the world, political leaders became increasingly sensitive to outside criticism about racial inequality in the United States. These factors, in combination, constituted a set of realities that made it increasingly evident that the southern way of life was inconsistent with the American liberal tradition of equality of rights for persons regardless of their race, sex, or ethnic background.

In sum, the black struggle for first-class citizenship proceeded on many fronts over a long period of time after *Plessy v. Ferguson.* Despite some successes, segregation was very much alive in the South. It would take the persistent efforts of black leaders throughout the 1950s and 1960s to induce members of Congress to pass effective civil rights legislation.

The Civil Rights Struggle and Congressional Action

Overcoming congressional barriers to racial equality after Reconstruction was a slow and difficult task for blacks. Some of the difficulty emanated from the division of sovereignty that gave the states, and denied the federal government, a comprehensive policing power with respect to the private rights of one individual against another. Furthermore, southern Democrats' control of key congressional committees and a conservative coalition between southerners and Republicans meant the graveyard for civil rights legislation for decades after Reconstruction. Even the campaign to enact federal laws to protect blacks against lynching met strong resistance in Congress. To illustrate, throughout most of the first half of the twentieth century Congress did not pass any federal antilynching legislation.[13]

The civil rights movement was the major impetus for change. Lunch counter sit-ins protesting segregated eating facilities, bus boycotts protesting laws requiring that blacks sit at the back of the bus, and freedom marches all captured the public's attention and revealed the contradiction between the American liberal tradition of equal rights for all and racial discrimination. Black protest activities during the 1950s met with some success when Congress passed two minor voting rights laws in 1957 and

1960. As insurgency activities gained momentum during the early 1960s, blacks were able to mount growing public support to get more civil rights issues placed higher on the national political agenda.[14]

Arguably, no single event galvanized public support for the civil rights cause more than the one that took place in Birmingham, Alabama, in 1963. In May public safety commissioner Eugene "Bull" Connor ordered police to unleash dogs to attack black demonstrators. The event was vividly portrayed in the media. National anger grew over the violent reactions by white segregationists to peaceful marches in Birmingham.[15] Photographs of fire hoses and police dogs turned on blacks were symbolic of the crisis.

The violence contributed to the civil rights cause in two important ways. First, President John F. Kennedy, a reluctant participant in the cause for civil rights before the summer of 1963, responded to the violence by moving civil rights legislation to the top of his priority list.[16] In June President Kennedy sent a comprehensive civil rights package to Congress, proposing that blacks be guaranteed access to public accommodations; that the federal government be allowed to file suit to desegregate public schools; that federal funds be cut off in areas using them for segregated programs; and that federal machinery be provided to prevent businesses receiving federal contracts from discriminating on the basis of race or national origin. Second, the Birmingham crisis contributed to the massive participation that summer, by both blacks and whites, to the "March on Washington," in which the Reverend Martin Luther King Jr. delivered his widely acclaimed "I Have a Dream" speech. The triumphant march on August 2, 1963, attracted 250,000 participants, one of the largest gatherings in the history of the nation's capital.

The events of that year, including the bombing and deaths of four black girls at the Sixteenth Street Baptist Church in Birmingham and the murder of Medgar Evers, state chairman of the NAACP in Mississippi, were major factors in propelling both President Kennedy and Congress into action despite southern opposition. Before Kennedy could see the final outcome of his plan, he was assassinated, on November 22, 1963, in Dallas, Texas. In memory of his predecessor President Lyndon Johnson stated:

> no memorial oration or eulogy could more eloquently honor President Kennedy's memory than the earliest possible passage of the civil rights bill for which he fought so long. We have talked long enough in this country about equal rights. We have talked for one hundred years or more. It is time now to write the chapter—and to write it in the books of law.[17]

In February of the following year the House, by a vote margin of 290 to 130, approved a bipartisan civil rights bill. Most of the opposition came from southern representatives. Of the 115 voting members of the southern House delegation, only 11 southern congressmen voted for the bill. The House bill was sent directly to the Senate floor, where southern senators began a filibuster against it. The major concern of proponents of the bill was whether there would be enough votes in the Senate to end the filibuster. In June, by a vote of 71 to 29, cloture was invoked and the filibuster ended. The cloture vote marked the first time in American history that a filibuster directed at blocking civil rights legislation had been broken. Subsequently, on June 19, 1964, the Senate approved the legislation by a roll call vote of 73 to 27.

The Civil Rights Act of 1964 represents the first attempt by Congress, and by far its best effort since the Civil Rights Act of 1875, to bring equal opportunity to black citizens. The landmark law was comprehensive in its coverage; its eleven sections: (1) strengthened voting laws to make it difficult to use devices such as literacy tests; (2) barred discrimination in public facilities and public accommodations; (3) authorized the attorney general to bring suit to desegregate public facilities; (4) authorized the attorney general to bring suit to desegregate public schools; (5) authorized the attorney general to bring suit for individuals incapable of doing so themselves and established a four-year Commission on Civil Rights; (6) barred discrimination in activities receiving federal assistance and provided for withdrawal of federal funds where noncompliance continued; (7) banned discrimination in employment by employers, employment, agencies and labor unions and created an Equal Employment Opportunity Commission; (8) required compilation of voter registration and voting statistics; (9) permitted the attorney general to intervene in any civil rights lawsuit begun in a federal court; (10) established a Community Relations Service; and (11) provided for jury trials and penalties for criminal contempt arising out of enforcement of the act.[18]

It is important to note that the amending stage was crucial to the strength and success of the 1964 Civil Rights Act. Diluting amendments had to be defeated and filibustering brought to an end. Even before the assassination of Kennedy, Congress deserves credit for initiating legislation to strengthen weak sections in the administration's bill. Under the Kennedy plan, for example, federal government authority to prohibit employment discrimination would only apply to businesses obtaining government contracts. Legislation initiated by House members added to the administration's proposal by extending the reach and scope of federal authority to ban discrimination in both the private and public sectors. Also, it was action in the House of Representatives that led to the establishment of the Equal Employment Opportunities Commission (EEOC) to investigate charges of employment discrimination.[19] The EEOC was later delegated powers to enforce fair employment practices.[20] The Senate also initiated actions to strengthen provisions in the law. Kennedy's original version contained language that would have "authorized" federal officials to cut off federal funds in local areas that used them for segregated programs. The Senate changed the language so that federal authorities would be "required," not just authorized, to cut off federal dollars. The change in language is significant because it provided the federal government with a powerful weapon to induce recalcitrant local public authorities to desegregate public schools in order to receive needed federal financial assistance.

Several civil rights bills have been enacted into law since the passage of the Civil Rights Act of 1964. The most notable ones pertain to fair housing and equal employment. The Civil Rights Act of 1968 prohibits discrimination in housing. More specifically, Title VIII of the act, commonly referred to as the Fair Housing Act of 1968, bans discrimination in the sale, rental, financing, or advertising of housing, based on race, color, religion, national origin, and, as amended in 1974, sex. Only dwellings of four units or fewer sold without the services of a broker were exempted from the law. The act was again amended in 1988 to extend coverage to the handicapped and to families with children. The Fair Housing Act of 1988 also gives the Department of Housing and Urban Development (HUD) the authority to penalize those who discriminate in the sale or rental of housing. Under the 1968 law HUD could only attempt to mediate disputes, while the Justice Department could bring suits against individuals for a pattern of housing discrimination. Fair housing laws cover more than three-fourths of all housing transactions. They do not cover apartment houses in which the owner maintains a residence, private clubs, and religious organizations providing housing for their members or homeowners selling their property without a real estate agent.

Another major piece of legislation is the Civil Rights Act of 1991, which focuses on employment discrimination. The bill was enacted into law after a two-year struggle between President George Bush and Congress. In 1990 Bush had vetoed job legislation by calling it a "quota" bill. The aim of the bill is to place a greater burden on employers to justify practices that adversely affect racial minorities and women. Employers must show that a discriminatory policy was a business necessity.

Continuing Discrimination

Since the 1960s Congress has passed legislation beneficial to African-Americans. Although congressional responsiveness to black interests has increased in recent decades, there remain signs of continuing white resistance to equal treatment for blacks. To be sure, most overt laws and practices have been eliminated.[21] But there is sufficient evidence to show that blacks face continuing discrimination in many areas they sought to correct during the civil rights movement.

Equal Educational Opportunity

In education the 1964 Civil Rights Act gave the Justice Department the authority to pursue school desegregation through litigation, negotiation, and federal fund termination in order to end government acts of discrimination—that is, de jure segregation. But in many school districts de facto school segregation (racial segregation that "in fact" exists but is not condoned by law) is widespread. Racially imbalanced schools are largely a function of residential segregation, and the problem is particularly acute in most metropolitan areas.[22] The migration of whites from inner cities to the suburbs, coupled with the withdrawal of white children from public to private schools, has resulted in central city schools being dominated by minority students and suburban schools being populated largely by white students. Often the quality of education suffers more in central city school districts because of a lack of funding. Since schools in many states generate much of their revenue from property taxes, and since the value of property tends to be higher in suburban areas of cities, this usually means suburban schools have more funds to spend on instructional materials for students and on repairs and maintenance of school buildings.[23]

The existence of separate central city and suburban schools districts has further exacerbated the problem of racial integration of the schools. In Boston, for example, school administrators were found guilty of deliberately building school facilities and drawing school districts "to increase racial segregation."[24] A major effect of de facto school segregation is that in many of the nation's cities there has been a dramatic decline in the number of white students in public schools. To illustrate, in Atlanta, Georgia, the number of white students in public schools fell from fifty thousand in the 1960s to four thousand by the early 1990s.[25]

Studies have also shown that, even where desegregation of schools does exist, "second-generation discrimination" (racial isolation in schools that give the outward appearance of racial balance) is becoming more prevalent in schools. The placing of a disproportionate number of blacks in underfunded classes for educable mentally retarded students infers a motivating factor of perpetuating second-class education for blacks. Placing black students in separate programs or classes from whites does not necessarily constitute concrete evidence of second-generation discrimination; however, there is evidence to suggest that such practices occur less frequently in school districts in which more blacks are on the school board and in other positions of authority.[26]

Remedial action to redress the problem of de facto segregation has frequently meant court-ordered busing of children to schools, especially when it can be demonstrated that school district lines have been defined in a discriminatory manner.[27] Otherwise, the courts have been reluctant to order cross-district busing to achieve racial balance in the schools.[28] As for the role of Congress, it has passed no law requiring the elimination of de facto segregation and on several occasions has come close to forbidding the use of federal funds to assist busing to achieve racial balance in schools.

Fair Treatment in Public Accommodations

The Civil Rights Act of 1964 prohibits discrimination in the area of public accommodations. All citizens are entitled to equal access to restaurants, bars, theaters, hotels, gas stations, and similar establishments serving the general public. Despite the success of the act in eliminating the most overt practices of discrimination, the practice of unfair treatment against blacks still continues. Some restaurants, stores, and hotels provide better service to white customers.[29] A vivid illustration of the continuing problem of prejudicial treatment in public accommodations is the incident involving a national restaurant chain. In the largest cash settlement to date in this area, Denny's restaurant chain, in 1994, agreed to pay over forty-five million dollars to black customers whose civil rights had been violated by the company. Over four thousand race-bias claims were filed on behalf of black plaintiffs, who charged that Denny's refused to serve them, required them to pay a cover charge on top of the cost of their meals, and asked them to pay before receiving their meals. One of the most damaging claims was filed after an incident in a Denny's in Maryland on April 1, 1993, when a group of black U.S. Secret Service agents were refused service while white agents at the same time were promptly served. Thousands of claims were filed nationwide, and the restaurant settled for a huge cash amount, yet the company insisted that it had no "discriminatory policies or practices."[30]

Fair Housing

The Civil Rights Act of 1968 makes it a crime to refuse to sell or rent a dwelling on the basis of race, religion, ethnicity, or sex. Even so, housing in the United States remains highly segregated. One major reason is the fact that the legacy of discrimination continues in America. One author sums up the problem in the following manner:

> The civil rights law seems to have had little impact on practice, since almost all residential areas are entirely black or white. Most whites prefer it that way . . . black Americans have no illusions about the hurdles they will face. If you look outside your designated areas, you can expect chilly receptions, evasive responses, and outright lies.[31]

A housing discrimination lawsuit filed by the Justice Department helps to illustrate the problem of discrimination in housing. In 1992 landlords of an apartment complex in Mount Clemens, Michigan, were charged with denying housing to blacks when openings were available. The government was able to gather evidence of racial bias by sending out "testers," both black and white, who posed as renters, to the apartments under investigation. Black applicants, or testers, were told by the landlords either that there were no vacancies or there was a long waiting list, whereas white testers were told units were readily available. In 1993 the owners and managers agreed to pay over $300,000 to victims, the largest settlement to date in a lawsuit by the federal government charging discrimination in housing.[32]

The problem of housing discrimination is exacerbated by the lending practices of banks and mortgage companies. A 1990 study by the Federal Reserve Board provides further evidence that racial bias is still a factor in the lending practices of banks. The study of nineteen major cities found that blacks were much more likely to be denied a mortgage loan than were whites, even when high-income black applicants were compared with high-income white applicants. The study found that banks rejected more than twice as many well-paid black applicants.[33]

Various techniques such as *steering, redlining,* and *blockbusting* are used to discriminate against racial minorities in housing. Steering is the practice by real estate agents of showing houses to African-Americans only in black, racially mixed, or deteriorating neighborhoods. Redlining is a cluster of activities engaged in by banks and mortgage companies to discriminate against loan applicants. The practice contributes to housing segregation because lenders are reluctant to grant loans and mortgages to black applicants who want to buy housing in a racially changing or white neighborhood. Blockbusting refers to unscrupulous realtors who sell a home to a black family in order to frighten white homeowners into selling at low prices. The realtor might concoct a tale to white homeowners of rising crime and deteriorating public schools once blacks move into the neighborhood. The "sell before it's too late" rumor causes whites to sell their homes at low prices out of fear of declining property value due to the influx of blacks moving into the area. As whites make an exodus from the neighborhood, the unscrupulous realtor then resells the homes to blacks at higher prices. Consequently, it is not uncommon to find a neighborhood that was previously all white go to being all black. Steering, redlining, and blockbusting are illegal practices, but they continue to be used. The principal effect of these practices is to perpetuate racial residential segregation in the United States.[34]

The Civil Rights Act of 1968 and its amendments in 1974 and 1988 are aimed at granting minorities the full enjoyment of housing opportunities. Although the enforcement provisions of the 1968 law were strengthened in 1988 (titled the Fair Housing Act), racial discrimination by bankers, real estate agents, and individual landowners has meant that the goal of equal access to housing has remained unfulfilled. Congressional attempts to further strengthen the law have often failed. One researcher describes the status of anti–housing discrimination legislation as containing "vague provisions and failing to state precisely what national policy is regarding equal housing opportunity or how it shall be implemented."[35]

Equal Employment Opportunity

Title VII of the Civil Rights Act of 1964 bans discrimination in the hiring, promotion, and wages of employees on the basis of race, religion, and sex. The act outlaws discrimination by both private and public employers. It covers employers with fifteen or more employees and unions. Fair employment laws brought an end to the most blatant discriminatory employment practices, but more subtle manifestations of discrimination still persist. A 1992 investigation by the EEOC found discriminatory practices existing among employment agencies. The federal agency discovered that code phrases were devised by employment agencies in order to screen out applicants for companies on the basis of race, sex, and age. An employment agency in Los Angeles, California, for example, was found to have discriminated against over thirty-five hundred applicants, many of whom were black.[36] Another example of employment discrimination involves Texaco Incorporated. On November 15, 1996, the oil company announced that it would spend $176.1 million to settle a two-year-old racial discrimination suit. The lawsuit, filed in 1994 on behalf of black employees, alleged prejudice in Texaco's treatment of minority employees. The suit claimed that senior Texaco officials had established informal rules that gave the best promotions and biggest raises to whites. Support for the plaintiffs' allegations came when it was disclosed that top executives had been caught on tape making disparaging comments about blacks and plotting to destroy crucial documents in the case. Texaco's settlement is the largest to date in a racial discrimination suit in the United States.[37] One author sums up the performance of Congress in the area of anti–job discrimination policies in the following way:

> Congress' support for fair employment has always been rather erratic and basically modest . . . the policy goal has never been decidedly defined, monitoring and enforcement of nondiscrimination standards have mostly been passive and limited, and the commitment of federal agencies to fair employment goals has varied by agency and over time.[38]

Title VII gave the foundation for rooting out employment discrimination. But one flaw in the provision was that the person filing job discrimination charges had the burden of showing deliberate discrimination as the cause of failing to get the job position or the training opportunity. Since an employer rarely admits to discriminating on the basis of race or sex, the complaining party faced the difficult task of showing job discrimination. Recognizing the defect in the law, the U.S. Supreme Court, in *Griggs v. Duke Power* (1971), allowed job victims (minorities and women) to make their case if they could show that an employer's hiring practices had the *effect* of exclusion. The Court's decision therefore shifted the burden of proof to the employer to show that his requirements were a "business necessity" that bore a relationship to the worker's success on the job.[39] In less than twenty years after the Court's decision in *Griggs v. Duke Power* the Rehnquist Court rendered a series of decisions restricting the reach and remedies of federal antidiscrimination laws by once again shifting the burden of proof back to workers. One of the Supreme Court's rulings that civil rights proponents found most objectionable was the 1989 case of *Wards Cove Packing Co. v. Atonio*.[40] In the decision the Court held that minority employees must prove that racial imbalances in the workplace have no valid business purpose. In effect, the decision overturned the Court's prior holding in *Griggs v. Duke Power*.

The major purpose of the Civil Rights Act of 1991 was to counter the Supreme Court's decision in *Wards Cove Packing Co. v. Atonio,* by again placing the burden of proof on employers to justify practices that adversely affect minority group members and women in the workplace. The act is a compromised version of an original proposal that would have provided stronger employment protection for racial minorities and women. The original bill, preferred by civil rights organizations, would have allowed workers to challenge a business's employment policies more generally rather than having to "pinpoint" specific causes of discrimination. Over the protests of liberal members of the House a weaker bill was substituted to appease the demands of wavering members in the lower chamber. In 1991 the substitute bill was enacted into law. The act shifts the burden of proof to employers, by requiring them to show that an exclusionary practice had a "substantial and manifest relationship" to job performance. Unless the court rules otherwise, however, workers are required to pinpoint specific tests or other business policies that caused the discrimination. Employees can no longer make a broad-based challenge to a wider range of screening criteria as they could for nearly twenty years after the *Griggs v. Duke Power* decision.

To summarize, since the 1960s Congress has passed legislation designed to breach barriers of traditional discrimination. While Congress has continued to address and pass civil rights legislation since the 1960s, the discussion in this section provides good evidence that the goal of equal opportunity for African-Americans has not been fully realized. A primary explanation for continuing discrimination is the waning commitment of Congress in passing effective legislation that would help eradicate existing unequal treatment. Since the mid-1960s the majority of the members of the House have been unwilling to support strong civil rights policies. The typical approach to decision making on racial equality issues has been to support compromised versions of civil rights bills. The structure and operations of Congress allow members numerous opportunities to dilute the strength of potentially effective civil rights legislation. The paradigm constructed in the first chapter can be used as a basis for showing the level of commitment of members of Congress to black policy preferences. The remaining sections are devoted to that objective.

Patterns of Legislator Responsiveness

In the preceding chapter federal voting rights measures were analyzed that together provided important information about congressional responsiveness to black voting rights. Unlike voting rights legislation, there is no orderly succession of civil rights bills that can be used to gauge legislator responsiveness to black policy preferences over time. Civil rights legislation is broad in its coverage, and there can be many different titles to antidiscrimination bills.[41] We can gain some understanding, however, about the quality of representation for African-Americans in this field by looking at crucial antidiscrimination legislation voted on in recent years. Measures of civil rights support are taken from roll call votes in the House of Representatives during which the Fair Housing Act of 1988 (100th Congress) and the Civil Rights Act of 1991 (102d Congress) were considered and passed. Clearly, equal employment and fair housing continue to be two of the most important areas of civil rights legislation. On the assumption that these two bills are good indicators of legislator support for civil rights, they are used to assess the extent to which representatives are responding to black interests.

Both civil rights bills passed in the House by wide margins. The Fair Housing Act of 1988 passed by a vote of 376 to 23 and the Civil Rights Act of 1991 passed by a margin of 381 to 38 in the House. At first glance one might assume that the two bills received strong bipartisan support throughout the legislative voting process. Yet an analysis of patterns of legislator support tells us quite a different story.

The overall levels and patterns of congressional support are displayed in figure 7 (Fair Housing) and figure 8 (Civil Rights). The figures also give a breakdown of representatives' mean support scores by party affiliation. Several important pieces of information can be derived from an examination of the bar graphs. First, the level of mean support for all members is higher on final passage than it is on amendments. This pattern holds true even when mean support scores are disaggregated by members' party affiliation. Second, the high levels of congressional support on final passage are virtually identical for both bills. As noted earlier, both bills received substantial bipartisan support on final roll calls. Third, Democrats are relatively consistent in giving high levels of support during both stages of legislative voting. The consistency level from amendment to final bill is one of stable and upper-range liberal voting for Democrats. In contrast, Republicans are far more willing to support final passage of civil rights legislation but less inclined to vote for amendments. The magnitude of differential voting between amendments and final roll call for Republicans is especially pronounced on votes for the 1991 civil rights law (fig. 8). On average only 6 percent of voting Republicans supported the amendments, and 81 percent did so on final roll call.

Differential voting becomes even clearer when one examines the patterns of voting behavior in figure 9 (Fair Housing) and figure 10 (Civil Rights). The bar graphs show the differences in levels of mean support between amendment voting and final passage voting for nonsouthern Democrats, nonsouthern Republicans, southern Democrats and southern Republicans. The first finding of note is that, relative to other regional party cohorts in the analysis, nonsouthern Democrats are the strongest supporters of civil rights legislation. This finding is consistent with what we observed in the previous chapter on federal voting rights legislation. Their mean support scores are no less than 90 percent on roll calls for fair housing and civil rights legislation.

A second finding of interest is that southern Democrats rank second

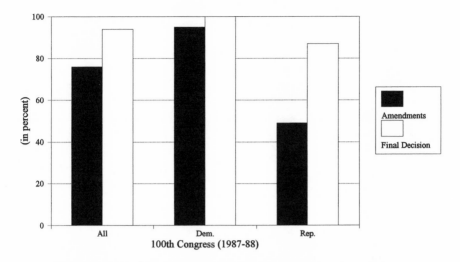

Fig. 7. Fair Housing Act of 1988 (mean support scores of representatives). (Note: Comparison of mean support scores of all voting members, voting Democrats (Dem.) and voting Republicans (Rep.). Computed by the author from data collected by the LCCR and *Congressional Quarterly Almanac*.)

to nonsouthern Democrats in support of black policy preferences. This is a dramatic transformation from three decades ago, when they were staunchly opposed to civil rights legislation. In 1964 over 90 percent of southern House Democrats voted against final passage of the Civil Rights Act. Three major factors help to account for this finding. First is the migration of the most conservative potential Democratic candidates to the Republican Party. This explanation is based on the assumption that there has been a significant party realignment in the South, driven by changes within the Democratic Party's position on civil rights. The South has traditionally been associated with the Democratic Party and racial conservatism, but, when the national Democratic Party began to infringe upon the extra sensitive issue of civil rights in the 1960s, many southern whites' satisfaction with the party began to deteriorate. As a consequence, the Republican Party has become a welcome alternative for a large proportion of the white southern electorate. It is interesting to note how southern House Democrats have become less conservative on civil rights issues across time, while southern House Republicans have remained conservative and their numbers have increased significantly in recent years.[42]

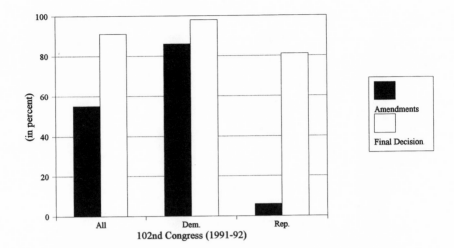

Fig. 8. Civil Rights Act of 1991 (mean support scores of representatives. (Note: Comparison of mean support scores of all voting members, voting Democrats (Dem.) and voting Republicans (Rep.). Computed by the author from data collected by the LCCR and *Congressional Quarterly Almanac.*)

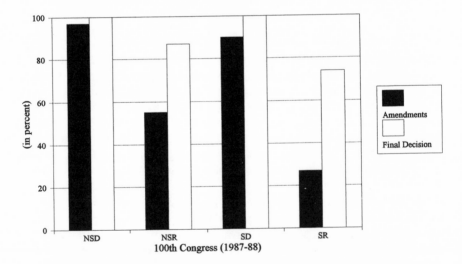

Fig. 9. Fair Housing Act of 1988 (mean support scores of representatives). (Note: Comparison of mean support scores of Nonsouthern Democrats (NSD), Nonsouthern Republicans (NSR), Southern Democrats (SD), and Southern Republicans (SR). Computed by the author from data collected by the LCCR and *Congressional Quarterly Almanac.*)

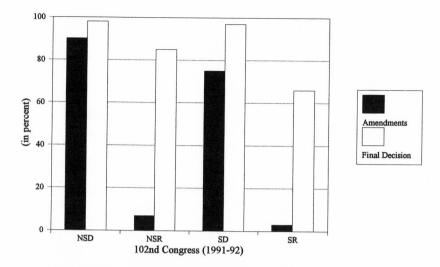

Fig. 10. Civil Rights Act of 1991 (mean support scores of representatives). (Comparison of mean support scores of Nonsouthern Democrats (NSD), Nonsouthern Republicans (NSR), Southern Democrats (SD) and Southern Republicans (SR). Computed by the author from data collected by the LCCR and *Congressional Quarterly Almanac*.)

The second factor is the changed behavior of southern Democrats brought on by the influx of blacks into the southern electorate. Research has demonstrated that long-term Democratic incumbents changed their behavior on black interest legislation in a liberal direction due in part to the empowerment of the southern black electorate.[43] As early as 1949, V. O. Key Jr. summed up the discourse on the role of race by pointing out, "whatever phase of the southern political process one seeks to understand sooner or later the trail of inquiry leads to the Negro."[44]

The final factor has to do with the voting behavior of nonsouthern Republicans. As mentioned earlier, the origins of this conservatism can be traced back to the racial voting alignment occurring in 1964. The 1964 election produced a large increase in the number of nonsouthern liberal Democrats at the expense of racially liberal nonsouthern Republicans.[45] As the findings here illustrate, this pattern of conservative voting on black policy preferences among House Republicans continues in the 1990s. Nonsouthern Republicans mean support scores are especially low on roll calls for civil rights amendments (7 percent) in 1991. The net effect of these changes has moved southern Democrats up in the rankings of support for civil rights.

The model constructed in chapter 1 predicts that nonsouthern Democrats and southern Republicans would be more consistent in their voting behavior than would be nonsouthern Republicans and southern Democrats. To some degree the patterns observed in figures 9 and 10 support this prediction. Relative to other party groupings, nonsouthern Democrats and southern Republicans are less likely to deviate in their roll call voting behavior than are southern Democrats and nonsouthern Republicans. The magnitude of difference between the two stages of legislative voting is fairly large, however, for southern Republicans (47 percent for fair housing, 63 percent for civil rights), suggesting a pattern of deviant voting behavior even for them. A detailed discussion for this observed pattern of voting behavior is forthcoming in the section on voting consistency. For now it suffices to note that, if a liberal civil rights proposal is watered down enough, representatives who are the least supportive of civil rights will vote for the measure. But further proof is needed to support this assertion. Before taking a closer look at voting consistency from amendment to bill, it would be useful to assess the strength of the relationships between civil rights legislation and relevant independent variables.

A More Systematic Investigation of Legislator Support for Civil Rights Legislation

The analysis that follows is similar to the one conducted on federal voting rights. The difference here is that the dependent variables have been changed from federal voting rights legislation to civil rights legislation, as measured by representatives' roll call voting decisions on fair housing legislation in 1988 and civil rights legislation in 1991. The two dependent variables are computed in the same fashion as the dependent variables for federal voting rights (see equation 1 for coding and measurements).[46] Two separate regression models are used for testing the relationships between legislator support for civil rights and party (coded 1 if Democrat, 0 if Republican), region (scored 1 for nonsouthern members, 0 for southern members), the percentage of the district's population that is black, and the percentage of the district's population residing in urban areas. Ordinary least squares regression is used for testing relationships in the amendment model, and logistic regression is used for the final passage model. It is expected that the relationships between the dependent variables and the independent variables will be significant and that the signs will be positive.

Table 7 (Fair Housing) and table 8 (Civil Rights) present the results of the analysis (see equation 1 for model specification). As can be seen, the regression and logit coefficients for the party and region variables are highly significant, and the signs are in the expected direction. The findings indicate that fair housing and civil rights legislation are significantly influenced by members' party and regional affiliation. Party is the most important explanatory variable in the models. In substantive terms the findings can be interpreted to mean that, on average, Democrats are much more likely to support civil rights legislation than are their Republican colleagues in the chamber. Likewise, nonsouthern members are more inclined to support black interest legislation than are representatives from the southern region of the country.

The findings for percent black and percent urban are not so easily explained. Although minor in comparison to the impact of party and region, congressional support for fair housing legislation (table 7) is significantly influenced by the percentage of blacks in districts. Yet percent black does not a have an impact on civil rights roll calls in 1991 (table 8). It is difficult to provide a precise explanation for why percent black significantly influences members' roll call voting behavior on some civil

TABLE 7.   Effects of Party, Region, Race, and Urbanization on House Members' Support for Fair Housing Legislation (1988)

Variables	Unstandardized	t-ratio
Votes on Amendments (regression estimates)		
Members' political party	45.907	17.005***
Region	17.577	5.172***
Percent black	.199	1.827*
Percent urban	−.124	.208
$R^2 = .49$		
$N = 365$		
Votes on Final Decision (logit estimates)		
Members' political party	3.274	3.724***
Region	2.477	3.133***
Percent black	.181	2.767***
Percent urban	−1.471	2.222**
−2 × log-likelihood = 111.48.		
Model chi square = 50.0, p < .0001.		
Percent correctly predicted = 94.05.		
Percent reduction in error = 0.		
$N = 365$.		

Source: Roll call data for fair housing legislation compiled from *Congressional Quarterly Almanac,* 1987–88.

***p < .01   **p < .05   *p < .10   (all one-tailed tests)

TABLE 8. Effects of Party, Region, Race, and Urbanization on House Members' Support for Civil Rights Legislation (1991)

Variables	Unstandardized	t-ratio
Votes on Amendments (regression estimates)		
Members' political party	78.747	46.531***
Region	10.785	5.585***
Percent black	.094	1.448
Percent urban	.054	2.477**
$R^2 = .86$		
$N = 407$		

	Votes on Final Decision (logit estimates)	
Members' political party	2.277	4.772***
Region	1.080	2.375**
Percent black	.016	.659
Percent urban	.238	.551

$-2 \times$ log-likelihood = 207.86.
Model chi square = 41.1, p < .0001.
Percent correctly predicted = 91.0.
Percent reduction in error = 0.
$N = 407$.

Source: Data for civil rights legislation derived from 1991 edition of *Congressional Quarterly Almanac.*
***$p < .001$ **$p < .05$ (all one-tailed tests)

rights issues, while on others it does not. As discussed in the previous chapter on federal voting rights, the failure of percent black to reach statistical significance may stem from the possibility that the effect of race on some civil rights issues may be working through partisan channels. Also, representatives' voting decisions may be guided by perceptions of their constituencies. That is, their roll call voting behavior may be strongly influenced by friends and family, interest groups, financial supporters, and, of course, white conservative constituency pressure. Furthermore, individual decision making may be a function of pressures coming from colleagues in Congress or from the president of the United States. Consequently, there may be a certain imprecision in the operational definition of *percent black.* But the most relevant point to be made about the findings presented here is that there is some evidence to suggest that the size of the black population in the district does constrain the voting behavior of representatives even after the powerful influences of party and region are controlled for in the model.

Interestingly, when percent black is significant in the models, percent urban is not. Or, in the case of final roll call voting on fair housing legislation (table 7), the percent urban variable has a negative impact. Without overstating the case, the negative relationship may be due to the differing urban character of constituencies of varying black populations. Urban districts are more likely to contain large (e.g., central cities) or small (e.g., suburbs) proportions of black citizens. Urban districts that contain large proportions of blacks are likely to exhibit a relatively liberal electorate. Urban districts with small proportions of black citizens are likely to be conservative, because they tend to be populated by white, middle- and upper-income voters who prefer the economic conservatism of the Republican Party. The negative impact of percent urban may be due to the conservative nature of some urban areas outside of central cities.

Overall the models tell us a good deal about what affects congressional support for civil rights issues.[47] The amount of variance explained in the amendment models is 50 percent for fair housing and 86 percent for civil rights. The model chi-square statistics reveal that the logistic models for fair housing and civil rights are statistically significant. The models, however, do not tell us much about voting consistency. The analyses in the remaining section are designed to shed some light on the subject.

Voting Consistency on Civil Rights Legislation

The figures presented earlier in this chapter revealed that House Republicans are more likely to deviate in their roll call voting behavior than are House Democrats. Further proof of policy deviation can be seen in table 9. It is clearly the case that supporting amendments and opposing the final bill (low final passage/high amendment category) is a nonfactor in congressional voting on legislation used for this analysis. The method of deviant voting used most often by representatives is to oppose one or more of the amendments and vote for the bill (low amendment/high final passage category).

There are two essential findings in table 9. First, on average Republicans are more likely to deviate in their voting behavior from amendment to final bill. On fair housing legislation the overall proportion of voting representatives displaying deviant behavior was 71 percent of southern Republicans, 68 percent of nonsouthern Republicans, 26 percent of southern Democrats, and 8 percent of nonsouthern Democrats. On civil rights legislation the proportion of regional party members deviating was 85 percent of nonsouthern Republicans, 75 percent of southern Democrats, 66 percent of southern Republicans, and 41 percent of nonsouthern Democrats. The second noteworthy finding is that the degree of voting variability

TABLE 9.   Degree of House Members' Support for Fair Housing and Civil Rights Legislation from the Amendment to the Final Bill (in percent)

	Oppose Amendments Support Final Bill				Support Amendments Oppose Final Bill				
	Fair Housing Legislation (1988)								
	-1.0^a	$-.75$	$-.50$	$-.25$	0.0	$+.25$	$+.50$	$+.75$	$+1.00$
NSD^b	$—^c$	—	2 (3)	6 (10)^d	92 (143)	—	—	—	—
NSR	10 (12)	16 (19)	20 (24)	22 (26)	31 (38)	—	—	—	—
SD	—	4 (2)	7 (4)	15 (9)	75 (44)	—	—	—	—
SR	9 (3)	38 (13)	18 (6)	6 (2)	24 (8)	—	—	—	—

	Civil Rights Legislation (1991)										
	-1.0^a	$-.80$	$-.60$	$-.40$	$-.20$	0.0	$+.20$	$+.40$	$+.60$	$+.80$	$+1.00$
NSD^b	$—^c$	—	—	5 (8)	35 (62)^d	58 (103)	—	—	—	—	—
NSR	68 (84)	5 (6)	7 (9)	5 (6)	—	12 (15)	—	—	—	—	—
SD	—	—	14 (10)	10 (7)	49 (35)	22 (16)	—	—	—	—	—
SR	55 (21)	11 (4)	—	—	—	29 (11)	—	—	—	—	—

Note: Support for fair housing and civil rights legislation on amendments is based on the position endorsed by the Leadership Conference on Civil Rights (LCCR).

[a]The number of amendments used in the analysis for fair housing was 4, for civil rights 5 (see app. B for description of amendments).

[b]NSD = nonsouthern Democrats, NSR = nonsouthern Republicans, SD = southern Democrats, SR = southern Republicans.

[c]Dash represents three cases or less in cell.

[d]Number of cases in parentheses.

was greater on civil rights legislation than it was on fair housing legislation. Table 9 shows that well over a majority of voting southern Republicans (55 percent) and voting nonsouthern Republicans (68 percent) opposed all of the civil rights amendments in the analysis and later decided to vote for the final bill. In contrast, the degree of deviant voting was considerably less on fair housing legislation. As the table reveals, only 9 percent of southern Republicans and 10 percent of nonsouthern Republicans exhibited this type of behavior.

Stronger evidence substantiating changing voting behavior (coded 1 if the legislator voted against a majority of the amendments but supported the bill, 0 if not) can be seen in table 10 (see equation 2 for measurements of variables). The model does a good job of predicting the voting behavior of representatives between the amendment stage and the final bill. Table 10 shows that the party variable has a significant positive effect on the probability of changing voting behavior between the two legislative stages. The findings suggest that House Republicans are far more likely to vote against amendments then vote for final passage of the bill than are House Democrats. As expected, the biggest impact of the party variable is on civil rights legislation, more than on fair housing legislation. Region also predicts the likelihood of legislators changing their voting behavior. Its sign is positive and is in the expected direction, suggesting that southern members are more apt to oppose amendments and support final passage than are representatives from the non-South. Finally, there is a small amount of statistical evidence to show that representatives change their behavior on the basis of the proportion of blacks residing in a congressional district. The proportion black variable is only statistically significant in the civil rights model, suggesting that representatives from districts with few blacks were less committed to civil rights overall.

The findings in tables 9 and 10 underscore the central point of this discussion. That is, a liberal civil rights proposal can undergo many revisions and modifications, to the point where even the most conservative members of Congress will support the bill on final action.

To understand fully the findings reported in tables 9 and 10 one must consider the political environment in which Congress has been making civil rights policy in recent decades. The Civil Rights Act of 1964 was a quintessential example of bipartisan and congressional-executive cooperation. As president, Johnson used his parliamentary skills and the lingering sympathy for John Kennedy to usher through the 1964 civil rights law. Since the mid-1960s Republicans and Democrats in Congress have been moving in different directions on civil rights. Furthermore, there has been less cooperation between the president and Congress. Both President Ronald Reagan and George Bush had confrontations with Democrats in Congress over civil rights legislation during their tenures in the White House.

Interbranch conflict was clearly present during debate over the 1991 civil rights bill. As previously mentioned, the bill stems from a series of court decisions that limited employee recourse in cases of employment discrimination. The original bill offered by House Democratic leaders was designed to reinstate the criteria from *Griggs v. Duke Power Co.,* along with provisions that would make it easier to punish racial harassment on the job and would permit women and religious minorities to be awarded unlimited monetary damages in cases of employment discrimination. In the 101st Congress (1989–90) Bush had vetoed a similar bill, contending that employers would be forced to hire specific numbers of minorities and women to avoid litigation. When the 102d Congress convened, proponents of the bill placed it high on the legislative agenda. Bush continued his efforts to make the bill a referendum on affirmative action by insisting that the bill would result in quota hiring. During debate in the House, Repub-

TABLE 10.   Effects of Party, Region, and Race on Behavioral Change among House Members from the Amendment to the Final Bill: Logit Estimates

Variables	Unstandardized	t-ratio
Votes on Fair Housing Act of 1988		
Members' political party	4.162	5.392***
Region	1.259	2.635***
Percent black	.001	.038

-2 log likelihood = 204.4.
Model chi-square = 92.3, p < .0001.
Percent correctly predicted = 86.8.
Percent reduction in error = 4.0.
N = 366.

Variables	Unstandardized	t-ratio
Votes on Civil Rights Act of 1991		
Members' political party	3.321	10.580***
Region	1.062	2.652***
Percent black	−.034	1.700*

-2 log likelihood = 320.9.
Model chi-square = 191.2, p < .0001.
Percent correctly predicted = 83.5.
Percent reduction in error = 46.8.
N = 408.

Note: Fair housing and civil rights legislation. Behavioral change is defined as roll calls on which a representative opposed a majority of the amendments in the analysis then voted for the final decision of the bill.

***$p < .001$ *$p < .10$ (one-tailed tests for party and region, two-tailed test for percent black)

licans supported Bush, claiming that if the bill passed it would clog the courts with job discrimination lawsuits and would also adversely affect small businesses.

Fearing a repeat of 1990, the strength of the bill was diluted to avoid a presidential veto. The most controversial aspect of the compromises is the criteria for proving job discrimination. The civil rights law of 1991 states that the burden of proof lies with employers and that all employment practices must be "job related for the position in question and consistent with business necessity." On the surface the bill appears to reinstate the standard from the *Griggs* case. Yet Congress made one important concession: it agreed to let the federal courts define what constitutes a "business necessity" when employers are sued by minorities and women for job discrimination. The decision to let the courts define *business necessity* is ironic because the bill was first introduced by Democrats (Edward

Kennedy of Massachusetts in the Senate, Augustus Hawkins of California in the House) to reverse the effects of Supreme Court decisions that had made it difficult for employees to bring job discrimination suits. The impact of the 1991 law may well depend on the ideological composition of the Supreme Court. Because of the conservative court appointments to the federal bench by Reagan and Bush, one is left with the impression that there will be a narrow interpretation of the civil rights laws.

Of course, virtually all legislative proposals undergo some revisions as they move through the various stages of congressional decision making. But do the revisions cause the bill to lose much of its original character? Clearly, the civil rights bill was watered down for the purpose of receiving more votes from members who had opposed many of its amendments. The long-term consequences of the Civil Rights Act of 1991 remain an open-ended question because of the inability of Congress to bring the issue surrounding the *Ward Cove* decision to a complete resolution.

Discussion

The refusal of Congress to pass civil rights laws for close to a century after the Civil War sent a clear message to segregationists that practices of discrimination were acceptable in the eyes of the law. Congress began to reverse its laissez-faire position toward the issue of racial inequality in the late 1950s, when it once again placed civil rights on the nation's policy agenda. But it was not until the passage of the Civil Rights Act of 1964 that the laws of Jim Crow segregation began to fall. Arguably the most significant civil rights legislation in American history, the 1964 act was instrumental in eradicating overt practices of discrimination in the areas of education, employment, housing, and public accommodations. But blacks continue to face subtle forms of discrimination, which raises the important question: What is the status of congressional responsiveness to black constituents thirty years after the landmark 1964 legislation?

The findings observed here provide some clues about the multifaceted business of legislative voting on black policy preferences in the contemporary period. Based on the evidence presented in this chapter, a sizable proportion of the House delegation is reluctant to support strong civil rights measures. As in the case in congressional decision making on federal voting rights, some members may be working hard behind the scenes to dilute the strength of a civil rights proposal then later decide to vote for the final bill to avoid being labeled anti–civil rights. Unfortunately, due to the nature of roll call votes, one cannot discern why members vote the way they do. We can say with some degree of confidence that the quality of a civil rights measure is affected before a final vote on the bill. Researchers should be cognizant of that fact when conducting their analyses on aspects of congressional behavior.

Civil rights was clearly at the top of the nation's policy-making agenda when the Civil Rights Act of 1964 and the Voting Rights Act of 1965 were written into the statute books. But this was a time when Democrats and Republicans in Congress worked in tandem to enact civil rights legislation, a time when the focus of civil rights was clearly on the plight of blacks, who were the victims of overt discrimination, and a time when there was a greater degree of cooperation between the executive and legislative branches of the national government.

Since the 1960s the political environment for civil rights has changed, and so have patterns of policy-making. In recent decades more groups in American society (e.g., Native Americans, Asians, Hispanics, women, gays, and the disabled) are seeking additional protection for their civil rights. In effect, this means that the civil rights agenda has expanded, resulting in greater competition between groups for scarce resources. Also, growing Republican strength in Congress has made it increasingly difficult to get strong civil rights measures enacted into law. Even though Republicans continue to emphasize that they are supporters of civil rights, the findings presented in this chapter contradict their claims. In the 105th Congress (1997–98) Republicans held a majority of the seats in the House and Senate. Their win represents the first time since the late 1920s that the Republican party held majority status in Congress twice in a row. If this trend of Republican growth continues or remains constant, one can expect fewer effective antidiscrimination bills to be enacted into law.

The most prevalent pattern in the 1980s and 1990s has been executive-congressional conflict over the issue of civil rights. Both Reagan and Bush were opposed to busing, affirmative action, and strong enforcement of civil rights laws. President Reagan, for instance, vetoed the Civil Rights Restoration Act of 1988.[48] In turn the House voted 292 to 133, and the Senate voted 73 to 24, to override Reagan's veto. As previously discussed, Bush originally vetoed the Civil Rights Act of 1990 before deciding to support a watered-down version of the bill in 1991 (102d Congress). President Clinton has been more supportive of civil rights than Reagan or Bush. He has, for example, nominated more Democrats to serve on the federal bench, who are more liberal than the nominees of Reagan and Bush, and a large percentage of them have been minorities and women. As of January 1995, 17 percent of Clinton's appointees to the federal district courts were African-Americans. In contrast, 7 percent of Bush's appointees to the federal district courts were African-Americans, and Reagan appointed only 2 percent.[49]

On the one hand, the findings suggest that congressional responsiveness to black policy preferences has weakened since the 1960s. On the other hand, the evidence presented indicates that congressional protection is still needed because subtle manifestations of discrimination against blacks continues in the United States. Civil rights proponents contend that the presence of more blacks in Congress will ensure that the concerns of blacks will not fade away from the national legislative agenda. But, from the perspective of substantive representation, does the race of the member really matter?

CHAPTER 4

The Color of Congress: The Impact of Race and the Role of Issues in Congressional Roll Call Votes

It is common knowledge that the history of American politics began with coalitions based on common interests involving economic, social, religious, and ethnic groups. In this context, the Congressional Black Caucus is not a maverick organization. . . . We are, therefore, interested in developing, introducing, and passing progressive legislation which will meet the needs of millions of neglected citizens.
—Congressman Louis Stokes, Congressional Black Caucus

It would be rare to find a social group whose members would not feel deprived if someone like themselves were not included in the representative assembly. The social composition of a representative body is important from a symbolic perspective because it demonstrates to groups in society that they are taken seriously by the government. Sociological similarity (descriptive representation) helps to promote good representation and political stability by increasing members of the group's faith and trust in government (symbolic representation).[1] Beyond the symbolic rewards a social group may receive from having someone like themselves in elective office, there should also be real and tangible policy benefits from increasing the group's representation in the assembly. The presumption is that representatives who share their constituents' sociological characteristics will work hard to speak for constituents' views and serve their constituents' interests in the governmental process. But is there a relationship between descriptive representation and substantive representation? In other words, is the quality of substantive representation for African-Americans affected by the racial composition within the congressional delegation? Or, bluntly put, does race really matter in congressional voting on black policy preferences? In view of the continuing controversy over racial redistricting to increase black congressional representation to better serve the policy interests of the black community, the issue of race takes on both political and legal significance.

The purpose of this chapter is threefold: first, to develop a theory for understanding the connection between race and legislator behavior; second, to determine whether race makes a difference in explaining black policy preferences; and, third, to take a closer look at the relevance of issues in congressional voting behavior on this important subject.

Theoretical Considerations

The extant literature on legislative elections and representation has paid little attention to the possible theoretical connection between the race of the legislator and the quality of representation that African-Americans will receive. The theoretical evidence that does exist in the larger literature on representation leads one to suspect that the race of the representative does not make a difference concerning matters of public policy. Hanna Pitkin, in her influential work on representation, defines political representation principally in substantive terms.[2] Likewise, Heinz Eulau and Paul Karps view other forms of representation as being less important than that of substantive representation.[3] David Vogler sums up the conventional view of the possible link between descriptive and substantive representation: "Sometimes background characteristics do influence a legislator's vote, but often they are of no relevance in explaining congressional behavior."[4]

Implicit in the theoretical literature on representation is the notion that representatives should be judged in terms of their legislative activities, not on the extent to which they mirror the social traits of the people they formally represent. From the perspective of traditional theory the race of the member ought *not* to affect his or her policy-making behavior. At first glance the theoretical evidence for hypothesizing that a relationship exists between race and representation is weak. Yet there is an alternative theoretical perspective grounded in the literature on group consciousness, the social psychology of race, and House members' political perceptions of their constituencies that points toward a different view of the race-representation connection.

Richard L. Hall and Colleen Heflin offer a theory concerning the relationship between racial group identification and minority substantive representation in Congress.[5] This theory is based on the proposition that historically blacks have been one of the most deprived and most discriminated-against groups in the United States. As discussed in the previous chapter, more subtle manifestations of racial discrimination appear to have replaced overt discriminatory laws and practices. Moreover, while integration has made some progress in the United States, race continues to be a major force shaping the lives of blacks. The economic deprivation and social isolation of blacks continue to be major features of the American political landscape. According to researchers who have analyzed the role of race from the standpoint of group consciousness, there should be a strong feeling of group attachment among African-Americans. Even though blacks are not monolithic in the political views they hold, these strong feelings of racial group identification should run deep within the African-American community and play a major role in determining how they view the political world. A sense of group consciousness should penetrate beyond the boundaries of the political behavior of the black masses (e.g., voting for party candidates) into the behavior of black political elites. Based on the socially constructed view of black elite attitudes, Hall and Heflin suggest that the policy interests of the black masses will be reflected in the legislative work of black representatives because of their common bond, resulting from shared past and present experiences.[6]

Michael Dawson, in *Behind the Mule: Race and Class in African-American Politics,* develops a theory that goes further to show that the psychology of social groups is critical in explaining group solidarity among African-Americans. Dawson's theory (termed *black utility heuristic*) places emphasis on perceptions of "linked fates" (perceived link between racial group interests and individual interests) and black economic subordination. That is, the social and economic opportunities of most African-Americans are so inextricably tied to being black that it is only rational for them to see racial group interests as a proxy for their individual interests. Thus, most blacks use racial group interests as a means by which they evaluate political candidates, political parties, and public policies. Furthermore, according to the author, the notion of linked fates transcends the boundaries of economic status within the black community. As suggested by Hall and Heflin (1994), this theory leads one to believe that the vast majority of black members of Congress will have a strong sense of racial identity, which will lead them to support policies of interest to black constituents. In some sense a spontaneous form of representation will emerge because of the development of a unique racial consciousness and belief system that makes black representatives predisposed to vote the way most blacks in the district would want the legislator to vote anyway. In essence their support for black policy preferences should be unparalleled in Congress because what's in the best interest of the black masses is also in the best interest of black policymakers.[7]

African-Americans, other minority group members, and women argue that their interests would be better served by increasing their representation in Congress. More specifically, civil rights advocates maintain that there is a need to increase black membership in Congress because there are many important issues that run along racial lines. Moreover, too often in the past elected officials have overlooked and disregarded the needs and concerns of African-Americans to the predictable end that blacks have been deprived of adequate representation. Once in office, civil rights proponents contend, African-Americans would be in a better position to place civil rights issues higher on the national political agenda to help fight continuing discrimination against people of color.

Implicit in the literature on the role of group consciousness is the assumption that black representatives will work diligently to improve the quality of substantive representation for fellow group members. Simply stated, there should be a strong link between descriptive and substantive representation. Undoubtedly, this was one of the major reasons for organizing the Congressional Black Caucus (CBC) in 1969. As one black representative who helped to organize the CBC states, "protecting black interests was the primary reason most of us were elected."[8]

The final line of theoretical reasoning focuses on the electoral link between the constituency and the political perceptions of the representative. This theoretical construction is based on the following question: Who does the representative think him- or herself responsive to on matters of public policy? The answer, to a large degree, lies in the member's own perception of the people who he or she thinks will provide the electoral support needed to win a seat in Congress. The importance of the electoral environment has been discussed throughout this book and extensively in the literature on congressional representation. Aside from the work of Hall and Heflin, however, the theoretical basis for linking black constituents to the political perceptions of the representative has received little attention. Hall and Heflin derive the theoretical foundation for hypothesizing the importance of such a relationship from the work of Richard Fenno, invoking his oft-cited passage in the introduction to *Home Style.* His study of eighteen House members at home in their districts led him to the following observations about their political perceptions of constituents:

> One question central to the representative-constituency relationship remains underdeveloped. It is: *What does an elected representative see when he or she sees a constituency?* And as a natural follow up, *What consequences do these perceptions have for his or her behavior?* The key problem is perception. And the key assumption is that the constituency a representative reacts to is the constituency he or she sees.[9]

The fundamental question Hall and Heflin derive from Fenno's observation is this: Is the correspondence between white representatives and their black constituents the same as it is for black representatives and their constituents? If the assumption can be made that a member's perception of the district is affected by his or her electoral needs, then it is believed that the answer is no. All things considered, black candidates need greater numbers of black votes to win a House seat than do white candidates. Hall and Heflin also call attention to Fenno's report of an exchange between a white congressman and his district staffer who were riding through a black neighborhood of a city. Fenno listened to the following exchange between the congressman and his staff member:

> *Congressman:* I concede the black vote.
> *Staffer:* I wouldn't want to be out there walking on the sidewalk.
> *Congressman:* It's like some Caribbean country.
> *Staffer:* It sure is a different country here.

To be sure, this is the view of only one representative and does not reflect the sentiments of all white lawmakers who represent multiracial districts. But this exchange suggests that, unlike the vast majority of black candidates, many white candidates do not have to rely heavily on the black vote to win a House seat. Black congressional candidates can ill afford to concede the black vote and expect to win a congressional race. Because of their greater need for black electoral support, the representational link between black representatives and their black constituents should be closer than the connection between white representatives and their black constituents. One possible consequence of this development is that black lawmakers will be more responsive to black policy preferences than white because they *see* black voters as a vital component of their electoral base, all things being equal.

Taken together, these factors provide a strong theoretical basis for hypothesizing that the race of the member will significantly affect the quality of substantive representation for African-Americans. As stated earlier, empirical investigation on the subject matter is virtually nonexistent. Recent findings, however, cast a shadow of doubt on whether race really matters in congressional roll calls on black policy preferences. Carol Swain, in her book *Black Faces, Black Interests: The Representation of African Americans in Congress,* finds little evidence that race impacts a legislator's substantive representation of black interests once the representative's party and regional affiliation are entered into the equation.[10] While the author acknowledges that her findings may not be generalized beyond her examination of the 100th Congress, nonetheless, the conclusions have profound implications for those wishing to improve the voice of historically underrepresented groups in society and for those who may wish to de-emphasize the significance of their membership in the legislature.

The purpose here is to conduct a thorough investigation to see if race makes a difference in the voting decisions of members of the House on civil rights–related issues. Before doing so, it would be useful to give a brief

overview of the history and current status of black congressional representation as well as the extant literature on white legislator responsiveness to
black constituents. The focus then shifts to an analysis of the role of race
and issues in congressional roll calls.

The Status of Black Congressional Representation

Congress has never been a sociological microcosm of the United States'
population. Throughout the nation's history it has been a haven for white
males. In all our history only ninety-nine blacks (1870–1997) have served
in Congress, four of them in the Senate and the rest in the House.[11] Nearly
one-third of them served during the Reconstruction era. During the
post–Civil War period all black members of Congress were Republicans,
loyal to the party of Abraham Lincoln. There were no blacks serving in
Congress from 1901 to 1928. In 1928 Oscar DePriest, a Republican from
the state of Illinois, was the first black to serve in Congress during the
twentieth century. Only four more blacks entered Congress before 1960
(Arthur W. Mitchell, Illinois; William L. Dawson, Illinois; Adam C. Powell Jr., New York; and Charles C. Diggs Jr., Michigan). In the years following the New Deal all but three blacks (Senator Edward W. Brooke of
Massachusetts and Representatives Gary Franks of Connecticut and J. C.
Watts of Oklahoma) have been Democrats.

Blacks have increased their congressional representation somewhat in
the past three decades primarily due to the Voting Rights Act of 1965 and
its extensions. In 1972 Barbara Jordan of Texas and Andrew Young of
Georgia were the first blacks elected in the South since 1900. Judicial interpretation of the act, as amended in 1982, brought additional black gains in
Congress. Court rulings mandated gerrymandering to maximize black
voting strength, which in turn created greater opportunities for black voters to elect representatives of their choice. As a result, black membership
in the House grew to over twenty members during the 1980s. Racial gerrymandering after the 1990 census led to the creation of twelve new black
majority districts. For the first time since Reconstruction blacks were
elected to Congress from Alabama, Florida, North Carolina, South Carolina, and Virginia. In 1992 thirty-nine members and one senator (Carol
Mosely-Braun, Illinois) were elected to serve in the 103d Congress. In 1994
thirty-nine African-Americans were elected to serve in the House in the
104th Congress. In proportional terms blacks who make up 12 percent of
the nation's population represented 9 percent of the House membership in
the 103d and 104th Congresses. After the 1996 elections thirty-nine
African-Americans were elected to serve (including nonvoting delegates)
in the House in the 105th Congress. They represent approximately 9.0 per-

cent of the membership in the House. A list of all black members of Congress serving throughout history to the present can be seen in table 11.

Despite black gains in Congress, the proportion of their membership in Congress remains below the proportion of African-Americans in the general black population. Black gains in Congress may be tenuous because the gerrymandering necessary to achieve black majority districts is being challenged in the courts. As shall be demonstrated in the next chapter, few blacks have been successful in winning congressional seats in white majority districts.[12] And, unless they are able to do so, future black gains in Congress may be short-lived.[13]

Past Research on White Congressional Responsiveness to Black Interests

Most research on legislator responsiveness to black policy interests has focused on the South, where blacks have faced the most resistance to their political participation. There is little doubt that the engine of change in the region has been the increase in black voter participation. As part of their strategy to win elective office, some white representatives have found it to be politically expedient to become more responsive to black interests. As discussed earlier, researchers are less certain about the exact nature of the relationship but agree that black voter participation has caused many southern House members to moderate their conservative policy views on racial issues.[14] A study by Kenny Whitby and Franklin Gilliam Jr. also found behavioral change occurring among southern white congressional Democrats over time. After analyzing the voting records of southern House members over a twenty-year period, it found a trend toward less conservative voting taking place in southern Democrats' voting behavior. The study also found that greater policy responsiveness from these legislators was due in part to the mobilization and participation of the southern black electorate.[15] The effects of black voter participation on white legislator responsiveness can also be interactive; that is, less conservative voting is in part caused by the interaction between the constituency variables race and urbanization.[16]

It should come as no surprise that past studies have found that partisanship plays a major role in congressional roll call voting on civil rights legislation.[17] Research on the impact of party has focused on both the South and the total membership of the House. Research reveals that partisanship is an important predictor of liberal voting.[18] Furthermore, according to previous findings, the predictive power of party has increased over time as a consequence of southern Democrats voting more like their party colleagues from the non-South.[19]

TABLE 11. African-American Members in Congress by Party, State, Year, and Congress, 1870–1997

Name	Party	State	Year	Congress
Senate				
Hiram R. Revels	R	Mississippi	1870–71	41st
Blanche K. Bruce	R	Mississippi	1875–81	44th–45th
Edward W. Brooke	R	Massachusetts	1967–79	90th–95th
Carol Mosely-Braun	D	Illinois	1993–	103d–
House				
Joseph H. Rainey	R	South Carolina	1870–79	41st–45th
Jefferson F. Long	R	Georgia	1870–71	41st
Robert B. Elliot	R	South Carolina	1871–74	42d–43d
Robert C. DeLarge	R	South Carolina	1871–73	42d
Benjamin S. Turner	R	Alabama	1871–73	42d
Josiah T. Walls	R	Florida	1871–76	42d–44th
Richard H. Cain	R	South Carolina	1873–75	43d–45th
			1877–79	43d–45th
John R. Lynch	R	Mississippi	1873–77	43d–47th
			1882–83	
James T. Rapier	R	Alabama	1873–75	43d
Alonzo J. Ransier	R	South Carolina	1873–75	43d
Jeremiah Haralson	R	Alabama	1875–77	44th
John A. Hyman	R	North Carolina	1875–77	44th
Charles E. Nash	R	Louisiana	1875–77	44th
Robert Smalls	R	South Carolina	1875–79	45th
			1882–83	47th–49th
			1884–87	
James E. O'Hara	R	North Carolina	1889–93	51st–52d
Henry P. Cheatham	R	North Carolina	1889–93	51st–52d
John M. Langston	R	Virginia	1890–91	51st
Thomsa E. Miller	R	South Carolina	1890–91	51st
George W. Murray	R	South Carolina	1893–95	53d–54th
			1886–97	
George H. White	R	North Carolina	1897–1901	55th–56th
Oscar DePriest	R	Illinois	1929–35	71st–73d
Arthur W. Mitchell	D	Illinois	1935–43	74th–77th
William L. Dawson	D	Illinois	1943–70	78th–91st
Adam C. Powell Jr.	D	New York	1945–67	79th–90th
			1969–71	91st
Charles C. Diggs Jr.	D	Michigan	1955–80	84th–96th
Robert C. Nix Sr.	D	Pennsylvania	1959–79	85th–95th
Augustus F. Hawkins	D	California	1963–90	88th–101st
John Conyers Jr.	D	Michigan	1965–	89th–
Louis Stokes	D	Ohio	1969–	91st–
William L. Clay	D	Missouri	1969–	91st–
Shirley Chisholm	D	New York	1969–83	91st–97th
George W. Collins	D	Illinois	1970–72	91st–92d
Ronald Dellums	D	California	1971–	92d–

TABLE 11—*Continued*

Name	Party	State	Year	Congress
Walter E. Fauntroy[a]	D	Washington, D.C.	1971–90	92d–101st
Ralph H. Metcalf	D	Illinois	1971–78	92d–95th
Parren J. Mitchell	D	Maryland	1971–87	92d–99th
Charles B. Rangel	D	New York	1971–	92d–
Yvonne B. Burke	D	California	1973–79	93d–95th
Cardis Collins	D	Illinois	1973–96	92d–104th
Barbara C. Jordan	D	Texas	1973–79	93d–95th
Andrew Young	D	Georgia	1973–77	93d–95th
Harold E. Ford	D	Tennessee	1975–96	94th–104th
Julian C. Dixon	D	California	1979–	96th–
William H. Gray III	D	Pennsylvania	1979–91	96th–102d
George T. Leland	D	Texas	1979–89	96th–101st
Bennett M. Stewart	D	Illinois	1979–81	96th
George Crockett Jr.	D	Michigan	1981–92	96th–102d
Mervyn M. Dymally	D	California	1981–92	97th–102d
Gus Savage	D	Illinois	1981–92	97th–102d
Harold Washington	D	Illinois	1981–83	97th–98th
Katie Hall	D	Indiana	1983–85	97th–98th
Charles A. Hayes	D	Illinois	1983–92	98th–102d
Major R. Owens	D	New York	1983–	98th–
Edolphus Towns	D	New York	1983–	98th–
Alan Wheat	D	Missouri	1983–94	98th–103d
Alton R. Walton Jr.	D	New York	1986–87	99th
Mike Espy	D	Mississippi	1987–93	100th–103d
Floyd Flake	D	New York	1987–	100th–
John Lewis	D	Georgia	1987–	100th–
Kweisi Mfume	D	Maryland	1987–96	100th–104th
Donald M. Payne	D	New Jersey	1989–	101st–
Craig Washington	D	Texas	1990–94	101st–103d
Eleanor H. Norton[a]	D	Washington, D.C.	1991–	102d–
Maxine Waters	D	California	1991–	102d–
Gary Franks	R	Connecticut	1991–96	102d–104th
William Jefferson	D	Louisiana	1991–	102d–
Barbara Rose-Collins	D	Michigan	1991–96	102d–104th
Lucien E. Blackwell	D	Pennsylvania	1991–94	102d–103d
Earl F. Hilliard	D	Alabama	1993–	103d–
Walter R. Tucker	D	California	1993–95	103d–104th
Corrine Brown	D	Florida	1993–	103d–
Carrie Meek	D	Florida	1993–	103d–
Alcee L. Hastings	D	Florida	1993–	103d–
Sanford Bishop	D	Georgia	1993–	103d–
Cynthia McKinney	D	Georgia	1993–	103d–
Bobby L. Rush	D	Illinois	1993–	103d–
Mel Reynolds	D	Illinois	1993–95	103d–104th
Cleo Fields	D	Louisiana	1993–96	103d–104th
Albert R. Wynn	D	Maryland	1993–	103d–

(continued)

TABLE 11—Continued

Name	Party	State	Year	Congress
Eva M. Clayton	D	North Carolina	1993–	103d–
Melvin L. Watt	D	North Carolina	1993–	103d–
James E. Clyburn	D	South Carolina	1993–	103d–
Eddie B. Johnson	D	Texas	1993–	103d–
Robert C. Scott	D	Virginia	1993–	103d–
Bennie G. Thompson	D	Mississippi	1993–	103d–
Chaka Fattah	D	Pennsylvania	1995–	104th–
Sheila J. Lee	D	Texas	1995–	104th–
J. C. Watts	R	Oklahoma	1995–	104th–
Jesse Jackson Jr.	D	Illinois	1995–	104th–
Elijah E. Cummings	D	Maryland	1996–	104th–
Juanita Millender McDonald	D	California	1996–	104th–
Julia M. Carson	D	Indiana	1996–	105th–
Danny Davis	D	Illinois	1996–	105th–
Harold Ford Jr.	D	Tennessee	1996–	105th–
Carolyn Kilpatrick	D	Michigan	1996–	105th–

Sources: Congressional Quarterly Weekly Report 49 (January 2, 1993), 10; Michael Barone and Grant Ujifusa, *The Almanac of American Politics, 1996* (Washington, D.C.: National Journal, 1995); *New York Times* (November 7, 1996).

[a]Nonvoting delegate.

It is undoubtedly true that party identification plays a major role in explaining the behavior of members on issues related to race. But is the impact of party so strong that race is an insignificant predictor of legislator behavior on black policy preferences? On the one hand, we have observed in this research that Democrats, especially nonsouthern Democrats, are supporters of black interest legislation. But, on the other hand, the findings show that some Democrats are reluctant to support civil rights legislation, especially during the amending process. Swain's analysis suggests that race matters little in explaining substantive representation for African-Americans primarily because of the influence of party. There is research to suggest otherwise. Empirical evidence can be found in Hall and Heflin's examination of the relationship between race and legislative voting behavior in the 101st and 102d Congress. In a study of elite attitudes Sidney Verba and Gary Orren find that, on equality issues, African-Americans are much more likely to be to the Left of other major social groups. Moreover, according to their research findings, black leaders also hold consistently more liberal views than other white Democratic leaders within the party's coalition.[20] There are theoretical reasons to suspect that the behavioral patterns exhibited by party leaders can manifest themselves in the voting patterns of members of Congress.

The Significance of Color in Congress

To investigate the dyadic relationship between race and representatives' policy views on black interest legislation, the roll call voting behavior of House members spanning a twenty-year time period (93d through 103d Congresses) is examined. The lengthy time period is needed because the content of civil rights bills vary from Congress to Congress. Furthermore, the analysis is comprehensive so that safe conclusions can be stated about the impact of race. To increase the small number of cases for black members and to lessen problems associated with redistricting, the research in this section is divided into four time periods: time period 1 = members serving in 1973–76 (93d–94th Congresses); time period 2 = representatives serving in 1977–82 (95th–97th Congresses); time period 3 = legislators serving in 1983–86 (98th–99th Congresses), and time period 4 = legislators serving in 1987–92 (100th–102d Congresses). Conducting the analysis in this manner also has the advantage of increasing the number of amendments and final roll calls.[21] Because of the relatively high number of blacks serving in the 103d Congress and the fact that it was the only Congress for which data were available for this investigation after the 1990s round of redistricting, it will be closely examined in the next section on the relevance of issues.

Two models are constructed—one including legislative proposals during the amending process and one incorporating final roll call bills. It is hypothesized that race is a predictor of legislator support for black policy preferences and that its effect will be greater on amendments than on final passage bills. On average black members of Congress will support legislation beneficial to black constituents regardless of the stage of the roll call voting process. It is white representatives who face the difficult task of deciding whether to support or vote against strong civil rights measures.

Congressional ratings compiled by the LCCR are used as the dependent variable in the two models to measure the extent to which House members support black interest legislation.[22] Civil rights bills cannot be used here to assess the behavior of representatives because they do not come up for consideration in every congress. As previously stated, in chapter 1, the LCCR index is used on a regular basis by researchers to measure legislator support for progressive civil rights proposals. Since the LCCR index was first computed in the late 1960s, it has the added value of giving the researcher the opportunity to examine the behavior of representatives on race-relevant issues over an extended period of time. A possible problem in using the LCCR scores in a longitudinal study of this nature is issue variance. That is, legislators' LCCR scores may vary from Congress to Congress because the nature of the bills may differ from year to year. One solution to this potential problem is to include only those members who serve from Congress to Congress in a chosen time period. Conducting the analysis in this fashion lessens the problems associated with issue variance by subjecting all members to the same issues and influences in a given time period.

Each of the two models considers five independent variables: political party, region, race of the member, the percentage of blacks in the district, and the percentage of urban residents. Unfortunately, high collinearity between the race of the member variable and the racial composition variable precludes a quantitative assessment of the complete model.[23] The high correlation between the two sets of independent variables is due to the fact that most black representatives come from districts with a large black population. The general problem with this strong statistical relationship between the percentage of blacks in the district and the representation of the district by a black lawmaker is that their parameter estimates are likely to be unreliable. Moreover, when high collinearity exists one runs the risk of accepting the null hypothesis when in fact there is a statistically significant relationship between the dependent and independent variables.[24] The prescription here is to drop one of the two independent variables from the model. Given the theoretical and substantive interest in this chapter on the race of the member, the decision here is to drop the proportion of blacks in district variable from the model.[25] Expressed in the form of an equation, the models take on the following forms:

$$Y = a + b_1 X_1 + b_2 X_2 + b_3 X_3 + b_4 b_4 + e \qquad (3)$$

where:

Y is the House member's LCCR score on amendments ranging from 0 (most conservative) to 100 (most liberal); and in the final passage model Y is the legislator's LCCR policy support score on final decision bills, operationalized in the same manner as amendments.

a is the constant.

b_1 is the representative's political party affiliation, coded 1 if Democrat, 0 if Republican.

b_2 is the member's regional affiliation, coded 1 if a representative is from the non-South, 0 if from the South.[26]

b_3 is the racial identity of the member, coded 1 if black, 0 if white.
b_4 is the proportion of the district that is urban.
e is the error term.[27]

The preceding considerations lead to the following expectations: $b_1 > 0$, $b_2 > 0$, $b_3 > 0$, and $b_4 > 0$; that is, the coefficient signs of party, region, race, and urbanization will be positive. It is also expected that each of the independent variables will have a statistically significant impact on policy responsiveness to black interests in both models. Ordinary least squares regression tests the impact of the explanatory variables.[28]

The results of the regression analysis are reported in tables 12 and 13. Unstandardized regression coefficients can be used to show the difference in mean policy support scores between blacks and whites, after the influences of party, region, and urbanization have been accounted for. The standardized regression coefficients (beta weights) are used to show the relative importance of the independent variable both cross-sectionally and across time periods.

Not surprisingly, party looms as the most important explanatory variable in the models. Mean support scores of Democrats are significantly different (.000 level) from the average support scores of Republicans, once the effects of region, race, and urbanization are controlled for. An examination of the unstandardized coefficients in the amendment model (table 12) reveals that differences in mean amendment scores between the two parties range from 40 percent (1973–76) to 52 percent (1983–86). Mean final roll call scores (table 13) range from 36 percent (1977–82) to 56 percent (1973–76). The findings clearly suggest that House Democrats, on average, are much more supportive of black interest legislation than are House Republicans. Moreover, as the standardized regression coefficients in both models show, the impact of party has grown over the two-decade period. Its weight ranges from .559 (1973–76) to .787 (1983–86) in the amendment model and varies from a low of .514 (1977–82) to a high of .755 (1987–92) in the final roll call model.

As hypothesized, region significantly influences (.000 level) the behavior of House members. But, as the strength of party has grown in recent years, the impact of region gradually weakens across time. Substantively, nonsouthern members continue to be more supportive of civil rights–related issues than their southern colleagues, but the gap among regional House members has declined. The drop in mean scores is about the same in both models, fluctuating between highs of 21 and 31 percent in the earliest time frame to lows of 11 and 15 percent in the more recent time periods. What the findings suggest is that party is becoming increasingly

TABLE 12. Effects of Party, Region, Race, and Urbanization on House Members' Support for Black Policy Preferences: Regression Estimates

Variables	Amendment Model		
	Unstandardized	Standardized	t-ratio
Members' Political Party			
1973–76[a]			
93d–94th Congresses	40.256	.559	22.287***
1977–82			
95th–97th Congresses	40.893	.610	31.188***
1983–86			
98th–99th Congresses	52.422	.787	38.644***
1987–92			
100th–102d Congresses	41.014	.744	42.022***
Region (Non-south/South)			
1973–76			
93d–94th Congresses	30.611	.379	14.891***
1977–82			
95th–97th Congresses	22.475	.299	15.104***
1983–86			
98th–99th Congresses	13.745	.185	9.149***
1987–92			
100th–102d Congresses	13.734	.221	12.566***
Race (Black/White)			
1973–76			
93d–94th Congresses	18.558	.097	3.863***
1977–82			
95th–97th Congresses	16.404	.091	4.663***
1983–86			
98th–99th Congresses	4.095	.024	1.157
1987–92			
100th–102d Congresses	5.010	.040	1.700*
Percent Urban			
1973–76			
93d–94th Congresses	.165	.110	4.240***
1977–82			
95th–97th Congresses	.219	.156	7.688***
1983–86			
98th–99th Congresses	.122	.083	4.015***
1987–92			
100th–102d Congresses	.130	.108	5.957***

Note: Members' support as measured by the Leadership Conference on Civil Rights (LCCR). Members' LCCR scores range from 0 (most conservative) to 100 (most liberal).

[a]1973–76 (R^2 = 49, N = 861); 1977–82 (R^2 = 54, N = 1293); 1983–86 (R^2 = .67, N = 837); 1987–92 (R^2 = .64, N = 1214).

***$p \leq .001$ *$p \leq .10$ (one-tailed tests)

TABLE 13. Effects of Party, Region, Race, and Urbanization on House Members' Support for Black Policy Preferences: Regression Estimates

Variables	Final Passage Model		
	Unstandardized	Standardized	t-ratio
Members' Political Party			
1973–76[a]			
93d–94th Congresses	56.236	.671	29.321***
1977–82			
95th–97th Congresses	36.031	.514	22.633***
1983–86			
98th–99th Congresses	47.731	.720	30.173***
1987–92			
100th–102d Congresses	42.414	.755	43.998***
Region (Non-South/South)			
1973–76			
93d–94th Congresses	26.261	.279	12.031***
1977–82			
95th–97th Congresses	20.781	.264	11.503***
1983–86			
98th–99th Congresses	10.539	.142	6.015***
1987–92			
100th–102d Congresses	15.041	.237	13.923***
Race (Black/White)			
1973–76			
93d–94th Congresses	6.811	.030	1.335
1977–82			
95th–97th Congresses	8.641	.045	2.000**
1983–86			
98th–99th Congresses	2.400	.014	.582
1987–92			
100th–102d Congresses	2.969	.023	1.289
Percent Urban			
1973–76			
93d–94th Congresses	.292	.167	7.049***
1977–82			
95th–97th Congresses	.187	.128	5.436***
1983–86			
98th–99th Congresses	.096	.066	2.707***
1987–92			
100th–102d Congresses	.140	.113	6.485***

Note: Per LCCR index.

[a]1973–76 (R^2 = .57); 1977–82 (R^2 = .37); 1983–86 (R^2 = .55); 1987–92 (R^2 = .66). See table 4.2 for N of cases.

***$p \le .001$ **$p \le .05$ (one-tailed tests)

influential in explaining legislator support of black policy preferences, but regional differences do remain a factor. The Civil Rights Act of 1964 and the Voting Rights Act of 1965 have been major factors in narrowing policy differences between northern and southern Democrats and sharpening those between the Democrats and Republicans in Congress. The findings do not mean, however, that southern Democrats are as responsive to black interests as their party colleagues in the non-South. They do imply that the southern congressional wing of the party has been slowly moving in the direction of the mainstream of the party on class-based socioeconomic issues.[29]

As expected, the constituency variable urbanization also helps to account for variation in black policy preferences. It is statistically significant in each of the time periods in the analysis. The findings are consistent with what we have observed in earlier chapters; that is, while urbanization is a predictor of support for black policy preferences, its predictive power is not as strong as party or region.

The relationship of particular interest is between the race of the member and black policy preferences. There are several noteworthy findings that can be deduced from the summary statistics in the tables. First, even after controlling for the powerful effects of region and party, race significantly impacts the behavior of House members in a positive direction. This finding can be interpreted to mean that the racial identity of the member matters in congressional voting for progressive civil rights proposals even when party and region are held constant. The difference in mean support scores between black and white legislators is approximately 9 percent (1977–82) in the final passage vote model, and average scores vary from 5 percent (1987–92) to 19 percent (1973–76) in the amendment vote model.

A second finding of note is that race has period effects. That is, based on the groupings of congresses for analysis, the average scores of black representatives in the 1983–86 time period in the amendment model are found not to differ significantly from the mean scores of their white colleagues. And, in the final passage vote model, the impact of race only shows up in the time period from 1977 to 1982. A more detailed explanation for the findings of period effects will follow in the next section. For now it suffices to note that the nature of the civil rights bills vary from Congress to Congress and can determine whether race will be a factor in explaining legislator responsiveness to black policy interests.

A third finding of interest is that the impact of race is stronger in the amendment model than in the final passage model. In each of the time periods in which race is found to be statistically significant, mean support scores are higher on roll call votes on amendments. The conclusion is that racial differences on black interest legislation are more likely to show up on roll calls during the amending process than on final passage.

Overall the goodness of fit in both models ranges in the low-moderate to high-moderate range. The major difference between the two models is the impact of race, whose effect is more pronounced on amendments than on final roll calls. The statistical analysis provides some evidence that race matters in representatives' voting decisions on civil rights–related issues. But the analysis does not tell us much about the actual conditions under which race is likely to be a significant predictor of civil rights support.

The Relative Importance of Issues

The main proposition here is that the saliency of race depends on the nature of the civil rights proposal being voted on by members of Congress. Civil rights bills vary in strength; some are controversial, and others are not. Civil rights bills that are relatively uncontroversial will produce roll calls that are unanimous or nearly unanimous in support or in opposition. They are weak tests of dimensionality—or, more specifically, support of black interest legislation—because they do not reveal anything about differences in issue positions among legislators. Even party, the strongest predictor of legislative voting on socioeconomic legislation, will not show up as a predictor of roll call voting behavior because of solid House support. Then there are civil rights proposals that produce cleavages along partisan lines—that is, unity within the Democratic or Republican Party for or against a bill. Here party becomes the major predictor of legislative behavior. Many civil rights bills do not produce racial cleavages because they are essentially moderate proposals designed to appeal to marginal supporters in the House. Finally, some civil rights proposals are controversial and are more likely to produce cleavages along racial lines in the House. These are the bills that provide a true test of the commitment of members to civil rights. The relevant point to be made here is that the relationship between descriptive representation and substantive representation of black interests is very much tied to the nature of issues. The more divisive the civil rights measure, the greater the likelihood that race will be a factor in explaining legislator behavior on African-American policy preferences.

One way to get a more complete explanation of the role of issues is to break down tables 12 and 13 into more discrete data. An examination of specific bills can help shed more light on the significance of issues in congressional voting along racial lines. Table 14 presents the proportion of voting members of the House supporting the LCCR position on the five most divisive bills in the LCCR indexes (see app. B). The data are displayed according to members' race, party, and regional affiliation for the

100th, 101st, 102d, and 103d Congresses. The findings reveal that black members of the House consistently occupy the Left position (most liberal) of the five groups, followed by white nonsouthern Democrats, southern Democrats, nonsouthern Republicans, then southern Republicans. Given the fact that the vast majority of African-Americans support policies of a redistributive nature, it is not surprising that black representatives would be to the Left of other members in the House. More than this, their position on socioeconomic policies is in accord with the theories proposed on the saliency of race in the House; that is, electoral considerations and a sense of group consciousness among blacks would lead one to expect that black lawmakers would cast their roll call votes in a manner consistent with the liberal policy views of the black masses.

In all cases white nonsouthern Democrats are supportive of the positions endorsed by the LCCR, but they are always to the Right of black representatives. Moreover, the distance between black members and white nonsouthern Democrats is greater on bills in the 101st through 103d Congresses than they are in the 100th Congress. The bills used to compile the LCCR scale during the 100th Congress include the Japanese-American Redress Act (and amendments to it); the Civil Rights Restoration Act (and amendments to it); Hate Crime Statistics Act; Pay Equity bill; Budget Resolution providing for increases in programs for the poor, impoverished children, medical insurance for the elderly and homeless; and the Fair Housing Bill of 1988 (and amendments to it). Of the five bills included in the table the greatest distance between the two cohorts occurs on two Japanese-American Redress bills, legislation designed to provide payments to Japanese-Americans interned during World War II.

The Lungren Amendment to the Japanese-American Redress Act was intended to strike a provision that gave restitution to Japanese-Americans for their hardships during World War II. The bill was opposed by the LCCR and rejected in the House by a vote of 162 to 237.[30] Black representatives who voted on the amendment gave their unanimous support, while 89 percent of voting white nonsouthern Democrats supported positions endorsed by the LCCR. The other bill was the adoption of the conference report that authorized payments of twenty thousand dollars in reparations to surviving Japanese-Americans interned during the war.[31] The LCCR endorsed the report, which was passed by a vote margin of 257 to 156 in the chamber. The proportion of black representatives supporting the bill was 100 percent, and for white nonsouthern Democrats the support level was 89 percent. The distance of 11 percent is relatively close and is even closer between the two liberal cohorts on votes for the other three most divisive bills in the LCCR index for the 100th Congress. The high lev-

TABLE 14. The Proportion of House Members Supporting the LCCR Position on the Five Most Divisive Votes in the LCCR Index

	BLK	WND	WSD	WNR	WSR
100th Congress					
Budget Resolution for low-income families	100.0	94.0	89.0	0.0	0.0
Amendment to Japanese-American Redress Act	100.0	89.0	45.0	38.0	12.0
Motion to Civil Rights Restoration Act	100.0	99.0	94.0	12.0	0.0
Adoption of Conference Report to Japanese-American Redress Act	100.0	89.0	41.0	50.0	10.0
Final Passage of Japanese Redress Act	100.0	94.0	44.0	42.0	15.0
101st Congress					
Habeas Corpus Amendment	95.0	78.0	13.0	33.0	3.0
Chapman Americans with Disabilities Amendment	95.0	81.0	23.0	22.0	5.0
Savings and Loan Redlining Amendment	100.0	82.0	30.0	31.0	3.0
Racial Justice Amendment	100.0	90.0	43.0	13.0	0.0
Olin Americans with Disabilities Amendment	95.0	86.0	34.0	27.0	34.0
102d Congress					
Balanced Budget Amendment	92.0	67.0	16.0	2.0	0.0
Unlimited Punitive Damage Amendment to the Civil Rights Act of 1991	96.0	63.0	20.0	2.0	5.0
Race-Based Sentencing Crime Amendment bill	95.0	77.0	26.0	6.0	5.0
Habeas Corpus Crime Amendment bill	95.0	86.0	50.0	6.0	0.0
Voting Rights Language Assistance Amendment	95.0	81.0	47.0	12.0	8.0
103d Congress					
District of Columbia Statehood bill	97.0	64.0	18.0	0.0	0.0
Balanced Budget Amendment	95.0	66.0	21.0	0.0	0.0
Gays in the Military Amendment bill	92.0	68.0	2.0	9.0	0.0
Adoption of Conference Report on Gun Control bill	92.0	78.0	46.0	35.0	23.0
Amendment to Racial Justice Crime bill	97.0	87.0	51.0	6.0	0.0

Note: BLK = black representatives; WND = white nonsouthern Democrats; WSD = white southern Democrats; WNR = white nonsouthern Republicans; WSR = white southern Republicans.

els of support and the close proximity of the two most supportive groups suggest that race was not a major factor.

In contrast, there are signs of racial cleavage on bills in the 101st through 103d Congresses. During the 101st Congress (1989–90) bills in the LCCR index included amendments to the Americans with Disabilities Act, Hate Crime Statistics Act, Minimum Wage Increase, amendments to the Civil Rights Act of 1990, a Savings and Loan Restructuring/Redlining amendment, the Family and Medical Leave Act (and amendments), and amendments to crime bills. During the 101st Congress the greatest distance between the two most supportive groups came on votes for a redlining bill and a crime bill. One of the more controversial bills was a savings and loans restructuring bill initially proposed by Senator Edward Kennedy of Massachusetts.[32] The bill was designed to help bank regulators combat the discriminatory practice of redlining used by some mortgage lenders to deny mortgage and other credit to racial minorities. The bill was endorsed by the LCCR and passed in the House by a vote of 214 to 200. The bill received the unanimous support of black representatives who cast roll call votes. The support level from white nonsouthern Democrats who cast a vote was 82 percent. The distance between the two cohorts was 18 percent.

Another illustration is a crime bill offered by Democrat William J. Hughes from New Jersey. The bill was endorsed by the LCCR. Provisions in the bill included, among other things, the requirement of competent counsel for death row prisoners filing federal habeas corpus petitions.[33] Although the bill was rejected in the House by a vote of 189 to 239, 95 percent of the black members who voted supported the bill, as compared to 78 percent of voting white nonsouthern Democrats. Thus, close to one-fourth of voting white nonsouthern Democrats voted in opposition to the position endorsed by the civil rights organization.

Debate over the issue of crime continued in the 102d Congress (1991–92). Two crime bills offered by Republican representative Henry J. Hyde made the list of the five most divisive bills in the LCCR index. The most divisive of the two was a proposal to eliminate a provision in a larger crime bill to allow death row prisoners to raise certain race-bias claims in federal habeas corpus appeals.[34] The Hyde amendment was adopted by a vote of 238 to 180. The LCCR opposed the proposal, as did all but one voting member of the black delegation, Republican Gary Franks from Connecticut. In comparison, 77 percent of white nonsouthern Democrats voted in opposition to the Hyde crime amendment. Even though over three-quarters of white nonsouthern Democrats supported the bill, they were still some distance away from the support level of 95 percent given by the black membership.

Race-based crime bills were not the only bills on which differences in voting among the two liberal voting groups can be seen. White nonsouthern Democrats were also some distance away from black legislators on a substitute amendment offered by Edolphus Towns of New York. The amendment would have provided for unlimited punitive damages for discrimination based on factors other than race (e.g., sex).[35] The bill was defeated by a vote margin of 152 to 277. The LCCR endorsed Towns's amendment. The only black member to oppose the bill was Gary Franks. Approximately two-thirds (63 percent) of voting white nonsouthern Democrats gave their support to the amendment. The distance between black legislators and white nonsouthern Democrats was fairly wide, at 33 percent.

Other bills included in the LCCR scale for the 102d Congress are Voting Rights Language Assistance (and amendments to it), Family and Medical Leave Act, National Motor Voter Registration, and a constitutional amendment to balance the federal budget. As table 14 shows, some racial cleavage between black representatives and white nonsouthern Democrats can be seen on votes for voting rights language assistance and the constitutional amendment to balance the federal budget.

During the 103d Congress (1993–94) the LCCR index included votes on the Elementary and Secondary Education Reauthorization Act, amendment and final passage of the Family and Medical Leave, National Motor Voter Registration bill, amendment to the Racial Justice Act, District of Columbia Statehood Bill, Balanced Budget Constitutional Amendment, gun control legislation (Brady Bill), Gays in the Military amendment, and bills on congressional compliance, violence against women, and employee protection. The most divisive votes came on bills to admit the District of Columbia into the union, a constitutional amendment to balance the budget, the Brady Bill, gays in the military, and racial discrimination in capital offenses. The distance between black members of the House and white representatives on these bills ranged from 10 percent to 33 percent. The greatest distance between black legislators and white nonsouthern Democrats came on final passage of a bill to admit the District of Columbia as the fifty-first state of the union.[36] The bill was rejected by a vote of 153 to 277. The LCCR endorsed the bill and 97 percent of the black congressional delegation gave its support. The only dissenting vote came from Gary Franks. White nonsouthern Democrats were less than enthusiastic about the idea of the District of Columbia becoming a state. Less than two-thirds (64 percent) of those who voted gave their support.

These findings are consistent with the model of voting behavior in this book. It is clear that black representatives constitute the most liberal cohort in the House on class-based socioeconomic issues. This, of course, clearly places them in the high amendment/high final passage category of voting behavior. White nonsouthern Democrats are on the liberal side, but they are outflanked by black members of the House. Furthermore, they are not as consistent as black members in giving high levels of support on policies of primary interest to African-Americans.

White southern Democrats are in the middle of the five groups, but their scores vary more widely than those of the other four groups. On some bills they give high levels of support. During the 103d Congress, for example, 86 percent of voting white southern Democrats supported the adoption of the conference report to require states to allow citizens to register to vote while applying for or renewing a driver's license either at agencies providing public assistance or through the mail. In comparison, 97 percent of black members, 96 percent of white nonsouthern Democrats, 13 percent of white nonsouthern Republicans, and 6 percent of southern Republicans supported the conference report, which was adopted by a vote margin of 259 to 164.

Southern Democrats were more tenuous in their opposition to an amendment designed to delete a provision in a racial justice bill to prohibit imposition of the death penalty if a criminal defendant could show racial discrimination. The bill was rejected by a margin of 212 to 217. The LCCR opposed the bill, as did 97 percent of the black delegation. The opposition score for white southern Democrats was in the moderate range, at 51 percent. Eighty-seven percent of white nonsouthern Democrats, 6 percent of white nonsouthern Republicans, and no southern Republicans voted in opposition to the bill. In contrast to their position on adoption of the "motor-voter" registration bill, white southern Democrats were opposed to granting statehood to the District of Columbia. As table 14 reveals, only 18 percent of the white southern House Democratic delegation gave support to the legislation. In sum, these examples give further support for the contention of policy deviation in the voting behavior of white southern Democrats. They do vote less conservatively than they did four decades ago, yet they are a good distance away from the consistent liberal roll call voting behavior manifested by black legislators.

Republicans are to the Right of Democrats on black policy preferences. In all cases southern Republicans are the most conservative. All things being equal, when it comes to opposing strong civil rights measures, Republicans are generally close-knit.

What are we to make of the findings in table 14? The evidence reported in this section points to two general conclusions. First, black representatives do a better job of representing the policy interests of black constituents than do white nonsouthern Democrats. Yet it is also true that the distance between the civil rights support scores of black representatives and white nonsouthern Democrats is not great, all things being equal. In substantive terms this means that the trade-off between gaining a black representative instead of a white nonsouthern Democrat will be relatively small. If one compares the mean civil rights support scores of black representatives to those of white nonsouthern Republicans, it becomes readily apparent that the policy distance between the two cohorts is substantial. As a consequence, blacks will reap the greatest policy benefits if a change in representation occurs, if a black Democrat replaces a Republican in the non-South. But, if gaining a black Democratic representative instead of a white nonsouthern Democrat means increasing the probability of a white nonsouthern Republican winning in an adjoining district, then the overall quality of substantive representation for black citizens may be adversely affected by the trade-off.

Second, the findings in table 14 point strongly to Hall and Heflin's argument that the race of the member matters mostly in the South, where blacks historically have been underrepresented in Congress.[37] On controversial black interest legislation the magnitude of the policy distance between black representatives and white southern Democrats is fairly substantial and is even greater between black representatives and white southern Republicans. But it is also the case that the drop-off in representation of black interests is substantial if the district moves from representation by a white Democrat to a white Republican in the region. Thus, the picture is less clear about the overall policy implications of increasing black congressional representation in the South—that is, if it is at the expense of a white southern Democrat.

More will be said about the potential trade-offs between descriptive representation and substantive representation in the next chapter. The major focus of this chapter is on the impact of the race of the representative on black policy preferences, and the evidence presented here indicates that the race of the member does matter in congressional voting. But further testing is needed on this important topic before more can be said about the relationship between race and representation.

The Impact of Race (101st–103d Congresses)

Having examined some of the issues in each of the individual congresses in time period 4, the hypothesis that the impact of the race of the member is conditioned by the controversial nature of bills becomes testable. Again, because of the high collinearity between the race of the member variable and the racial composition variable, the latter was dropped from the model.[38] Based on the examination of specific issues in the preceding section, the race variable should be a statistically significant predictor of black policy preferences in the 101st, 102d, and 103d Congresses. Furthermore, the effect of race should be greater on votes during the amending process than on final roll calls.

The results are reported in tables 15 and 16. The tables essentially break down the data in time period 4 more discretely into individual congresses. As expected, there are sizable differences between the two parties on social and economic legislation. On average Democratic support is at least five times greater than that of Republican support. Also as expected, House members from the non-South are more supportive of civil rights than are legislators from the South. Regional differences are anywhere from 13 to 23 percent in the four congresses under investigation. Percent urban fails to pass statistical significance in the 100th Congress but does contribute to the explanation of civil rights support in the other three congresses. The findings show that there are measurable differences between the mean scores of party and region. In fact, the smallest gap between the mean scores of party and the mean scores of region in a given Congress is 32 percent (final passage model, 100th Congress). The party, region, and urbanization variables are highly statistically significant at the .000 level. But it is abundantly clear that party is the key variable in explaining black policy preferences.

As for the race variable, it is statistically insignificant in both models for the 100th and 101st Congresses. As for the 100th Congress, this finding is to be expected, since votes on bills were relatively undivisive. The findings also support what Swain (1993) observed in her multivariate analysis of the 100th Congress. For the 102d and 103d Congresses the race variable is statistically significant at the .000 level in the amendment model. After controlling for the impact of party and region, racial differences are significant and range from 10 to 12 percent in the model. Race failed to reach statistical significance in the 100th through 102d Congresses in the final passage model. Moreover, racial differences are not as pronounced in the final passage model as they are in the amendment model, again confirming the hypothesis that voting on amendments is a more demanding test of legislator support for black policy preferences than votes on final roll calls.

The evidence presented in tables 15 and 16 indicates that race has an impact on civil rights proposals, but its impact is periodic; in other words, in some years it has a significant impact but not others. A plausible interpretation of this finding is that the impact of race will depend on the nature of the issues, which can vary from Congress to Congress. The results also reveal that the race variable has a stronger relationship with voting on amendments than on final passage.

The investigation shows some evidence of congressional voting along racial lines after other explanatory factors have been controlled for. It

TABLE 15. Effects of Party, Region, Race, and Urbanization on House Members' Support for Black Policy Preferences: Regression Estimates for Individual Congresses

| | Amendment Model | | |
Variables	Unstandardized	Standardized	t-ratio
Members' Political Party			
1987–88[a]			
(100th Congress)	50.863	.753	23.798***
1989–90			
(101st Congress)	57.573	.725	25.170***
1991–92			
(102d Congress)	62.803	.784	28.625***
1993–94			
(103d Congress)	72.096	.845	39.868***
Region (Non-South/South)			
1987–88			
(100th Congress)	18.831	.244	7.775***
1989–90			
(101st Congress)	23.174	.261	9.127***
1991–92			
(102d Congress)	16.696	.184	6.798***
1993–94			
(103d Congress)	12.666	.136	6.516***
Race (Black/White)			
1987–88			
(100th Congress)	1.920	.012	.718
1989–90			
(101st Congress)	6.681	.033	1.106
1991–92			
(102d Congress)	12.138	.070	2.508**
1993–94			
(103d Congress)	10.195	.097	4.468***
Percent Urban			
1987–88			
(100th Congress)	.044	.029	.916
1989–90			
(101st Congress)	.342	.197	6.739***
1991–92			
(102d Congress)	.229	.129	4.593***
1993–94			
(103d Congress)	.236	.124	5.771***

Note: Per LCCR index.

[a]1987–88 (R^2 = .62, N = 398); 1989–90 (R^2 = .68, N = 412); 1991–92 (R^2 = .72, N = 394); 1993–94 (R^2 = .82, N = 426).

***$p \leq .001$ **$p \leq .01$ (one-tailed tests)

TABLE 16. Effects of Party, Region, Race, and Urbanization on House Members' Support for Black Policy Preferences: Regression Estimates for Individual Congresses

Variables	Final Passage Model		
	Unstandardized	Standardized	*t*-ratio
Members' Political Party			
1987–88[a]			
(100th Congress)	48.540	.767	24.853***
1989–90			
(101st Congress)	46.681	.723	22.820***
1991–92			
(102d Congress)	58.512	.784	27.123***
1993–94			
(103d Congress)	63.806	.792	32.104***
Region (Non-South/South)			
1987–88			
(100th Congress)	16.968	.234	7.666***
1989–90			
(101st Congress)	15.926	.221	7.014***
1991–92			
(102d Congress)	16.233	.193	6.723***
1993–94			
(103d Congress)	14.945	.171	6.995***
Race (Black/White)			
1987–88			
(100th Congress)	3.706	.024	.762
1989–90			
(101st Congress)	.870	.005	.169
1991–92			
(102d Congress)	4.796	.029	1.008
1993–94			
(103d Congress)	7.361	.074	2.936***
Percent Urban			
1987–88			
(100th Congress)	.029	.021	.676
1989–90			
(101st Congress)	.190	.135	4.172***
1991–92			
(102d Congress)	.156	.094	3.183***
1993–94			
(103d Congress)	.323	.179	7.190***

Note: Per LCCR index.

[a]1987–88 (R^2 = .64); 1989–90 (R^2 = .61); 1991–92 (R^2 = .68); 1993–94 (R^2 = .76). See table 15 for N of cases.

***$p \leq .001$ (one-tailed test)

could be argued, however, that some of the issues in the LCCR index are tangential to black interests, thus affecting the findings. For instance, legislation pertaining to the Japanese Reparations Act is not directly indicative of black interests. Nor, for that matter, is the amendment pertaining to gays in the military.

Because some of the votes may not be directly related to black interests, a variant of the multivariate models displayed in tables 15 and 16 is constructed. The reconstructed models drop from the LCCR indices votes that do not directly pertain to the social and economic policy interests of African-Americans. Determining which votes to exclude is open to multiple, qualitatively different interpretations by the analyst. The decision here is to drop votes on the Japanese Reparations bills (100th Congress), American with Disabilities bills (101st Congress), Voting Rights Language bills and the Balanced Budget Amendment (102d Congress), and Gays in the Military bill and the Balanced Budget Amendment (103d Congress).

Tables 17 and 18 present the estimates of the multivariate models. The first observation to be made is the considerable stability of the results across the two different versions of the models. While the magnitudes of the coefficients undergo some change, the essential findings remain the same. What accounts for these findings? A plausible interpretation is that blacks are consistent in taking the liberal positions on civil rights issues, even if the issues are tangential to black interests. The issue of gays in the military, for example, is not an issue that directly pertains to black interests. Even so, black-white differences can be seen on the issue of gay rights. On a related question, in a 1992 NES survey respondents were asked if they favored laws to protect homosexuals from discrimination. In the case of whites 59 percent favored the law. As for blacks, 70 percent favored protecting homosexuals from discrimination.

Racial differences can be seen in the voting behavior of members on the Meehan amendment (103d Congress) to strike the provision in the Fiscal Year 1994 Defense Authorization Bill codifying a ban on homosexuals in the military. The LCCR endorsed the amendment, as did 92 percent of black members who voted on the bill. In contrast, 68 percent of white nonsouthern Democrats, 2 percent of white southern Democrats, 9 percent of white nonsouthern Republicans, and no southern Republicans cast their votes for the bill. In essence the inclusion of tangential bills in the LCCR index does not significantly alter the results in this chapter.

Discussion

Proponents of descriptive representation argue that the quality of substantive representation for blacks will improve if more of them are elected to

TABLE 17. Effects of Party, Region, Race, and Urbanization on House Members' Support for Legislation More Reflective of Black Interests: Regression Estimates for Individual Congresses

Variables	Amendment Model		
	Unstandardized	Standardized	*t*-ratio
Members' Political Party			
1987–88[a]			
(100th Congress)	52.332	.761	23.802***
1989–90			
(101st Congress)	62.650	.759	27.266***
1991–92			
(102d Congress)	62.763	.779	28.176***
1993–94			
(103d Congress)	76.858	.872	43.253***
Region (Non-South/South)			
1987–88			
(100th Congress)	16.958	.216	6.806***
1989–90			
(101st Congress)	22.201	.241	8.705***
1991–92			
(102d Congress)	16.727	.184	6.708***
1993–94			
(103d Congress)	10.291	.107	5.388***
Race (Black/White)			
1987–88			
(100th Congress)	1.524	.009	.278
1989–90			
(101st Congress)	8.360	.041	1.450
1991–92			
(102d Congress)	12.071	.069	2.500**
1993–94			
(103d Congress)	8.682	.080	3.873***
Percent Urban			
1987–88			
(100th Congress)	.010	.002	.896
1989–90			
(101st Congress)	.290	.161	5.670***
1991–92			
(102d Congress)	.247	.138	4.902***
1993–94			
(103d Congress)	.179	.091	4.471***

Note: Per LCCR index.

[a]1987–88 (R^2 = .61); 1989–90 (R^2 = .70); 1991–92 (R^2 = .71); 1993–94 (R^2 = .84). See table 15 for *N* of cases.

***$p \leq .001$ **$p \leq .01$ (one-tailed tests)

TABLE 18.   Effects of Party, Region, Race, and Urbanization on House Members' Support for Legislation More Reflective of Black Interests: Regression Estimates for Individual Congresses

Variables	Final Passage Model		
	Unstandardized	Standardized	t-ratio
Members' Political Party			
1987–88[a]			
(100th Congress)	50.418	.788	25.799***
1989–90			
(101st Congress)	55.692	.748	24.659***
1991–92			
(102d Congress)	59.869	.800	28.418***
1993–94			
(103d Congress)	51.124	.766	29.034***
Region (Non-South/South)			
1987–88			
(100th Congress)	14.603	.199	6.594***
1989–90			
(101st Congress)	18.368	.221	7.327***
1991–92			
(102d Congress)	14.016	.166	5.944***
1993–94			
(103d Congress)	10.928	.151	5.774***
Race (Black/White)			
1987–88			
(100th Congress)	2.307	.015	.474
1989–90			
(101st Congress)	1.624	.009	.286
1991–92			
(102d Congress)	3.242	.020	.698
1993–94			
(103d Congress)	6.898	.084	3.105***
Percent Urban			
1987–88			
(100th Congress)	.009	.007	.229
1989–90			
(101st Congress)	.209	.128	4.150***
1991–92			
(102d Congress)	.167	.101	3.497***
1993–94			
(103d Congress)	.288	.193	7.240***

Note: Per LCCR index.

[a]1987–88 ($R^2 = .65$); 1989–90 ($R^2 = .64$); 1991–92 ($R^2 = .70$); 1993–94 ($R^2 = .73$). See table 15 for N of cases.

***$p \leq .001$ (one-tailed test)

serve in Congress. This assumption is based upon the notion that questions of race have political implications. As a consequence, most civil rights leaders look to the number of people of color in Congress to assess its representativeness. There is a theoretical basis to support their assertions, which can be found in the social science literature on group consciousness and representatives' political perceptions of their constituencies. The first view posits that strong feelings of group attachment brought on by shared historical and life experiences can influence the substantive legislative activities of black lawmakers. In the words of black congressman Louis Stokes of Ohio, "We're carrying the load for 25 million black people."[39] Those words infer a sense of group consciousness among black members of Congress that transcends the boundaries of constituents in their congressional districts. The second view holds that legislative behavior will be influenced by representatives' perceptions about who will optimize their chances for reelection. Thus, there is a strong theoretical basis for hypothesizing that African-American representatives will be most responsive to black interests.

Using data from eleven congresses coupled with an examination of bills in the more recent congresses, the analysis here finds evidence for the hypothesis that race matters even after controlling for the strong impact of party and region. These findings indicate that it is misleading to state or infer that race is a nonfactor in legislative voting on issues of primary interest to the black community. As the results reveal, the significance of race as a predictor of black policy preferences will depend on the nature of the bills.

By now it should be clear that the two major political parties are polarized on class-based socioeconomic issues. The complaint that there is not a "dime's worth of difference" or that the two parties play Tweedledum and Tweedledee does not apply to roll call voting on civil rights. The evidence presented here suggests that the race of the member will matter most when the Democratic Party holds a slim majority of the seats in the House, all things being equal. Because the parties are more united in opposition to each other than at any time since World War II, each party is more dependent on its own members for votes. Within the Democratic Party this translates into greater bargaining power for the Black Caucus, which can use its leverage to bargain successfully for more social programs of importance to its constituents. Conversely, the caucus will have little influence in a Congress with a Republican majority because of its small Republican membership and the fact that black constituents are not a major component of the electoral coalition of Republican candidates.

While the two parties are clearly polarized on issues of primary interest to African-Americans, there are some important internal differences with the Democratic Party on civil rights legislation. All things being equal, black representatives are the most supportive of black interests, followed by white nonsouthern Democrats. While both are in the high final passage/high amendment category, on balance there is a good deal of space between the two groups on some important issues. The variation in the support level of white nonsouthern Democratic support gives more credence to the hypothesis that race matters in the decision calculus of the representative.

Racial differences in congressional voting are much more pronounced in the South, where the proportion of blacks in the House is low relative to the proportion of the regional population. Some success has been made in this area as the result of the 1990s round of redistricting, which brought in a record number of black representatives to serve in the 103d, 104th, and 105th Congresses. Even so, representation of blacks is still not comparable to the proportion in the region. The analysis indicates that researchers should exercise caution when interpreting the voting behavior of white southern Democrats. While southern Democrats are less conservative than they were three decades ago, on average they are some distance away from the support levels of black representatives or nonsouthern Democrats.

There are reasons to believe that the findings in this chapter may underestimate the effects of member race. This statement is based on an important observation made by Hall and Heflin regarding the censoring of civil rights proposals by the party leadership in Congress. As they rightfully point out, the types of policies most African-Americans would like to see enacted into law lie far to the Left of the median voter in Congress. This is especially true of congresses in which the Republican Party holds a majority of the seats. With the data in table 14 in mind, consider the following example. Suppose that there is a normal distribution of voting preferences on civil rights proposals in the House. Now suppose that black representatives are on the far Left (most liberal), followed by white nonsouthern Democrats (liberal), southern Democrats (moderate), nonsouthern Republicans (conservative), and southern Republicans (most conservative). Assume also that the Rules Committee and leaders of both parties censor civil rights proposals before they are considered on the floor. If the gross assumption can be made that they censor civil rights proposals with the thought in mind of winning enough votes on the floor for passage, then many liberal proposals will not be considered for floor action because they are likely to be defeated, because of a lack of majority support on the floor of the House. If liberal proposals do come up for a vote on the floor, they will likely produce cleavages along racial lines in the legislative chamber. More important, one is likely to see the emergence of member race as a predictor of roll call voting behavior on black interest legislation.[40]

The findings presented here have potentially important political consequences. There is more to the election of African-Americans than symbolism or the color of skin. The color of Congress has implications for the quality of substantive representation for African-Americans. The high level of support among black lawmakers is unmatched by any other cohort in the assembly. Civil rights advocates have long argued that the racial composition of Congress and districts significantly affects the quality of representation for blacks. As a consequence, they have called for legal remedies to enhance the electoral fortunes of black congressional candidates. The course of action sought most often to elect more blacks to legislative assemblies has been benign racial redistricting, a subject for analysis in the next chapter. Their efforts have met with some success, as a record number of black representatives were elected after the 1990 round of redistricting. But in the wake of *Shaw v. Reno* (1993), *Miller v. Johnson* (1995), and *Bush v. Vera* (1996), which question the merits of reapportionment based on race, recent gains made by blacks through racial redistricting may be temporary. At the very least those who are interested in increasing the number of historically underrepresented racial minorities in Congress should take some comfort in knowing that opponents cannot deny the importance of color in Congress based on substantive reasoning.

CHAPTER 5

Racial Redistricting and the Representation of Black Interests

As long as members of racial groups have the commonality of interest . . . and as long as racial bloc voting takes place, legislators will have to take race into account in order to avoid dilution of minority voting strength in districting plans they adopt.
　　—Justice David H. Souter, dissenting opinion in *Miller v. Johnson*

The process of redrawing congressional district boundary lines in response to a reapportionment of congressional seats among the states is called redistricting. It is one of the most important political processes in the United States. The process occurs after the decennial population census, and it is usually in the hands of legislatures and governors to determine the configuration of district boundary lines. Redistricting is crucial because it can help determine whether the House will be dominated by Democrats or Republicans. It can also help determine whether people of color will increase their numbers in a legislative assembly.

The round of redistricting completed after the 1990 census has caused a wave of controversy in academic, legal, and political circles unlike any since the passage of the Voting Rights Act of 1965. Much of the controversy centers around the extent to which district lines were redrawn to accommodate more racial minorities so that they would be better able to elect members of their choice to Congress. The analysis in this chapter focuses on one specific aspect of this controversial topic: What impact has the creation of majority-black districts had on the quality of representation for African-Americans?

The preceding chapter presents evidence that the race of the member in Congress does matter to the representation he or she will give to policies of interest to blacks. A major contention among many civil rights proponents is that race-conscious drawing of constituency boundary lines is needed so as to elect more black candidates to Congress in order to better serve the needs and interests of black constituents. But do blacks undermine their own substantive political interests when they seek to maximize their numbers in Congress through the creation of majority-minority districts? To what extent should race be used as a factor in creating majority-minority districts? In an attempt to provide some answers to these important questions, this chapter examines the impact of partisan seat change and racial demographic change in congressional districts on the roll call voting behavior of House members.

Racial Gerrymandering

The redrawing of electoral districts to enhance the political fortunes of a party, candidate, or group is called gerrymandering. The term originated in 1811 when Massachusetts governor Elbridge Gerry was alleged to have designed a district resembling a salamander in shape to promote his party's interests. Gerrymandering is a political process, and politicians have long recognized the value of drawing district lines adroitly to produce desired electoral outcomes. Beyond the purview of party, gerrymandering can be viewed in terms of racial and ethnic groups in society. Racial gerrymandering can be of the negative or positive variety. The negative variety is defined in terms of any redistricting plan that minimizes or dilutes the voting strength of racial minorities. The Voting Rights Act and its extensions ban redistricting plans that dilute the voting strength of black communities. Section 5 of the Voting Rights Act mandates the Justice Department to preclear redistricting plans in all or parts of Alabama, Arizona, Georgia, Louisiana, Mississippi, South Carolina, Texas, Virginia, California, Connecticut, Florida, New Mexico, New York, and North Carolina. Under Section 5 the Justice Department can reject any redistricting plan that dilutes the voting strength or in any other way discriminates against racial minorities.[1]

Even though redistricting for the purpose of racial discrimination is expressly forbidden by law, state and local public officials have devised redistricting schemes to dilute black voting strength. The more common techniques of negative racial gerrymandering include "cracking," "stacking," and "packing."[2] *Cracking* involves the redrawing of district lines to divide and disperse a concentrated black population within a district. The usual outcome of this redistricting scheme was the dispersal of the black population through two or more districts with majority-white populations.

Nowhere was the practice of cracking more blatantly used than in the state of Mississippi. Historically, the black population in Mississippi was clustered in the western half of the state, in the area known as the Delta. From 1882 until 1966 the Mississippi legislature drew congressional district boundary lines so that blacks would constitute a majority within the district. Although the district's black population was about 66 percent, white congressmen continued to be elected during this long period mainly because blacks were denied the right to register and vote. As black voter registration and voter participation increased, after passage of the Voting Rights Act of 1965, the Mississippi legislature began the practice of drawing district boundary lines to minimize black voting strength by splitting up the heavily black population area of the Delta into four of the five congressional districts in the state. This gerrymandering scheme was preserved in the Mississippi redistricting plans of 1972 and 1981 and was instrumental in preventing any black from being elected to Congress until 1986, when Mike Espy became the first black representative since Reconstruction to be elected in the state.

As noted earlier, other pejorative techniques of racial gerrymandering include stacking and packing. *Stacking* occurs when a large and concentrated black population is diluted by combining part of it with a greater white population to create a majority-white district; *packing* is defined as creating a black supermajority district to prevent blacks from having a majority or near majority in adjacent districts. The gerrymandering techniques of cracking and stacking have been declared unconstitutional and discriminatory. Packing has not been declared unconstitutional, although there is a wealth of information to show that it is a strategy used to minimize black influence over the political process.[3]

In the 1970s the Supreme Court began to extend the reach of the Voting Rights Act to cover both federal and state legislative redistricting plans (see *Georgia v. United States* [1973]).[4] In extending the reach of the law, the Court began to move in the direction of rejecting congressional redistricting plans that gave the appearance of diluting the voting strength of racial minorities (see, e.g., *White v. Regester* [1973]).[5] In *United Jewish Organizations v. Carey* (1977), a case involving the redistricting of Brooklyn state legislative districts so as to create an additional black majority district, the Supreme Court upheld the race-conscious redistricting on the grounds that the Voting Rights Act was not only a remedial tool but also a device to increase the opportunities for people of color to elect more of their fellow group members to legislative assemblies.[6]

Three years later, in the case of *City of Mobile v. Bolden* (1980), the Court narrowed the reach of the Voting Rights Act in protecting against minority vote dilution.[7] The case involved a challenge to the at-large system of electing city commissioners in the city of Mobile, Alabama. By a vote of 6 to 3 the high Court ruled that lawsuits alleging dilution of black voting power must demonstrate that a questioned practice or law was implemented or maintained with racially discriminatory intent. The fact that no black had been elected under the city's at-large system was insufficient proof of racial discrimination. The main effect of the *Mobile* decision was that districting arrangements could be found illegal only if they were intentionally drawn to dilute minority voting strength.

The *Mobile* decision set off an immediate protest by civil rights advocates claiming that the Court had misinterpreted the voting rights law, making it virtually impossible to prove minority vote dilution. Their efforts met with some success when Congress amended the Voting Rights Act in 1982 and included a "results test" for proof of discrimination. Congress overturned the *Mobile* decision by revising Section 2 of the law to say that any practice that has the effect of discriminating against blacks or other minorities is unconstitutional.

Four years later the Supreme Court applied the results test in *Thornburg v. Gingles* (1986).[8] In *Thornburg* the Court ruled that six of North Carolina's multimember districts were impermissible under the Voting Rights Act because they diluted black voting power. Through broad interpretation of the act's mandate, as expressed in the *Thornburg* case, the Court has ruled that the states should create majority-minority districts wherever possible to elect more people of color to legislative assemblies. Furthermore, in its ruling the Court set out three criteria that, if met, should lead to the creation of a majority-minority districts: Is the minority group large and geographically compact enough to constitute a majority in a single district? Is the group politically cohesive? Is there evidence of racially polarized voting by the white majority that prevents minority preferred candidates from winning elective office?

As a consequence of their application of the results test, both the Justice Department and the federal courts have charged state legislatures with evading constitutional standards of equality. After the 1990 census the initial plans of several states—including Georgia, Mississippi, and North Carolina—were rejected by the Justice Department and the federal courts on the grounds that their congressional redistricting plans were devised to erode minority political gains.

In 1992, in the first election held after the new district congressional district boundary lines were drawn, thirteen new black representatives were elected to the House; none of them was defeated in the 1994 election.[9] Overall the number of black majority districts grew from seventeen in 1990 to thirty-two in 1992, a record number for districts of this variety. Of the thirty-two black majority districts, thirty-one (97 percent) were represented by African-Americans in the 103d Congress. Thomas M. Foglietta, a Democrat from Pennsylvania, was the only white member elected to represent a black majority district in the 103d, 104th, and 105th Congresses. The thirty-one African-Americans elected from majority-black districts constituted 82 percent of the total black membership of the House in the

103d and 104th Congresses (thirty-eight members with a vote on the floor of the House in each Congress). Under federal court order, some states with majority-black districts had to redraw their district boundary lines before the November 1996 elections. As a result, Georgia's majority-black districts were reduced from three to one, in Florida from three to two, in Louisiana from two to one, and in Texas from two to zero. When the 105th Congress convened in January 1997, African-Americans from black majority districts comprised 65 percent of the voting black delegation in the House. Eighty-six percent of them came from majority-minority districts. Five African-American representatives (Democrats Corrine Brown of Florida, Julia Carson of Indiana, and Sanford Bishop Jr. and Cynthia McKinney of Georgia; Republican J. C. Watts of Oklahoma) elected after the 1996 elections were from majority-white districts. They represent close to 14 percent of the black voting delegation in the House. The data here suggest that the increase in the number of black representatives in the House during the first three congresses of the 1990s is highly related to the size of the black population in the particular district rather than to any changes in the willingness of white voters to support black candidates.[10]

Proponents of the creation of majority-minority districts argue that they are needed to compensate for historical and ongoing discrimination against racial minority groups. Advocates of such districts also contend that the drawing of district boundary lines has been tolerated in the past as a way of promoting the interests of political parties and incumbents; consequently, gerrymandering to favor candidates from disadvantaged groups in society should also be considered acceptable. Opponents of racial redistricting contend that it is unconstitutional because it amounts to reverse discrimination against white voters. Opponents argue that lawmakers are elected to represent all the constituents of a district, not a particular ethnic group or faction. They maintain that the requirement that district boundaries be drawn to favor racial minorities goes against a Constitution that is supposed to be color-blind. Civil rights advocates counter by arguing that the color-blind argument is inconsistent with the nation's long history of discrimination against African-Americans and other minority groups. As evidence to support their contentions, proponents point to the fact that the creation of black majority districts has contributed to the election of black representatives from the states of Alabama, Florida, North Carolina, South Carolina, and Virginia for the first time since the turn of the century (see table 11). Thus, a policy that is so effective in correcting past and present injustices should not be abandoned without careful scrutiny.

More recently, the U.S. Supreme Court has expressed a strong dislike for elongated and highly contorted districts. In the process the Supreme

Court has opened the way for challenges by opponents to the drawing of majority-minority districts. In a potential setback for civil rights advocates the Supreme Court, in the 1993 *Shaw v. Reno* decision, invited a wave of lawsuits by white voters to challenge the constitutionality of drawing majority-black electoral districts. In *Shaw v. Reno*, a case involving claims by white plaintiffs in North Carolina that their constitutional rights had been violated by efforts to create two majority-black congressional districts, the Court's majority was highly critical of districts that were highly irregular in form, noncontiguous, and unconnected to traditional political jurisdictions.[11] In the five-to-four majority opinion Justice Sandra Day O'Connor, author of the controversial 1993 decision, decried redistricting authorities' abandonment of the traditional standards of compactness and contiguity. But, as dissenting justice John Paul Stevens noted, "there is no independent constitutional requirement of compactness or contiguity." As noted earlier, state legislatures throughout the course of the nation's history have created oddly shaped districts for a variety of purposes, including, but not limited to, the creation of majority-minority districts.

In the case of *Miller v. Johnson* (1995) the Supreme Court continued to question the constitutionality of racially motivated redistricting. In the *Miller* case the major issue raised by the Court was that of race being the primary basis for the creation of a black majority district in the state of Georgia. In this five-to-four decision the high court struck down the redistricting plan in the 11th District in Georgia. The Court referred to the 11th District as a "monstrosity" connecting "widely spaced urban centers that have absolutely nothing to do with each other." The Court further stated that, while race could be a consideration in redistricting decisions, it could not be the "predominant factor." According to the Court's majority, when a state assigns voters on the basis of race, "it engages in the offensive and demeaning assumption that voters of a particular race, because of their race, think alike, share the same political interests, and will prefer the same candidates at the polls." By stating that this justice department–directed plan to create a third black majority district in Georgia violated the equal protection rights of white voters because race was used as a predominant factor in drawing district lines, the Court put at risk similar redistricting plans throughout the nation by ruling that districts must all be "narrowly tailored to achieve a compelling [state] interest."[12]

In June 1996 the U.S. Supreme Court continued its assault on race-conscious redistricting when it struck down 3 majority-minority districts in the state of Texas. In *Bush v. Vera* (1996), decided by a five-to-four vote, the high court rule that the 18th and 30th black majority districts and the 29th Hispanic majority district in Texas were unconstitutional racial gerrymanders because race was used as the predominant factor in drawing their district boundary lines.[13] Just how the lower courts are to determine whether race is a predominant factor in the configuration of district boundaries is not spelled out in *Miller* nor *Bush*. As a result we can expect substantial litigation concerning this question over the next few years.

The question of whether the federal government should assist in requiring state legislatures to create majority-black districts is only one aspect of the redistricting wars. Within the confines of the controversy there is much debate in academic and legal circles over the efficacy of advancing minority representation through the creation of majority-minority districts. With very few exceptions African-American politicians and activists have argued strongly for creating black majority districts "safe" enough to elect black legislators to office. Some academicians contend, however, that civil rights proponents overestimate the percentage of blacks that is needed for fair black congressional representation. Some even doubt the necessity of drawing black majority districts in order to ensure black membership in the House. Carol Swain argues that black candidates can win election to the House by devising campaign strategies to build biracial coalitions rather than concentrating on winning elections through the aid of "affirmative" redistricting.[14] In a similar vein Timothy O'Rourke and Abigail Thernstrom oppose racial redistricting as an effective means of advancing minority representation. O'Rourke maintains that black candidates can win elective office without the assistance of black majority districts but provides little evidence to support his claims.[15] Thernstrom, a critic of federal review of redistricting plans under Section 5, also argues that there are other routes to elective office for black candidates than through black majority constituencies.[16]

But there is another view that suggests that the creation of majority-black districts is an important factor in determining whether blacks will be elected to Congress. Bernard Grofman and Lisa Handley provide evidence showing that race matters in the election of black candidates. In their examination of the relationship between the proportion of racial minorities and the electoral success of representatives during the 1980s, the authors show that black legislators benefit from the creation of majority-minority districts rather than from any changes in the willingness of white voters to support them.[17] David Lublin, in his study of 4,406 congressional elections between 1972 and 1992, supports the findings of Grofman and Handley. His findings show that the racial composition of a congressional district is a strong predictor of the race of its representative.[18]

One solution that has been offered by the Courts over the necessary percentage for fair black representation is the "65 Percent Rule." In *Kirsey v. Board of Supervisors of Hinds County, Mississippi* (1977), a federal district court proposed that a 65 percent minority percentage is needed for blacks to elect officials of their choice.[19] Critics of the 65 Percent Rule argue that the rule should not be a standard guide for determining the proportion of blacks needed in a majority black district for fair representation. Opponents of the percentage argue that creating 65 percent black districts would waste black votes and should not be used as a rule of thumb for creating black majority districts. David Butler and Bruce Cain, in their book *Congressional Redistricting: Comparative and Theoretical Perspectives* state: "it is . . . worth remembering that, in some situations, a minority may exercise more influence by having substantial blocks of voters putting pressure in a number of white districts than by having a single representative of their own."[20] Instead of mandating a national standard black percentage when creating these districts, some academicians suggest that the proportion of blacks in a district should reflect the particular election circumstances regarding the black voter registration and participation rates in a district.[21]

As the debate over racial gerrymandering will undoubtedly continue, there is one fact that is clear about the impact of creating a black majority district: it can change the racial composition in adjoining districts. If the overall goal is to increase the level of substantive representation for African-Americans, then the creation of the greatest number of majority-black districts might undermine that objective. This scenario can take place as a result of redistricting to make some districts "blacker" while in the process making other districts "whiter." In other words, adjusting district boundary lines to accommodate more blacks necessitates "bleaching" adjoining districts, thus making them more conservative and more Republican. The key question becomes: Does the creation of more majority-black districts decrease the overall level of policy responsiveness from white representatives? The issue of racial redistricting to increase black representation in Congress is likely to become more important in the 1990s and beyond as ethnic and racial minorities continue to make claims before the courts that it is a principal means of improving the quality of representation that they receive from legislative bodies. The purpose here is to provide some answers on this controversial subject.

Racial Change, Behavioral Change, and Partisan Change in Congressional Districts in the South

The southern states that created majority-black districts can be examined to gauge the impact of racial redistricting on support for black interests. There are several important reasons for choosing the South for the analysis. First, voting rights laws developed over the past twenty years have been specifically aimed at preventing the states from implementing redistricting plans that would dilute minority voting strength. There can be little debate that the South has led the way in attempting to minimize the voting power of blacks by redrawing congressional district lines in such a way as to fragment the black population. In this respect the South can be used as a barometer for determining whether racially motivated redistricting to benefit historically disadvantaged groups is an effective means of enhancing black representation. Second, the South provides a good case study for analysis because of what actually occurred in the region as a result of redistricting. Of the fifteen new black majority districts drawn for the 1992 election, twelve were located in eight southern states (one each in Alabama, Louisiana, South Carolina, Texas, and Virginia; two each in Georgia and North Carolina; and three in Florida). Before the 1990s round of redistricting, blacks constituted a majority in only four congressional districts (Georgia's 5th, Louisiana's 2d, Mississippi's 2d, and Tennessee's 9th) in the eleven states of the "Old Confederacy." The resulting majority-black districts helped to elect twelve first-term blacks to Congress. Third, racial gerrymandering became an issue in the South because of the dispersal of the black population throughout each state. This meant that some odd-shaped district lines had to be drawn to encompass a majority of black constituents in a single district. The extent to which district lines were drawn to include more racial minorities in the South was one of the major concerns raised in *Shaw v. Reno.* Finally, from the perspective of party politics, concentrating African-Americans into black-dominated districts offers the possibility of eviscerating the biracial power bases of many southern white Democrats. Initially, Democrats assumed that minority-controlled districts would ensure the election of Democratic members to Congress. Republicans, however, have supported these efforts, reasoning that, if black voters were packed into a few districts, Democratic strength in other districts would erode and enhance Republican congressional candidates' prospects in adjoining districts. With these reasons in mind the South offers researchers a good means by which they can assess the political consequences of racial redistricting.

Table 19 displays summary statistics related to changes in district racial compositions across the 1990 redistricting period. Districts in the states of Alabama, Florida, Georgia, Louisiana, North Carolina, South Carolina, Texas, and Virginia are used as the units for the analysis. Overall the results show that the mean black population fell by 4.9 percentage points in white majority districts. The average white Democrat saw the percentage of blacks in his or her district drop by 4.5 percentage points between 1992 (before redistricting) and 1993 (after redistricting). The table also reveals a decline in the black population in districts held by Republicans. In fact, the average 5.1 percentage point drop for southern Republicans is the largest among the two party cohorts. This finding is noteworthy for two reasons. First, a fair share of the black population needed to create new black majority districts came from districts already represented by Republicans. Drawing blacks from Republican-controlled districts serves to lessen the severity of eroding the power bases of white Democratic candidates. Second, the results suggest that removing blacks from Republican-held districts makes them safer for Republican incumbents. In terms of the substantive impact for blacks the trade-off is not that great, because the size of the black population appears to have little positive impact on the behavior of Republicans.

Turning to Table 20, the findings reveal that a decline in black population size in districts does not appear to have had a negative impact on the behavior of white Democrats. On average mean LCCR scores actually rose by 12 percentage points from the 102d Congress (1991–92) to the 103d Congress (1993–94). As for districts represented by Republicans, mean LCCR scores fell by 7.1 percentage points.

The state of Georgia can be used as an example to shed more light on the political consequences of racial redistricting. The following analysis is based on the configuration of districts before the Supreme Court declared Georgia's 11th District unconstitutional in *Miller*. As Butler and Cain note, in order for racial gerrymandering to be an issue in a particular state the black population must be of some critical size and concentration level.[22] Both conditions were factors during the 1990 redistricting debate

TABLE 19. Changes in Racial Composition in White Majority Districts (in percentage)

	Mean Black Population (1993)	Mean Black Population (1992)	Mean Difference
All	12.1	17.0	–4.9
White Democrats	14.6	19.1	–4.5
Republicans	9.4	14.5	–5.1

TABLE 20. Changes in LCCR Scores in White Majority Districts (in percentage)

	Mean LCCR (1993–94)	Mean LCCR (1991–92)	Mean Difference
White majority districts	40.0	39.0	+1.0
White Democrats	62.0	50.0	+12.0
Republicans	17.0	24.1	–7.1

TABLE 21. **District Profiles of Changes in Racial Composition and LCCR Support Scores in the State of Georgia (in percentage)**

Districts	Percent Black Population (1990)	Percent Black Population (1992)	LCCR (1991–92)	LCCR (1993–94)
	Democratic districts losing black population in redistricting and going Republican			
1	32	23	43	14
3	35	18	21	14
4	25	12	86	14
	Democratic districts losing black population in redistricting and remaining Democratic			
5	67	62	93	100
8	36	21	29	43
9	5	4	57	21
10	23	18	14	43
	Democratic districts gaining black population in redistricting			
2	37	57	43	79
7	9	13	43	57
	Republican districts remaining Republican			
6	20	6	7	14
	Newly created majority-black district			
11	—	64	—	100

in Georgia and appear to have affected black substantive representation. The proportion of blacks (27 percent) in the state is the fourth largest in the region. Of the eleven congressional districts created in the state (see fig. 11) for the 1992 elections, three were majority-black. Of the three districts containing a black-majority population, only the 5th District, which includes metropolitan Atlanta, met the traditional standard of compactness and contiguity for drawing district boundaries. As figure 11 shows, the other two black majority districts (2d and 11th Districts) were neither compact nor contiguous because of assymetrical residential patterns among blacks in the state.

The creation of the three black majority districts in Georgia required removing blacks from some adjoining districts. Table 21 presents data illustrating the different possible outcomes of racial redistricting. First, the districts that shifted from being Democratic to being Republican after redistricting saw the percentage of the black population drop by no less than nine percentage points. As can be seen in the table, there is also a fall-off in civil rights support that accompanies this partisan seat change. If partisan control of a district changes in this manner as a result of redistricting, then legislative support for civil rights will decrease. In the three Republican districts support for black interest legislation plummeted to 14 percent each. In the 4th Congressional District the decline in support for the LCCR legislation (72 percent) was substantial.

It is interesting to note that the policy trade-off varies substantially when a district moves from representation by a white southern Democrat to a white Republican. This is because some white southern Democrats have relatively high LCCR support scores, while others have moderate to low civil rights support scores. This finding is in line with the results in the previous chapters, which reveal that there continues to be a blend of conservatism and liberalism among white southern Democratic representatives. Second, the table shows cases of black population losses in districts controlled by Democrats. The decrease in the black population in these districts vary from a low of 1 percent (District 9) to a high of 15 percent (District 8). In terms of policy responsiveness there is no evidence to show that legislators voted more conservatively once blacks were removed from districts controlled by Democrats across the redistricting period. Third, in Democratic-held districts that gained black constituents after the 1990 redistricting, the LCCR scores of representatives increased. Fourth, in the Republican-held 6th District of Newt Gingrich (speaker of the House in the 104th and 105th Congresses) LCCR scores remained in the low range from the pre-redistricting Congress (102d Congress) to the post-redistricting Congress (103d Congress). Finally, a comparison could not be done of pre- and post-redistricting behavior in the 11th District because it was first created in 1992. There is, however, one noteworthy observation. The member who represented the district, Cynthia McKinney, had a LCCR rating of 100 in the 103d Congress. Thus, for those who favor creating majority-minority districts, redistricting had the desired policy effect.

It must be emphasized that Georgia represents an extreme example of the shift in partisan control from being Democratic controlled to being Republican controlled. In 1990, before redistricting, Democrats held a 9-to-1 seat margin in the state of Georgia; after Representative Nathan Deal switched to the Republican Party, in 1995, the delegation became 8–3 Republican. The only Democratic representatives from

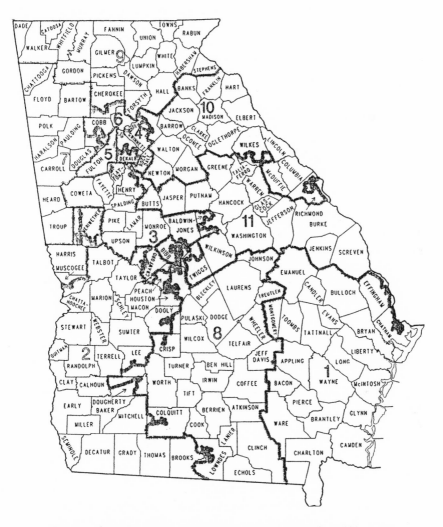

Fig. 11. Georgia district boundaries created after the 1990 census. (Reprinted from U.S. Department of Commerce, Economic and Statistics Administration, "Population and Housing Characteristics for Congressional Districts of the 103d Congress, Georgia," *Bureau of the Census,* G-2 Georgia.)

Georgia in the 104th and 105th Congresses were African-Americans. In the state of North Carolina, for instance, the loss of Democratic seats wasn't as severe from 1990 (102d Congress, 7–4 seat margin) to 1996 (105th Congress, 6–6 seat margin), even though two black majority districts were created (1st and 12th Districts) in the state.

The state of Georgia is an interesting case, which serves to illustrate the potential policy consequences of racial redistricting. As noted previously, the configuration of the 11th District was challenged in the case of *Miller v. Johnson* and disallowed by the Supreme Court in 1995. After remanding the case to lower courts for further adjudication, a three-judge panel of the United States Court of Appeals for the 11th Circuit drew a new congressional map in Georgia that significantly alters the racial composition in districts in the state (see fig. 12).[23] In a 2-to-1 decision the majority of the panel decided that the district map created after the 1990 census was unconstitutional because race was the predominant factor in the design of the districts. If the December 1995 court decision is upheld, only the 5th District in metropolitan Atlanta will maintain its majority black population status. Under the new redistricting plan the 2d District is 35 percent black compared to 57 percent under the old district. The black population in the old 11th District was 64 percent; it is 33 percent under the new plan.[24]

It is too soon to tell what will be the long-term impact of the new map on black representation or partisan politics. The new plan increases Georgia's black population among several districts, therefore giving Democrats an opportunity to reverse some of the gains made by Republicans in the early 1990s. After the 1996 elections, the partisan distribution of seats in the state remained unchanged from the previous Congress. Three Democrats (all African-Americans) and eight Republicans represent the state in the House in the 105th Congress. As stated earlier, two African-Americans won House seats in majority-white districts in Georgia. On the surface, their election undermines the argument that black majority districts are critical to the success of black congressional candidates. It is important to point out, however, that Representatives' Sanford Bishop Jr. and Cynthia McKinney are incumbents, and incumbents rarely lose their bids for reelection. Consequently, by spreading out the black population in this manner, the new map is likely to cause some problems for black congressional candidates in districts in which the black voting-age population is no longer in the majority or near a majority. Furthermore, with Republicanism clearly on the rise in Georgia, the new plan could also give Republicans a greater opportunity to pick up two additional seats in Congress in future elections.

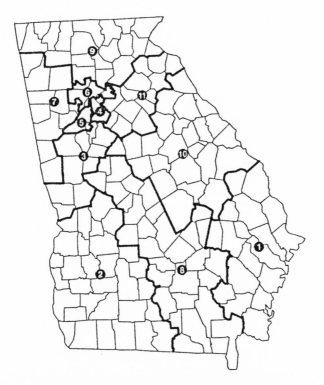

Fig. 12. Court redistricting plan for Georgia, 1995. (Adapted from Congressional Quarterly Weekly Report, "Several Minority-Majority Districts," *Congressional Quarterly Almanac* (February 24, 1996): 456; and "Housing Characteristics for Congressional Districts of the 103d Congress, Georgia," *Bureau of the Census,* G-2 Georgia.)

A More Systematic Investigation

The findings in table 21 indicate that there is a representational trade-off for blacks in creating majority-black districts. It is important to stress that districts in the state of Georgia represent only a small sample of those in the analysis. A more systematic level of analysis of all the districts in this investigation can tell us more about the political consequences of creating majority-black districts. To date, the only published scholarly work that relates to this research is Charles Bullock's analysis of the policy consequences of racial redistricting.[25] The model specification presented here differs from that used by Bullock. The primary focus of Bullock's research was on the impact of the changing racial composition of congressional districts on legislative behavior calculated by subtracting LCCR support scores for the 102d Congress from the 1993 LCCR scores.[26] The focus here is on how district profiles influence legislator behavior. To accomplish this objective this research examines the effect of change in party seat control along with the impact of racial change in districts and other relevant independent variables on post-redistricting voting behavior of House members. The units of analyses are congressional districts in the eight southern states that created majority-black districts. The following model is used to test the relationships:

$$Y = a + b_1 X_1 + b_2 b_2 + b_3 b_3 + b_4 b_4 + b_5 b_5 + e \qquad (4)$$

where:

Y is the LCCR score of the member representing the district in the 103d Congress (1993–94).

   a is the constant.

   X_1 is the 1991–92 LCCR score of the member in the district prior to the redistricting. That is, as a baseline against which to measure members' post-redistricting voting behavior, LCCR scores in the 102d Congress are utilized.

   X_2 is the explanatory variable that measures the level of change in the black population in each legislator's district. It is operationalized by subtracting the percentage of blacks in the district prior to redistricting (1990) from the percentage of blacks in the district after redistricting (1992). Districts in which the black population increased will generate positive values, and those in which the black population dropped will have negative values.

   X_3 is a dummy variable used to measure House seats shifting from Democratic controlled to Republican controlled, taking the value of 1 if the seat shifted from Democratic to Republican controlled, 0 if otherwise.

   X_4 is a dichotomous variable for Democrats replacing an incumbent Democrat.

   X_5 is a dummy variable for a Republican replacing an incumbent Republican.

   e is the error term.

This model predicts that $b_1 > 0$; that is, a strong positive relationship will exist between 1991–92 and 1993–94 LCCR scores.[27] It is hypothesized that $b_2 > 0$; if legislative voting behavior responds to variations in the size of the black population in a district, then the change in the percent black variable should be statistically significant, and its coefficient sign should be positive. It is expected that $b_3 < 0$; that is, the coefficient sign of the partisan shift variable should be negative and statistically significant, indicating that, if the district goes from being Democratic controlled to being Republican controlled, then a fall-off in support for civil rights should occur. Previous research reveals that legislative behavior is a function of generational replacement. Greater support for black policy preferences may be the result of new Democrats replacing old Democrats, and more conservative voting may be due to new Republicans replacing more senior Republicans.[28] If so, the coefficient sign of the Democratic replacement variable should be positive ($b_4 > 0$), and the coefficient sign of the Republican replacement should be negative ($b_5 < 0$). Ordinary least squares regression tests and evaluates the impact of the explanatory variables on behavioral change among House members.

The findings reported in table 22 show that the racial composition variable is strongly positively significant. Other things being equal, for each gain of 1 percent black as a consequence of redistricting, LCCR scores increase by 1.018 percentage points. Conversely, the findings indicate that a loss of black constituents contributes to lower LCCR scores. As for the partisan shift variable, if the district moves from the Democratic to the Republican column, there will be a loss in representation of black interests. On average the 36-point shift to the right represents those

TABLE 22. Impact of Racial Change and Partisan Change in Districts on Changing Behavior of Southern Representatives, Controlling for Other Factors: Regression Estimates

Variables	Unstandardized	Standardized	t-ratio
1992 LCCR score	.481	.502	7.351***
Change in percent black	1.018	.359	5.046***
Partisan seat change	−36.045	−.308	4.463***
Freshman Democrat	11.937	.078	1.138
Freshman Republican	−24.889	−.181	−2.712**
Constant	29.254		
	$R^2 = .60$	$N = 97$	

Note: Per LCCR index.

***$p < .001$ **$p < .01$ (one-tailed tests)

Republicans who replaced Democrats in the district immediately after the 1990 redistricting. The 36 percent drop in support for LCCR legislation is significant because it complicates the desirability of going to great lengths to create majority-minority districts to increase the number of black representatives in Congress. The findings show that senior Republicans were less conservative than newly elected Republicans. Although the sign is positive and in the right direction, there was no significant difference between the behavior of freshmen Democrats and incumbent Democrats, once other factors are controlled for in the equation. Overall the model performs moderately well, explaining 60 percent of the variance in the change in civil rights support.

Tables 23 and 24 analyze the behavior of Democrats in the region.[29] As expected, the impact of the change in the percent black variable for all Democrats (table 23) is similar to the one observed in the full model. It is no surprise that black population size is a factor in helping to explain changing roll call voting behavior across the redistricting period. The real significance of the finding for Democrats is revealed when black Democrats are removed from the analysis. As table 24 shows, once black representatives are excluded from the analysis of southern Democrats, the racial

TABLE 23.   Impact of Racial Change in District on Changing Behavior of Southern Democrats, Controlling for Other Factors: Regression Estimates

Variables	Unstandardized	Standardized	t-ratio
1992 LCCR scores	.314	.394	3.642***
Change in percent black	.876	.503	4.562***
Freshman Democrats	2.541	.031	.275
Constant	47.663		
	$R^2 = .40$	$N = 56$	

Note: Per LCCR index.
***$p < .001$

TABLE 24.   Impact of Racial Change in District on Changing Behavior of Southern White Democrats, Controlling for Other Factors: Regression Estimates

Variables	Unstandardized	Standardized	t-ratio
1992 LCCR score	.382	.505	3.767***
Change in percent black	.092	.028	.214
Freshman Democrats	−2.409	−.026	.199
Constant	41.271		
	$R^2 = .26$	$N = 45$	

Note: Per LCCR index.
***$p < .001$

composition variable becomes statistically insignificant. What accounts for this finding? It would appear that behavioral change is due to increases in the black population in districts represented by African-Americans, not white Democrats. In other words, the significance of the racial district variable appears to be the result of black representatives becoming more liberal than what they had been previously or what their predecessors had been in the 102d Congress. To some degree the move further to the left served to obviate the gains made by Republicans due to some districts shifting from the Democratic column to the Republican column.

In sum, once the analysis is conducted separately for white Democrats, the findings offer no evidence for the contention that white Democrats changed their voting behavior on civil rights as a consequence of losses in black constituents in their districts.

Discussion

Even though the one-person, one-vote, standard is firmly grounded, debate over what constitutes fair representation for racial and ethnic groups continues in American society. Although the Voting Rights Act prohibits the dilution of minority vote influence, it was not until after the 1982 extension of the Voting Rights Act and the U.S. Supreme Court ruling in the 1986 *Thornburg v. Gingles* case that the issue of majority black districts emerged front and center in the redistricting battles over representation.

Reapportionment after the 1990 census gave the states of the Old Confederacy a net gain of nine seats. The completion of the 1990 redistricting resulted in the creation of fifteen new black majority districts. Twelve of these types of districts were created in the South, the region in which blacks had long been underrepresented relative to their proportion in the general population. These new black districts, along with existing ones, led to a record number of thirty-eight black voting representatives being elected to the 103d and 104th Congresses, and thirty-seven in the 105th Congress. While civil rights advocates have generally applauded the results, there may be unintended political consequences. The creation of black majority districts is usually done at the expense of reducing the proportion of blacks in other districts. This supposition may promote a conflict between the need, on one hand, to create black-majority districts in order for African-Americans to receive more than token representation in Congress and, on the other hand, the possibility of a partisan shift to the Right, which would lead to less support for civil rights legislation. Put another way, the political expediency of increasing black representation might be at the expense of reducing the overall level of policy responsiveness from white lawmakers and the possibility that more Republicans will be elected to Congress who generally are less sensitive to black concerns.

The initial finding revealed that districts that lost black voters because of the 1990 redistricting did change their voting behavior. Upon further probing, it became clear that white members, on average, did not alter their voting patterns in response to racial redistricting. Any behavioral change that has occurred appears to be due to the election of more blacks, who were able to move the Democratic Party to the Left on civil rights–related issues.

Even though the approach used here to investigate relationships differs somewhat from Bullock's, both studies reach similar conclusions. Several factors may help to account for why southern white Democrats did not change their behavior as a result of racial redistricting. First, the fact that white members did not alter their voting behavior is consistent with the earlier works of Aage Clausen and John Kingdon, who maintain that lawmakers have a tendency to develop frameworks for issue voting early in their congressional careers and do not deviate in any measurable way over time.[30] Instead, when a systematic pattern of behavioral change does occur, it is more apt to happen across the different stages of the legislative voting process. Second, the argument that black majority districts for the 1992 elections were created at a major expense to white Democrats is an overexaggeration. In fact, more than one-third of white Democrats actually saw only slight increases in the proportion of blacks in their districts after the 1990 redistricting cycle. In a good proportion of districts in which white Democrats lost black constituents, the decline in the percentage of blacks in their districts was relatively small. In a similar vein, through adroit cartography a good proportion of blacks were removed from districts already represented by Republicans. While it is true that the decline in the proportion of blacks in Republican districts make them safer for Republican incumbents, it is also the case that African-Americans lose very little in terms of their substantive representation, since Republicans, especially from the South, are generally insensitive to black policy preferences in the first place.

Even though the analysis shows the absence of a statistically significant relationship between racial change in districts and the roll call voting behavior among white Democrats, the creation of majority-black districts may hurt black representation in another important way. That is, "bleaching" adjoining districts so as to increase black descriptive representation may lead to a shift in partisan control. All things being equal, if a Democratic seat is lost to a Republican as a result of fashioning a new majority-black district, then a fall-off in black substantive representation will occur.

Republican successes after the 1994 and 1996 congressional elections raise some troubling issues about the benefits of creating majority-minority districts. For the first time in the South the Republican Party captured a majority of the House seats. In the 104th Congress (1995–96) Republicans held 65 (62 percent) of the 125 House seats allocated to the eleven states of the Old Confederacy. They continued their dominance in the region after the 1996 elections. To be sure, some of the change in partisan control can be attributed to racial redistricting. But it would be a mistake to suggest that aggregate Democratic losses were due solely to the way congressional district boundary lines were redrawn. There is ample evidence to suggest that the political evolution of the South, so evident in recent presidential voting behavior, has not left the world of southern congressional politics untouched. In other words, the South is undergoing a period of party realignment that is driven by social cleavages in the electorate.[31] The gradual shift of white voters to the Republican Party can be traced back to the mid-1960s, when the national Democratic Party no longer formally espoused the segregationist racial views held by a large faction of the southern white electorate. In a recent study by John Petrocik and Scott Desposato of the partisan effects of creating majority-minority districts, the authors demonstrated that a variety of factors helped to contribute to the losses of Democratic congressional candidates in 1992 and 1994. Some of the factors include: a decline in black voter turnout, a reduction in the Democratic affiliation of white Southerners, and an anti-Democratic tide, which defeated Democratic incumbents.[32] Kevin Hill, in his study of the partisan consequences of racial redistricting in the South, found that some Democratic districts did move to the Republican column in 1992 as a result of racial redistricting. But, as the author notes, "not all Republican gains in the South were related to racial redistricting."[33]

The creation of majority-minority districts clearly suggests that there are representational trade-offs to increasing black descriptive representation. On the one hand, blacks do reap substantive benefits from having black membership in Congress because the race of the member matters on many important issues that run along racial lines. Based on the evidence presented in this chapter, it does not appear at this time that changes in the racial composition of congressional districts cause white Democrats to alter their voting behavior in a manner detrimental to black substantive interests. On the other hand, if district lines are drawn in a way that would result in new conservative Republican districts and a Republican majority in the House, then blacks may well undermine their own substantive political interests.[34]

CHAPTER 6

Epilogue: Black Policy Preferences, Congressional Behavior, and the Future of Representation for African-Americans

The preceding chapters have presented an investigation of legislative voting behavior on policies of primary interest to blacks. In the investigation we have looked at voting patterns, tested models, and examined evidence, all for the purpose of assessing the overall quality of representation for blacks in Congress. This concluding chapter looks at the implications of the results in this book and speculates about the level of congressional responsiveness to black interests in the future.

The Ebb and Flow of Congressional Responsiveness to Black Interests

It would be useful to place the analysis into a historical perspective in order to better understand what might lie ahead. Since the Civil War there has been an ebb and flow of congressional responsiveness to black policy preferences within the political system. Specifically, there have been four distinct periods of congressional responsiveness and unresponsiveness. During the period of Reconstruction Congress was in the vanguard of policy responsiveness. Neither judicial nor executive action could match or interfere with Congress' protection of the constitutional rights of freed slaves. For instance, when President Andrew Johnson sought to interfere with Congress' plan for Reconstruction, he was impeached and missed conviction by only one vote. Further testimony to Congress' commitment to civil rights for freed blacks was passage of the Civil War Amendments, followed by several civil rights laws. The major consequence of this expansion of federal power was the curtailment of states' rights and the nationalization of civil rights for blacks in America.

The second period, from about 1883 to 1957, constitutes the quintessential model of congressional unresponsiveness to the needs and interests of black Americans—a supreme example of unrepresentative democracy. One of the major reasons why Reconstruction fell woefully short of its

135

goal of achieving civil rights equality for black Americans is because Congress refused to pass any civil rights statutes for nearly three-quarters of a century after the early 1880s. Congressional inaction sent a clear message to institutions and people that the protection of civil rights for blacks was not the business of the United States government.

Signs of a renewed federal legislative concern with racial issues began when Congress passed the Civil Rights Act of 1957. In this century congressional responsiveness to black policy interests reached its apex when the Civil Rights Act of 1964 and the Voting Rights Act of 1965 were enacted into law. They represent the most sweeping antibias legislation enacted since the period of Reconstruction. Numerous compromises had to be made in order to get the bills through Congress. Ironically, compromises that were made on the civil rights bill actually strengthened it beyond what President Kennedy had initially requested. In the end it was a sound piece of legislation containing titles dealing with voting rights, public accommodations, desegregation of public facilities, desegregation of public education, and the creation of governmental enforcement agencies empowered to carry out the law. But this was a period when civil rights issues were in the spotlight of public attention, at the cutting edge of social debate. It was a time when the focus was clearly on the plight of blacks, the victims of overt racism and discrimination. It was also the time of bipartisan cooperation in Congress, a time of executive-legislative cooperation to ensure passage of strong civil rights legislation.

Since the 1960s Congress has addressed civil rights issues on many occasions, but it would be misleading to conclude that congressional responsiveness to black policy preferences is at a comparable level to that of the 1960s. To be sure, racial issues continue to arouse intense feelings in America. It is also true that there have been some notable accomplishments by Congress over the past three decades, including extensions of the Civil Rights Act and the Voting Rights Act, Martin Luther King Jr. Holiday (1983), South Africa Sanctions (1985–86), Fair Housing Act (1988), and the National Voter Registration Bill (1993). But behind these accomplishments is the realization that a sizable proportion of the House delegation is unwilling to support strong civil rights measures that would help to combat subtle forms of discrimination against racial minorities and women. Here it is important to emphasize the utility of the paradigm in supporting the claim of waning congressional responsiveness to black interests. Based on the theoretical model, the evidence in this book shows that the political parties are more polarized than ever on the issue of civil rights. Even though the Democratic members are far more supportive of civil rights than are their Republican colleagues, this does not mean that the Democratic Party has become internally cohesive. The analysis provides strong evidence for a pattern of deviant voting behavior within the party. A sizable proportion of the white southern Democratic delegation, as well as a few white nonsouthern Democrats, are reluctant to support liberal proposals.

In assessing the level of congressional responsiveness to black policy interests in recent years, one concludes from the findings in this book that the overall policy record of Congress is basically modest. The usual approach to congressional decision making on racial issues is to make minor to moderate modifications in existing civil rights laws.

The political environment for black civil rights has changed since the mid-1960s, becoming more politicized and partisan. Republican gains in Congress, recalcitrant Democrats, executive-congressional conflict, and the fact that more social groups are seeking additional protection for their civil rights will make it increasingly difficult to get legislation of primary interest to most African-Americans enacted into law. The structure and operations of the policy-making process allow members of Congress numerous opportunities to water down civil rights proposals to render them virtually ineffective. Moreover, in a governmental body in which a single vote can decide the fate of a measure, there is all the more reason to suspect that it will be difficult for Congress to come to grips and deal effectively with the kinds of social and economic hardships that fall disproportionately on disadvantaged citizens.

Yet over the past two decades there have been some successes in legislative enactments. Congress deserves some credit, especially in the wake of recalcitrant presidential administrations and a conservative majority on the U.S. Supreme Court. At present the recalcitrance of the other two branches of the national government is all the more reason to underscore Congress' role as being in the vanguard of policy articulation on racial issues.

One of the goals of this research was to conduct a systematic investigation of several facets of congressional responsiveness to black interests. This study has included research on federal voting rights, race and racial redistricting, as well as the general field of civil rights.

Black Voting Rights

The Voting Rights Act of 1965 was originally targeted at dismantling the Jim Crow system, which for decades had been effective in preventing many blacks from participating in the voting process. There is strong evidence to show that the act has been effective in dismantling first-generation overt barriers to black voter participation. In fact, one researcher predicts that black and white voter registration rates will most likely converge sometime in the 1990s.[1] So, too, has there been an increase in the number of black elected officials. African-Americans now hold elective offices at virtually all levels of government. Between 1970 and 1992 their numbers increased fivefold, from 1,469 to over 7,552.[2] The act was a success mainly because of the high level of commitment by Congress toward protecting black voting rights.

Some academicians and politicians interpret increasing levels of black voter registration and the election of more black public officials to mean that racial minorities no longer need the protection of the Voting Rights Act. Abigail Thernstrom, one of the leading critics of federal voting rights protection, argues that electoral systems used to disadvantaged minority voters are no longer a major factor in minority vote dilution. There is, however, ample empirical evidence to show that second-generation voter discrimination is prevalent in America.

In the United States there are three kinds of electoral systems: at-large (contested seats on a governing body are chosen by all of the voters within a jurisdiction); single-member districts (an electoral district from which a single legislator is chosen, usually by plurality); and mixed systems (some of the seats on a governing body voted on at-large and some by district). The conventional wisdom is that minority candidates are disadvantaged by at-large elections because they have more difficulty winning elective office in majority-white jurisdictions. In other words, the tendency for whites to engage in bloc voting in at-large elections diminishes the likelihood that minority candidates will be elected to office. In one of the most comprehensive analyses of the impact of electoral systems on minority representatives undertaken since the inception of the Voting Rights Act, the findings of the authors and contributors of the *Quiet Revolution in the South* offer strong support for the biasing effect of at-large elections. In their longitudinal analysis of over one thousand cities in eight southern states spanning a three-decade period (1965–89), the researchers found that, in hundreds of small towns across the region, minority vote dilution continues to be a reality in the United States.[3] The authors of the book conclude that, while "the Voting Rights Act has wrought a "quiet revolution" in southern politics and is perhaps the single most successful civil rights bill ever passed, the need for it is far from over."[4]

At present areas covered by the act may make no change in voting practices without preclearance by the attorney general or the United States Court of Appeals for the District of Columbia. Examples of voting and election practices that must be precleared include changes in the composition of the electorate such as changes from ward to at-large elections or changes in voting districts' boundary lines, changes in candidacy requirements and qualifications such as filing deadlines, and changes in the locations of polling places. Under current law these changes cannot be pre-cleared by local federal district judges because of the fear that they might succumb to local political pressures.

Controversy over what constitutes minority vote dilution and the issue of federal preclearance will undoubtedly continue in the future. As stated earlier, in 1981 when the act came up for a vote in the House, south-ern Republicans sought to remove the federal preclearance provision, claiming that it unjustly singled out southern states for voting rights viola-tions. Although they insisted there was no need for the provision, the fed-eral government had vetoed hundreds of proposed changes in their voting laws or practices. In essence the future of black voting rights seems to be tied to federal voting rights protection.

Members' Race

The evidence reported in this book points to the conclusion that race is a factor in congressional roll call voting on black policy preferences. The results of this research demonstrate that the election of blacks to Congress goes beyond the notion of descriptive and symbolic representation into the substantive area of public policy. Policy pay-offs may come in the form of more effective antidiscrimination policies in the areas of education, employment, and housing. Or policy rewards may come from higher increases in minimum wages and unemployment compensation to help alleviate some of the economic hardships that fall disproportionately on blacks and other minorities.

The Congressional Black Caucus has seen its membership swell from nine members in 1970 to thirty-nine (including nonvoting delegate and senator) in the 105th Congress. With this growth comes the potential for more political clout in Congress and, subsequently, better policy represen-tation for blacks. As a unit, the Black Caucus can use its size to place race-relevant issues higher on the national political agenda. The Black Caucus can use its size in House deliberations to emphasize the need for increased spending on social and economic programs beneficial to blacks, women, and minorities. As a consequence of its increased size and leverage, the CBC should be in a better position to bring relevant issues to the House floor for action, eventually to be passed in the chamber.

Another important factor that might increase the political influence of black representatives in the future is the fact that some of the more senior members in the House are black. The creation of majority-minority districts enhances the electoral fortunes of black incumbents. As of the 105th Congress, there are five black representatives whose careers extend beyond twenty years. Several other members have been in Congress for at least ten years (see table 11). More important, accompanying this longevity is the opportunity for blacks to chair more committees and sub-committees. In the 103d Congress, for example, four African-Americans served in important leadership positions: John Conyers Jr. (chair of Government Operations Committee), Ronald V. Dellums (chair of Armed Services Committee), William L. Clay (chair of Post Office and Civil Service), and John R. Lewis (chief deputy majority whip). Although these positions do not guarantee influence, they do give African-Americans additional leverage in advancing black-favored legislation. If this trend continues, African-American legislators can reach new levels of political influence and power. Of course, their opportunity to chair committees and subcommittees is contingent on their party's control of the chamber.

As a result of the 1994 congressional elections, Republicans took control of both the Senate and the House for the first time in more than forty years. There was no change in the balance of power after the November 1996 congressional elections. The Democrats' loss of the House has diminished the caucus's influence to some degree in the 104th Congress. The transfer of power meant that black lawmakers had to relinquish their leadership positions. The Republican Party leadership also cut off the caucus's funds for salaries and operations. Nonetheless, as a solid bloc of Democratic votes in an assembly in which one vote can make the difference in the outcome of a legislative proposal, the CBC can continue to make its presence felt on a variety of issues.

As the CBC has grown, its membership has become more diverse. The Black Caucus can no longer be considered a small cadre of liberals from big cities with an urban perspective. Some members come from urban districts, while others represent the interests of rural constituencies or a mix of the two. Some represent districts that are more impoverished than others. Furthermore, as of the 105th Congress, one of the members of the Black Caucus is a Republican (J. C. Watts of Oklahoma). There were two black Republicans in the 104th Congress. Increased size and differences within the group may lead to internal conflict. If so, then there is the possibility that the overall quality of substantive representation for African-Americans may be adversely affected. Former chairman of the CBC, Kweisi Mfume, of Maryland, acknowledged the potential for schism within the organization when he noted: "I realize this is a challenge . . . but I honestly believe that the task is manageable. We can grow and diversify and evolve while at the same time increasing our effectiveness."[5]

To be influential and effective black representatives, like other members, have to negotiate, bargain, compromise, and follow congressional norms and procedures. In short, to get black interest legislation passed in the chamber, they need votes. Their success depends on the assistance they can get from their colleagues. In an attempt to fulfill its objectives, in 1984, the Black Caucus began accepting white associate members. These members work to draft and frame legislation to advance the interests of minority citizens. And their roll call voting behavior reveals that they are supportive of black-favored legislation. While there is ample evidence to show that there are white members in the chamber who support black policy preferences, the findings in this book reveal that there is no cohort in Congress that represents the views, values, or interests of the black community better than black members of Congress.

Racial Redistricting

Since the passage of the Voting Rights Act of 1965, civil rights activists have argued that the creation of majority-black districts is necessary for increasing black representation in order for blacks to have a more effective voice in the chambers of Congress. There is evidence in this book to show that the policy interests of most African-Americans are better reflected in the legislative activities of black lawmakers.

Thus far civil rights advocates have been successful in impressing their view on Congress and the courts. But the 1990s round of redistricting has spawned a storm of controversy unlike any before. The length to which redistricters went to draw some majority-minority districts has incurred the wrath of the U.S. Supreme Court (*Shaw v. Reno* [1993]; *Miller v. Johnson* [1995]; *Bush v. Vera* [1996]). In particular, the Court expressed a strong dislike for majority-minority districts with elongated, contorted boundaries. Although justification for the drawing of district lines to include more majority-minority populations can be found in the Voting Rights Act (as amended in 1982) and *Thornburg v. Gingles* (1986), nonetheless, critics contend that the creation of these districts constitutes federal encroachment into state affairs and is a form of "political apartheid." It is interesting to note that oddly configured boundaries are nothing new to the American political landscape. Incumbents and party candidates have long recognized the advantages of constructing boundary lines as a means of enhancing their electoral fortunes. Consequently, one is left with the impression that the Court was willing to tolerate contorted boundary lines until racial minorities gained enough political clout to claim their spoils in the political system.

Beyond the question of whether the creation of these districts is an unwarranted intervention of the federal government into state prerogatives is the perennial question: What is the best electoral strategy for maximizing black congressional representation? One alternative electoral strategy that has been proposed is that African-Americans should focus more on building biracial strategies instead of concentrating on creating black majority districts. An advocate of the biracial campaign strategy is Carol Swain, who states that "districts with black majorities are clearly not the black politician's only route to Congress . . . a more promising strategy is to elect blacks in districts without black majorities."[6] She contends that black candidates can win in non–majority black districts if they can supply white voters with plenty of information about themselves and their campaigns to overcome any predisposition to vote on the basis of race. Intuitively, the biracial campaign strategy makes sense because of the relatively small size of the black population and its distribution and concentration level in the United States. Ideally, the biracial campaign is the best-case scenario and should be carefully considered by candidates running for elective office. The major defect of the biracial campaign strategy is that it discounts the significance of racially polarized voting in the United States. There is still little empirical evidence to support the conclusion that black congressional candidates can win on a consistent and long-term basis in districts that contain a majority of non-Hispanic white voters. For example, of the six major party black congressional challengers who ran against a white candidate in non–majority black districts during the general election campaign of 1994, only one, Republican J. C. Watts of Oklahoma, was victorious.[7] After the 1996 elections, Democratic candidate Julia Carson of Indiana was the only black nonincumbent candidate elected from a solid majority-white district. It must be kept in mind that four of the five black congressional candidates (Sanford Bishop Jr. and Cynthia McKinney of Georgia, Corrine Brown of Florida, and J. C. Watts of Oklahoma) who won in majority-white districts in November 1996 were incumbents. The electoral advantage of incumbency is well-known in academic and political circles. Typically, more than 90 percent of House incumbents win reelection in a given year. In November 1996, for example, 94 percent of them won their reelection bid. The only black congressional incumbent to lose his bid for reelection was Republican Gary Franks of Connecticut. What these numbers suggest is that the number of blacks in Congress is almost invariably related to the proportion of blacks in a district. Their probability of winning is greatly enhanced when the district is either majority black or majority-minority. Therefore, until there is more evidence to show that racially polarized voting has declined and more black nonincumbent candidates can win in majority-white districts, the campaign strategy of building a biracial coalition is unlikely to produce the desired results.

Another alternative electoral and political arrangement that has been offered as a means of maximizing black representation is called "cumulative voting." Awareness of this proposal was heightened during the controversy in 1993 surrounding the failed nomination of civil rights attorney Lani Guinier as assistant attorney general for civil rights. Guinier is critical of the current electoral system for what she attacks as being the "triumph of tokenism."[8] Guinier's reform proposal is based on the premise that the system of plurality voting in single-member districts greatly advantages white majorities and in turn dilutes minority voting strength. The logic is that the majority usually garners a higher share of seats than votes cast under this system. Because of the bias in the electoral system toward majority majority-white constituencies, seats held by racial minorities will be smaller than their share in either the general or voting-age population.

As an alternative to the single-member plurality system of elections, Guinier proposes a form of proportional representation that gives each voter a number of votes equal to the position to be filled. For instance, if there were ten congressional seats, each voter would have ten votes. Each voter would then be allowed to cast his or her votes among the candidates in any manner desired. Thus, a voter could cast one vote for each of ten candidates, ten votes for only one candidate, eight votes for one candidate and two for another, or any other collectivity chosen by the voter. On the one hand, proponents contend that cumulative voting will allow more opportunities for racial minorities to gain representation, by pooling their votes behind candidates of their choice. Advocates of this system also argue that cumulative voting has the advantage of being a nonracial means to increase minority representation.[9] In other words, the government does not have to engage in race-conscious districting for minorities to gain congressional representation. Furthermore, the contention is that a proportional representational system corrects for some of the defects under the current system such as wasted and diluted votes. On the other hand, critics maintain that this system violates the egalitarian principles imbedded in the judicial criterion of "one person, one vote" rule of governance. It is important to note that Guinier does not totally abandon majority-minority districts as a means of advancing black congressional representation. Yet, according to her, race-conscious districting would be unnecessary if a more equitable electoral system is placed in effect.

The merits of different electoral systems is beyond the scope of this book. The discussion is only to point out the direction of future debate. At present no member in Congress has proposed cumulative voting to replace the current single-member plurality district electoral system. It would seem that the best strategy for electing more black representatives is the creating of majority-minority districts.

The creation of these districts is designed to compensate for the discriminatory nature of the electoral system. It is also a justiciable means of controlling "majority tyranny"—that is, the potential of a majority to monopolize power for its own gain and to the detriment of minority rights and interests. In creating these districts, however, there is the risk of eviscerating the biracial power bases of white liberal Democrats if district lines are drawn in a manner that substantially reduces the proportion of blacks in their districts. A confluence of factors may produce this effect, including excessive packing of black voters and the precision with which district lines are drawn by political cartographers. Unfortunately, the Voting Rights Act's extension in 1982, or the post-1982 vote diluting caselaw, gave little direction to planners in addressing electoral arrangements for redistricting. The 65 Percent Rule appears to be too simple a solution to a complex issue. In the future it would seem that more careful consideration should be given to other factors, including the sociodemographic composition in the area (e.g., percentage of blacks with a high school or college education), the black voting-age population and black voter registration data, and the overall history of black voting in the area.

Those liberals who are opposed to the creation of black majority districts on the grounds that it would undermine the overall substantive objectives of minorities must keep in mind that for most of this nation's history blacks have been without a voice in the halls of Congress. At some point it becomes a subjective decision about the representational trade-offs in creating these types of districts. As one researcher on the topic of racial redistricting notes:

> the effects must be weighed against the losses in system legitimacy and stability when minority voices are not well represented. This is a judgement call well within the range of normal democratic choices.[10]

Looking Ahead

The purpose of this research was to enrich our understanding of policy responsiveness to blacks using the most central actor in lawmaking, the United States' Congress. It is also hoped that this research has laid the groundwork for systematic investigation into some important questions in the future. How far must political cartographers go to create a majority black or Hispanic district in a state? What are the political trade-offs in using race as a driving force in drawing district lines? How large must a majority-black or majority-minority district be in order to be acceptable? These are just a few of the perennial questions to be resolved in the future. What policymakers decide on these questions will have an important impact on future race relations and the quality of life for people of color in America.

Appendixes

Description of Voting Rights Measures during Amending Phase

I. Voting Rights Act Extension of 1982
1. Butler amendment (HR 3112) — an amendment that would transfer jurisdiction for bail-out suits from the District of Columbia Federal District Court to local federal district courts. Rejected, 132–277. A favorable vote was against the amendment.
2. Campbell amendment (HR 3112) — an amendment that would have weakened the "bail-out" provision by permitting states to bail out even though some counties in the state did not meet the bail-out requirements. Rejected, 95–313. A vote in support of black voting rights was one against the amendment.
3. McClory amendment (HR 3112) — an amendment introduced to repeal the bilingual provisions of the measure. Rejected, 128–284. A favorable vote was against the amendment.

II. Voting Rights Act Extension of 1975
1. Butler amendment (HR 6219): an amendment making it easier for states covered by the Voting Rights Act to exempt, or "bail-out," from its requirements. Rejected, 134–279. A favorable vote was one against the amendment.
2. McClory amendment (HR 6219): an amendment eliminating extension of the Voting Rights Act protection to non-English-speaking American citizens. Rejected, 104–305. A vote in support of civil rights was one against the amendment.
3. Hyde amendment (HR 6219): an amendment to repeal the provision requiring preclearance of election law changes. Rejected, 105–300. A vote in support of black voting rights was against the amendment.

III. Voting Rights Act Extension of 1970
1. Republican Substitute amendment of 1969 offered by Gerald Ford of Michigan (HR 4249): a substitute amendment con-

taining provisions that would weaken the Voting Rights Act. Adopted, 208–204. A vote against the amendment was a favorable one.

2. Matsunaga Motion (HR 4249): a motion for the House to accept the Senate version of a bill that would add new provisions strengthening and extending the Act to 1970. Rejected, 224–183. A vote for the motion was a favorable one.

3. Amendment in the Nature of a Substitute (HR 4249): amendment in the nature of a substitute offered by the Nixon administration to amend the Voting Rights Act of 1965. Adopted 234–179. A favorable vote was against the substitute.

IV. Voting Rights Act of 1965

1. Boggs amendment (HR 6400): an amendment providing weak penalties for falsifying voting or registration information. A favorable vote was against the amendment. Rejected, 155–262. A vote against the amendment was in support of strengthening federal voting rights.

2. Collier Motion (HR 6400): a motion with instructions to the committee to submit a Republican substitute amendment providing remedies to voter discrimination on a county-by-county basis rather than statewide for "massive discrimination." Rejected, 171-248. A favorable vote was one against the motion.

3. Gilbert Amendment (HR 6400): amendment to stipulate that a person could not be denied the right to vote because of an inability to read or write English if he demonstrated that he or she successfully completed the sixth grade. Rejected, 202–216. A vote in support of black voting rights was against the amendment.

4. Cramer Amendment (HR 6400): amendment to provide penalties of up to ten thousand dollars in fines/or up to five years imprisonment for falsifying voting or registration information. Passed, 253–165. A favorable vote was against the amendment.

V. Civil Rights Act of 1960

1. Rule for Debate (HR 359): an open rule providing debate on a civil rights bill. Adopted, 313–93. A favorable vote was one for the rule.

2. McCulloch/Cellar amendment (HR 8601): an amendment for court-appointed referees to help blacks register and vote when the court found a "pattern or practice" of discrimina-

tion existed. Adopted, 295–124. A favorable vote was one for the amendment.

3. Voting Records amendment (HR 8601): an amendment requiring the preservation of voting records by officials. Adopted, 311–109. A vote in support of federal voting rights protection was one for the amendment.

VI. Amendments to the Civil Rights Act of 1957

1. Poff Motion (HR 6127): a motion to insert a provision for jury trial in any criminal contempt action arising under the legislation. Rejected, 158–251. A favorable vote was against the motion.

2. Madden Motion (HR 6127): a motion to end debate on a provision amending the Senate's jury trial amendment. Adopted, 274–101. A vote in support of ending the motion was a favorable one.

3. Adoption Motion (HR 6127): adoption of the modified jury trial provision. Passed, 279–97. A yes vote was a supportive one.

4. Open Rule for Debate (H Res 259): rule to debate federal voting rights. Adopted, 291–117. A favorable vote was for the rule to debate.

Description of Amendments

Description of Fair Housing Amendments in 1988

1. Shaw amendment (HR 1158): to delete the provision barring discrimination in housing because a family has young children. Rejected, 116–289. A right vote was against the amendment.
2. McCollum amendment (HR 1158): to require that only 10 percent, rather than 100 percent, of any new multifamily housing project to meet federal standards for the handicapped. Rejected, 78–330. A right vote was against the amendment.
3. Hyde amendment (HR 1158): to provide that nothing in the bill requires, permits, or authorizes any preference in the provision of any dwelling based on race, color, religion, gender, or national origin. Rejected, 139–265. A favorable vote was against the amendment.
4. Burton motion (HR 1158): to recommit the bill to the House Judiciary Committee with instructions to report it back with an amendment excluding those with AIDS from the definition of handicapped. Rejected, 63–334. A right vote was against the motion.

Description of Civil Rights Amendments in 1991

1. Wheat motion (HR 1): to order the previous question on the rule to provide for House floor consideration of the bill to reverse or modify a series of Supreme Court rulings that narrowed the reach and remedies of job discrimination laws and to authorize compensatory and punitive damages for victims of discrimination based on sex, religion, or disability. Passed, 259–165. A right vote was for the motion.
2. Adoption of Rule (HR.1): adoption or rule to provide for House floor consideration of the bill to reverse or modify a series of Supreme Court rulings that narrowed the reach and remedies of job discrimination. Passed, 247–175.

3. Towns' substitute amendment (HR.1): to provide for unlimited punitive damages for discrimination based on sex, religion, or disability as opposed to the $150,000 cap provided for in the Brooks amendment. Rejected, 152–277. A favorable vote was for the Towns' substitute.

4. Administration's Substitute (HR.1): to substitute the Bush administration's civil rights bill. The substitute would remove compensatory and punitive damages for job discrimination based on sex, religion, or disability but allow up to $150,000 for cases involving harassment; define "business necessity" as a practice that has a manifest relationship to the employment or that serves a legitimate employment goal; allow challenges to consent decrees; ban the use of race-based adjustments to hiring test scores; and make other changes. Rejected, 162–266. A right vote was against the Administration's Substitute.

5. Brooks's substitute (HR.1): to place a cap of $150,000 on punitive damages for victims of intentional job discrimination on the basis of sex, religion, or disability or the amount of compensatory damages, whichever is greater; define "business necessity" as a practice that must bear a significant manifest relationship to the requirements for effective job performance; ban the use of race-based adjustments to hiring test scores; include a provision explicitly prohibiting the use of quotas; and for other purposes. Passed, 264–166. A right vote was for the Brooks's substitute.

APPENDIX C

Description of Bills as They Appear in Table 14

100th Congress

1. Budget Resolution (H Con Res 93): bill providing increases in selected programs for the poor, the homeless, and impoverished children and medical insurance for the elderly. Passed, 230–192. LCCR endorsed the resolution.
2. Lungren Amendment (HR 442): bill designed to remove the authorization of payments to Japanese Americans interned during World War II. Rejected, 162–237. LCCR opposed the amendment.
3. Motion (S. 557): a motion to order the previous question (ending debate and the possibility of amendment) on the rule (Civil Rights Restoration Act) to provide for House floor consideration of the bill to restore broad coverage of civil rights laws. Approved, 252–158. LCCR supported the motion.
4. Japanese-American Redress Act (HR 442): adoption of the Conference Report to provide reparations to Japanese Americans who were relocated to internment camps during World War II. Adopted, 257–156. LCCR supported the adoption.
5. Japanese-American Redress Act (HR 442): Final passage of the bill to provide payments to Japanese Americans interned during World War II. Passed, 243–142. LCCR endorsed the bill.

101st Congress

1. Habeas Corpus Amendment (HR 5269): bill requiring competent counsel for death row prisoners, and to reduce from one year to six months the time in which death row prisoners must file federal habeas corpus petitions after direct appeals have been exhausted. Rejected, 189–239. LCCR supported the amendment.
2. Americans with Disabilities Act (HR 2273): Chapman amendment to give employers discretion in moving employees with communi-

cable diseases. Adopted, 199–187. LCCR opposed the amendment.

3. Savings and Loan Restructuring/Redlining (HR 1278): amendment to require federal bank and thrift regulators to disclose the ratings and evaluation they give financial institutions under the 1977 Community Reinvestment Act and to require mortgage lenders to disclose the race, gender, and income of loan applicants and recipients. Adopted, 214–200. LCCR supported the amendment.

4. Racial Justice (HR 5269): Sensenbrenner amendment to strike the provision of the bill that bans execution of prisoners who demonstrate that the death sentence was imposed because of racial discrimination. Rejected, 204–216. LCCR opposed the amendment.

5. Americans with Disabilities Act (HR 2273): Olin amendment to limit the bill's coverage through the definition of undue hardship. Rejected, 187–213. LCCR opposed the amendment.

102d Congress

1. Balanced-Budget Constitutional Amendment (HJ Res 290): passage of the joint resolution to propose a constitutional amendment that would prohibit deficit spending unless a three-fifths majority of both chambers of Congress approve a specific deficit amount or there is a declaration of war or declaration of national military emergency enacted into law. Rejected, 280–153. A two-thirds majority of those present is needed in the House (289 in this case). LCCR opposed the constitutional amendment.

2. Unlimited Punitive Damages Amendment to Civil Rights Act of 1991 (HR1): Towns' substitute amendment to provide for unlimited punitive damages for discrimination based on sex, religion, or disability. Note: unlimited punitive damages for discrimination based on race already included in civil rights legislation. Rejected, 152–277. LCCR supported the amendment.

3. Race-based Sentencing Amendment in Omnibus Crime Bill (HR 3371): Hyde amendment to strike the provisions that allow death row prisoners to raise certain race bias claims in habeas corpus appeals. Adopted, 238–180. LCCR opposed the amendment.

4. Habeas Corpus Omnibus Crime Amendment (HR 3371): Hyde amendment to prohibit federal habeas corpus appeals in cases that had a "full and fair" hearing at the state level; limit death row prisoners to one federal habeas corpus petition that must be filed within six months of appeal; and set time limits for consideration

of habeas corpus petitions. Rejected, 208–218. LCCR opposed the amendment.

5. Voting Rights Language Assistance Amendment (HR 4312): Condit amendment to require federal grants to cover the cost of providing bilingual voting assistance to counties that are required to provide assistance. Rejected, 184–186. LCCR opposed the amendment.

103d Congress

1. District of Columbia (D.C.) Statehood Bill (HR 51): passage of the bill to admit D.C. into the union as the state of New Columbia. Rejected, 153–277. LCCR endorsed the bill.

2. Balanced-Budget Constitutional Amendment (HJ Res 103): joint resolution to propose a constitutional amendment to require a balanced budget by 2001 or the second fiscal year after ratification by three-fourths of the states, whichever is later. Congress could waive the balanced-budget requirement if three-fifths of the House and the Senate approve deficit spending. Rejected, 271–153. A two-thirds majority vote of those present and voting (283 here) is required to pass a joint resolution proposing an amendment to the Constitution. LCCR opposed the constitutional amendment.

3. Gays in the Military (HR 2401): Meehan amendment to strike the provisions in the Fiscal Year 1994 Defense Authorization Bill classifying a ban on homosexuals in the military. Rejected, 169–264. LCCR supported the amendment.

4. Brady Bill (gun control legislation, HR 2401): adoption of the conference report to require a five-business-day waiting period before an individual could purchase a handgun to allow local officials to conduct a background check. Adopted, 238–187. LCCR endorsed the amendment.

5. Racial Justice Amendment: McCollum amendment to remove the provisions that would have prohibited imposition of the death penalty if a criminal defendant could show racial discrimination in capital sentences. The amendment would have substituted provisions banning the use of such statistics. Rejected, 212–217. LCCR opposed the amendment.

Notes

Chapter 1

1. Gunnar Myrdal, *An American Dilemma* (New York: Harper and Brothers, 1944). For more recent discussions on the problem of the racial dilemma in America, see Jennifer L. Hochschild, *What's Fair? Americans Beliefs about Distributive Justice* (Cambridge: Harvard University Press, 1981), 1; Sidney Verba and Gary R. Orren, *Equality in America: The View from the Top* (Cambridge: Harvard University Press, 1981), 15; Jennifer L. Hochschild, *Facing Up to the American Dream: Race, Class, and the Souls of the Nation* (Princeton: Princeton University Press, 1995).

2. The racial dilemma can also be seen in the behavior of Thomas Jefferson, whose sweeping statement that "all men are created equal" was inconsistent with his practice as a slaveholder. For a discussion of the Declaration of Independence and the place of blacks in American society, see Carl L. Becker, *The Declaration of Independence* (New York: International Publishers, 1958), 100–110; John Hope Franklin, *From Slavery to Freedom: A History of Negro Americans* (New York: Vintage Books, 1969), 129–30; John Chester Miller, *Thomas Jefferson and Slavery* (New York: Free Press, 1977).

3. Gerhard Lowenberg, "Comparative Legislative Research," in *Comparative Legislative Behavior: Frontiers of Research,* ed. Samuel C. Patterson and John C. Wahlke (New York: John Wiley, 1972), 12.

4. Hanna F. Pitkin, *The Concept of Representation* (Berkeley: University of California Press, 1967).

5. Ibid., 209.

6. See Heinz Eulau and Paul D. Karps, "The Puzzle of Representation: Specifying Components of Responsiveness," in *The Politics of Representation,* ed. Heinz Eulau and John C. Wahlke (Beverly Hills, Calif.: Sage Publications, 1978).

7. Ibid., 62–67.

8. For a discussion and analysis of dyadic and collective representation, see Robert Weissberg, "Collective vs. Dyadic Representation in Congress," *American Political Science Review 72* (1978): 535–47.

9. John Adams, "Thoughts on Government," in *American Political Writings during the Founding Era, 1760–1805,* ed. Charles S. Hyneman and Donald S. Lutz (Indianapolis: Liberty Press, 1983), 1:403.

10. John Wahlke, Heinz Eulau, William Buchannan, and Leroy Ferguson, *The Legislative System: Explorations in Legislative Behavior* (New York: John Wiley, 1962), 253.

11. Leroy N. Rieselbach, *Congressional Politics: The Evolving Legislative System* (Boulder: Westview Press, 1995), 391.

12. See Karlyn Bowman, "What We Call Ourselves," *Public Perspective* 5 (1994): 29–31; Richard Morin, "From Colored to African American," *Washington Post,* January 21, 1994, A17.

13. Jennifer L. Hochshild, *Facing Up to the American Dream: Race, Class, and the Souls of the Nation* (Princeton: Princeton University Press, 1995), 6–7; Paula D. McClain and Joseph Stewart Jr., *Can We All Get Along?* (Boulder: Westview Press), 5.

14. Gerald David Jaynes and Robin M. Williams, eds., *A Common Destiny: Blacks and American Society* (Washington, D.C.: National Academy Press, 1989); Howard Schuman, Charlotte Steeh, and Lawrence Bobo, *Racial Attitudes in America* (Cambridge: Harvard University Press, 1985); Floris W. Wood, ed., *An American Profile—Opinions and Behavior, 1972–1989* (New York: Gale Research, 1990).

15. Data on poverty levels, income levels, and unemployment rates were collected from the U.S. Department of Commerce, U.S. Bureau of the Census, Statistical Abstract of the United States (Washington, D.C.: Government Printing Office, 1996), 394, 462, 472.

16. A 1988 survey by the National Opinion Research Center General Social Surveys (NORC-GSS) found on the question of discrimination that, among whites who had an opinion, only 39 percent agreed with the idea that the worsening condition of blacks was mainly due to discrimination; by contrast, 80 percent of blacks blamed discrimination.

17. There is little doubt that upper-status blacks feel the impact of class in their political predispositions, like any other ethnic or racial group. For research on the topic, see the works of William J. Wilson, *The Declining Significance of Race* (Chicago: University of Chicago Press), 1980; Alvin F. Pouissant, "The Price of Success," *Ebony* 10 (1987): 76–80. Even so, there is ample evidence to show that upper-income blacks are more likely to identify with their race than with their social class. For instance, higher-class status blacks are less likely to identify with the Republican Party than are whites of upper-class status. See, for example, Katherine Tate, *From Protest to Politics: The New Black Voters in American Elections* (Cambridge: Harvard University Press, 1993). Furthermore, there is evidence to suggest that upper-class status blacks are much more supportive of redistributive policy issues than are their white upper-status peers. See Franklin D. Gilliam Jr. and Kenny J. Whitby, "Race, Class, and Attitudes toward Social Welfare Spending: An Ethclass Interpretation," *Social Science Quarterly* (1989): 88–100; Michael C. Dawson, *Behind the Mule: Race and Class in African-American Politics* (Princeton: Princeton University Press, 1994).

18. For a few studies employing the use of the Leadership Conference on Civil Rights (LCCR) index on the topic, see Charles S. Bullock III, "Congressional Voting and the Mobilization of a Black Electorate in the South," *Journal of Politics* 43 (1981): 662–82; and "Congressional Roll-Call Voting in a Two-Party South," *Social Science Quarterly* 66 (1985): 789–804; Kenny J. Whitby, "Voting Behavior of Southern Congressmen: The Interaction of Race and Urbanization," *Legislative*

Studies Quarterly 10 (1985): 505–17; Kenny J. Whitby and Franklin D. Gilliam Jr., "A Longitudinal Analysis of Competing Explanations for the Transformation of Southern Congressional Politics," *Journal of Politics* 53 (1991): 504–18; Carol M. Swain, *Black Faces, Black Interests: The Representation of African Americans in Congress* (Cambridge: Harvard University Press, 1993).

19. For research comparing the correlation between the LCCR index and other interest group scales, see Bullock, "Congressional Voting," 662–82; Kenny J. Whitby,"Measuring Congressional Responsiveness to the Policy Interests of Black Constituents," *Social Science Quarterly* 68 (1987): 367–77; Swain, *Black Faces, Black Interests.* For further analysis on the relevancy of interest group ratings in legislative research, see Keith Krehbiel, "Deference, Extremism, and Interest Group Ratings," *Legislative Studies Quarterly* 19 (1994): 61–77.

20. Malcolm E. Jewell and Samuel C. Patterson, *The Legislative Process in the United States* (New York: Random House, 1966), 416.

21. For a good discussion of strategies involved in congressional decision making, see John W. Kingdon, *Congressmen's Voting Decisions,* rev. ed. (New York: Harper and Row, 1989). For a good summary on voting procedures in the House, see Walter J. Oleszek, *Congressional Procedures and the Policy Process* (Washington, D.C.: Congressional Quarterly Press, 1996), 161–97.

22. Jerrold Schneider, "Analyzing Votes in Congress," in *Congress and Public Policy,* ed. David C. Kozak and John D. Macartney (Homewood, Ill.: Dorsey Press, 1982), 333.

23. James M. Enelow and David H. Koehler, "The Amendment in Legislative Strategy: Sophisticated Voting in the U.S. Congress," *Journal of Politics* (1980): 397; James M. Enelow, "Saving Amendments, Killer Amendments, and Expected Utility Theory of Sophisticated Voting," *Journal of Politics* 43 (1981): 1063–73.

24. Merle Black, "Racial Composition of Congressional Districts and Support for Federal Voting Rights in the American South," *Social Science Quarterly* 59 (1978): 440.

25. Kingdon, *Congressmen's Voting Decisions,* 35–43.

26. Ibid., 274.

27. For examples of this literature, see Aage Clausen, *How Congressmen Decide* (New York: St. Martin's Press, 1973); Herbert Asher and Herbert Weisberg, "Voting Change in Congress: Some Dynamic Perspectives on an Evolutionary Process," *American Journal of Political Science* (1978): 391–425; Kingdon, *Congressmen's Voting Decisions.*

28. Kingdon, *Congressmen's Voting Decisions,* 276.

29. Steven S. Smith, *The American Congress* (Boston: Houghton Mifflin, 1995), 245.

Chapter 2

1. See, for example, Gabriel A. Almond and Sidney Verba, *The Civic Culture: Political Attitudes and Democracy in Five Nations* (Princeton: Princeton University Press, 1963).

2. August Meier and Elliot Rudwick, *From Plantation to Ghetto* (New York: Hill and Wang, 1966), 69.

3. Everette Swinney, "Enforcing the Fifteenth Amendment, 1870–1877," *Journal of Southern History* 27 (1962): 202–18; James M. McPherson, *The Struggle for Equality: Abolitionists and the Negro in the Civil War and Reconstruction* (Princeton: Princeton University Press, 1964); William Gillette, *The Right to Vote: Politics and the Passage of the Fifteenth Amendment* (Baltimore: Johns Hopkins Press, 1965); Eric Foner, *Reconstruction, 1863–1877: America's Unfinished Revolution* (New York: Harper and Row, 1988).

4. *United States v. Reese,* 92 U.S. 214 (1876).

5. *United States v. Cruikshank,* 92 U.S. 542 (1876).

6. For a cogent discussion of the Jim Crow system after Reconstruction, see V. O. Key Jr., *Southern Politics in State and Nation* (New York: Knopf, 1949); Donald R. Matthews and James W. Prothro, *Negroes and the New Southern Politics* (New York: Harcourt, Brace and World, 1966); John Hope Franklin, *Reconstruction: After the Civil War* (Chicago: University of Chicago Press, 1961); J. Morgan Kousser, *The Shaping of Southern Politics: Suffrage Restriction and the Establishment of the One-Party South, 1880–1910* (New Haven: Yale University Press, 1974); Steven F. Lawson, *Black Ballots* (New York: Columbia University Press, 1976); Bernard Grofman and Chandler Davidson, eds., *Controversies in Minority Voting: The Voting Rights Act in Perspective* (Washington, D.C.: Brookings Institution, 1992).

7. Key, *Southern Politics.*

8. Pat Watters and Reese Cleghorn, *Climbing Jacob's Ladder* (New York: Harcourt, Brace and World, 1967).

9. Lester M. Salamon and Steven Van Evera, "Fear, Apathy, and Discrimination: A Test of Three Explanations of Political Participation," *American Political Science Review* 67 (1973): 1288–1306; J. Morgan Kousser, *The Shaping of Southern Politics: Suffrage Restriction and the Establishment of the One-Party South, 1880–1910* (New Haven: Yale University Press, 1974); David J. Garrow, *Protest at Selma* (New Haven: Yale University Press, 1974).

10. C. Vann Woodward, *The Strange Career of Jim Crow,* 2d ed. (New York: Oxford University Press, 1966).

11. Based on data reported in *The American Negro Reference Book* (Englewood Cliffs: Prentice-Hall, 1966).

12. Lawson, *Black Ballots.*

13. Donald S. Strong, *Negroes, Ballots and Judges: National Voting Rights Legislation in the Federal Courts* (Tuscaloosa: University of Alabama Press, 1968).

14. Richard J. Timpone, "Mass Mobilization or Government Intervention? The Growth of Black Registration in the South," *Journal of Politics* 57 (1995): 425–42. For additional research on the Voter Education Project as the primary impetus for black voter registration in the South before the 1965 Voting Rights Act, see Watters and Cleghorn, *Climbing Jacob's Ladder;* Harrell R. Rodgers Jr. and Charles S. Bullock III, *Law and Social Change: Civil Rights Laws and Their Consequences* (New York: McGraw-Hill, 1972); Earl Black and Merle Black, *Politics and Society in the South* (Cambridge: Harvard University Press, 1987); Harold W. Stanley,

Voter Mobilization and the Politics of Race: The South and Universal Suffrage, 1952–1984 (New York: Praeger, 1987); Edward G. Carmines and Robert Huckfeldt, "Party Politics in the Wake of the Voting Rights Act," in *Controversies in Minority Voting: The Voting Rights Act in Perspective,* ed. Bernard Grofman and Chandler Davidson (Washington, D.C.: Brookings Institution, 1992); James E. Alt, "The Impact of the Voting Rights Act on Black and White Voter Registration," in *Quiet Revolution: The Impact of the Voting Rights Act 1965–1990,* ed. Chandler Davidson and Bernard Grofman (Princeton: Princeton University Press, 1994).

15. Carmines and Huckfeldt, "Party Politics."

16. Data were taken from Everett Carll Ladd Jr., "Negro Politics in the South: An Overview," in *Negro Politics in America,* ed. Harry A. Bailey Jr. (Columbus: Charles E. Merrill, 1967), 245.

17. See David J. Garrow, *Protest at Selma* (New Haven: Yale University Press, 1974).

18. For some good literature on the Voting Rights Act and its consequences, see Lawson, *Black Ballots;* Gayle Binion, "The Implementation of Section 5 of the 1965 Voting Rights Act," *Western Political Quarterly* (1979): 155–73; Twiley W. Barker Jr. and Lucius J. Barker, "The Courts, Section 5 of the Voting Rights Act, and the Future of Black Politics," in *The New Black Politics,* ed. Michael B. Preston, Lenneal J. Henderson Jr., and Paul Puryear (New York: Longman Press, 1982), chap. 3; Richard Scher and James Button, "Voting Rights Act: Implementation and Impact," in *Implementation of Civil Rights Policies,* ed. Charles S. Bullock III and Charles M. Lamb (Monterey: Brooks/Cole, 1984), 20–54; Lorn S. Foster, ed., *The Voting Rights Act: Consequences and Implications* (New York: Praeger, 1985); Steven F. Lawson, *In Pursuit of Power: Southern Blacks and Electoral Politics, 1965–1982* (New York: Columbia University Press, 1985); Bernard Grofman, Lisa Handley, and Richard G. Niemi, *Minority Representation and the Quest for Voting Equality* (Cambridge: Cambridge University Press, 1992); Chandler Davidson and Bernard Grofman, eds., *Quiet Revolution in the South* (Princeton: Princeton University Press, 1994).

19. Lawson, *Black Ballots,* 331.

20. *City of Mobile v. Bolden,* 446 U.S. 55 (1980).

21. Davidson and Grofman, *Quiet Revolution.*

22. Despite all that has been said and written on the subject of federal voting rights, few systematic longitudinal studies have been conducted to chart and explain the roll call voting behavior of House members on the topic. Previous studies have had a tendency to use a descriptive approach to examine the legislative history of voting rights legislation. See Richard Scher and James Button, "Voting Rights Act: Implementation and Impact," in *Implementation and of Civil Rights Policies,* ed. Charles S. Bullock and Charles M. Lamb (Monterey: Brooks/Cole, 1984); Lawson, *Black Ballots.* Other researchers have focused exclusively on specific voting rights bills usually from the perspective of the role of the courts (see, e.g., Binion, "Implementation of Section 5," 155–73). One good longitudinal analysis is offered by M. Black, "Racial Composition of Congressional Districts," 435–50. Black's research, however, focuses only on final passage votes of southern

representatives prior to the 1982 extension of the Voting Rights Act. For a comprehensive examination of the impact of the Voting Rights Act on voter registration, voter participation, and minority representation in eight southern states, see Davidson and Grofman, *Quiet Revolution.*

23. M. Black, "Racial Composition of Congressional Districts," 435–50.

24. Ibid., 433.

25. Key, *Southern Politics,* 3–12; Donald R. Matthews and James W. Prothro, *Negroes and the New Southern Politics* (New York: Harcourt, Brace and World, 1966), 115–20; David Knoke and N. Kyriazis, "The Persistence of the Black-Belt Vote: A Test of Key's Hypothesis," *Social Science Quarterly* 57 (1977): 900–906; Earl Black and Merle Black, *Politics and Society in the South* (Cambridge: Harvard University Press, 1987), 9–12.

26. M. Black, "Racial Composition of Congressional Districts," 445.

27. A favorable vote on amendments for the 1981, 1975, and 1970 extensions of the act was one endorsed by the LCCR. Because the LCCR index was not computed before the 91st Congress convened (1969), *Congressional Quarterly*'s listing of major voting rights bills was used as the criteria for collecting data on earlier amendment votes. For amendments selected, a favorable vote for 1957, 1960, and 1965 amendments was one supported by African-American members of Congress.

28. See Julius Turner, *Party and Constituency: Pressures on Congress* (Baltimore: Johns Hopkins Press, 1951), for an early comprehensive analysis of party behavior in Congress. For examples of more recent studies, see David Mayhew, *Party Loyalty among Congressmen* (Cambridge: Harvard University Press, 1966); W. Wayne Shannon, *Party, Constituency and Congressional Voting* (Baton Rouge: Louisiana State University Press, 1968); Aage Clausen, *How Congressmen Decide* (New York: St. Martin's Press, 1973); Morris Fiorina, *Representatives, Roll Calls, and Constituencies* (Lexington: Lexington Books, 1974); John Kingdon, *Congressmen's Voting Decisions* (Ann Arbor: University of Michigan Press, 1989).

29. Edward G. Carmines and James A. Stimson, *Issue Evolution: Race and the Transformation of American Politics* (Princeton: Princeton University Press, 1989), 76–82.

30. Steven F. Lawson, *Running for Freedom* (New York: McGraw-Hill, 1991).

31. There were seven voting Republicans in 1957, seven in 1960, eleven in 1965, twenty-six in 1970, and twenty in 1975.

32. For analysis of white southern voters' dissatisfaction with the Democratic Party and their migration to the Republican Party, see Jack Bass and Walter Devries, *The Transformation of Southern Politics* (New York: Basic Books, 1976); Barbara Sinclair, *Congressional Realignment* (Austin: University of Texas Press, 1982); John R. Petrocik, "Realignment: New Party Coalition and Nationalization of the South," *Journal of Politics* 49 (1987): 347–75; Kenny J. Whitby and Franklin D. Gilliam Jr., "A Longitudinal Analysis of Competing Explanations for the Transformation of Southern Congressional Politics," *Journal of Politics* 53 (1991): 504–18.

33. See, for example, Joe R. Feagin, "Civil Rights Voting by Southern Congressmen," *Journal of Politics* 34 (1972): 484–99; M. Black, "Racial Composition

of Congressional Districts"; Bullock, "Congressional Voting"; Whitby, "Voting Behavior"; Davidson and Grofman, *Quiet Revolution.*

34. A reliability test was first conducted to determine if the items (amendments) scaled properly for analysis. The minimum standard for acceptability was .60. The results of the reliability test yielded the following information: 1957–58 (alpha = .90), 1959–60 (alpha = .91), 1965–66 (alpha = .71), 1969–70 (alpha = .80), 1975–76 (alpha = .85), and 1981–82 (alpha = .86).

35. John H. Aldrich and Forrest D. Nelson, *Linear Probability, Logit, and Probit Models* (Beverly Hills, Calif.: Sage Publications, 1984).

36. For examples of this literature, see David Mayhew, *Party Loyalty among Congressmen* (Cambridge: Harvard University Press, 1966); Shannon, *Party, Constituency and Congressional Voting;* Feagin, "Civil Rights Voting"; Fiorina, *Representatives, Roll Calls, and Constituencies.* For literature pertaining to the impact of urbanization of black interests, see Whitby, "Voting Behavior"; and "Measuring Congressional Responsiveness"; Swain, *Black Faces, Black Interests.*

37. Richard Fenno, *Home Style: House Members in Their Districts* (Boston: Little, Brown, 1978).

38. Lawrence Bobo and Franklin D. Gilliam Jr., "Race, Sociopolitical Participation, and Black Empowerment," *American Political Science Review* 84 (1990): 377–94.

39. Michael Combs, John R. Hibbing, and Susan Welch, "Black Constituents and Congressional Roll Call Votes," *Western Political Quarterly* 37 (1984): 424–34; Whitby, "Voting Behavior"; and "Measuring Congressional Responsiveness."

40. Whitby and Gilliam, "Longitudinal Analysis."

41. Urbanization is excluded from the analysis because there is no compelling reason to believe that voting variability on federal voting rights will occur on the basis of the proportion of urban residents in a district.

42. *Congressional Quarterly Weekly Report* (1981): 415–16. For a good discussion of first- and second-generation voting discrimination, see Davidson and Grofman, *Quiet Revolution.*

43. *Congressional Quarterly Weekly Report* (1992): 27.

44. J. Morgan Kousser, "The Voting Rights Act and the Two Reconstructions," in *Controversies in Minority Voting: The Voting Rights Act in Perspective,* ed. Bernard Grofman and Chandler Davidson (Washington, D.C.: Brookings Institution, 1992), 176.

45. Ibid.

Chapter 3

1. *Slaugherhouse Cases,* 16 Wallace 36 (1873); *Civil Rights Cases,* 109 U.S. 3 (1883); *Hurtado v. California,* 110 U.S. 516 (1884); *Plessy v. Ferguson,* 163 U.S. 537 (1896).

2. See *Gideon v. Wainwright,* 372 U.S. 335 (1963). For relevant court cases associated with the movement toward nationalization of the Bill of Rights before

Gideon v. Wainwright, see *Gitlow v. New York,* 268 U.S. 652 (1925), *Powell v. Alabama,* 287 U.S. 45 (1932).

3. The watershed ruling on school desegregation in *Brown v. Board of Education,* 349 U.S. 294 (1954), was the major court case to begin the slow process of ending segregation.

4. *Guinn v. United States,* 238 U.S. 347 (1915).

5. Doug McAdam, *Political Process and the Development of Black Insurgency, 1930–1970* (Chicago: University of Chicago Press, 1982), 78.

6. Thomas R. Brooks, *Walls Come Tumbling Down: A History of the Civil Rights Movement, 1940–1970* (Englewood Cliffs: Prentice-Hall, 1974), 17.

7. Thomas R. Dye, *The Politics of Equality* (New York: Bobbs-Merrill, 1971), 22.

8. McAdam, *Political Process,* 78–87.

9. Exec. Order 8802, *Federal Register* 6 (1941): 3109.

10. Exec. Order 9981, *Federal Register* 12 (1948): 4313.

11. P. H. Vaughn, "The Truman Administration's Fair Deal for Black America," *Missouri Historical Review* 70 (March 1976): 291–305.

12. See McAdam, *Political Process,* 65–77.

13. C. Vann Woodward, *The Strange Career of Jim Crow* (New York: Oxford University Press, 1966), 143.

14. For some good works on the civil rights movement, see Thomas R. Brooks, *Walls Come Tumbling Down: A History of the Civil Rights Movement, 1940–1970* (Englewood Cliffs: Prentice-Hall, 1974); Richard Kluger, *Simple Justice: The History of Brown v. Board of Education and Black America's Struggle for Equality* (New York: Knopf, 1975); Lucius J. Barker and Jesse J. McCrory Jr., *Black Americans and the Political System* (Cambridge: Winthrop, 1976); Harvard Sitkoff, *The Struggle for Black Equality, 1954–1980* (New York: Hill and Wang, 1981); Doug McAdams, *Political Process and the Development of Black Insurgency* (Chicago: University of Chicago Press, 1982); Aldon D. Morris, *The Origins of the Civil Rights Movement* (New York: Free Press, 1984); Rhoda Lois Blumberg, *Civil Rights: The 1960s Freedom Struggle* (Boston: Twayne, 1984); Manning Marable, *Black American Politics: From Washington Marches to Jesse Jackson* (London: Verso, 1985); Hanes Walton Jr., *Invisible Politics: Black Political Behavior* (Albany: SUNY Press, 1985); Jack M. Bloom, *Class, Race, and the Civil Rights Movement* (Bloomington: Indiana University Press, 1987); Taylor Branch, *Parting the Waters: America in the King Years, 1954–63* (New York: Simon and Schuster, 1988).

15. For a vivid account of this event and others during the civil rights movement, see the film documentary *Eyes on the Prize,* pt. 1.

16. Critical assessments of John F. Kennedy's performance on civil rights can be found in the books of Victor Navasky, *Kennedy Justice* (New York: Atheneum, 1971); Pat Watters and Reese Cleghorn, *Climbing Jacob's Ladder: The Arrival of Negroes in Southern Politics* (New York: Harcourt, Brace and World, 1967). Less critical works of Kennedy's performance is the research of Carl Brauner, *John F. Kennedy and the Second Reconstruction* (New York: Columbia University Press,

1977); Harris Wofford, *Of Kennedys and Kings: Making Sense of the Sixties* (New York: Farrar, Strauss and Giroux, 1980).

17. Merle Miller, *Lyndon: An Oral Biography* (New York: G. P. Putnam's Sons, 1980).

18. For cogent discussions of the politics behind the enactment of the 1964 Civil Rights Act, see Gary Orfield, *Congressional Power: Congress and Social Change* (New York: Harcourt, Brace, Jovanovich, 1975); Charles Whalen and Barbara Whalen, *The Longest Debate: A Legislative History of the 1964 Civil Rights Act* (New York: New American Library, 1986); Edward G. Carmines and James A. Stimson, *Issue Evolution: Race and the Transformation of American Politics* (Princeton: Princeton University Press, 1989), chap. 3.

19. This provision became Title VII of the Civil Rights Act of 1964, 78, Stat. 241.

20. Title VI section of the 1964 Civil Rights Act, 78, Stat. 241.

21. See Howard Schuman, Charlotte Steeh, and Lawrence Bobo, *Racial Attitudes in America* (Cambridge: Harvard University Press, 1985); Gerald David Jaynes and Robin M. Williams Jr., eds. *A Common Destiny* (Washington, D.C.: National Academy Press, 1989); Andrew Hacker, *Two Nations: Black and White, Separate, Hostile, Unequal* (New York: Charles Scribner's Sons, 1992); Douglas S. Massey and Nancy A. Denton, *American Apartheid* (Cambridge: Harvard University Press, 1993).

22. Gary Orfield and Franklin Monforth, "Status of School Desegregation: The Next Generation," a report to the National School Board Association; reprinted in Karen DeWitt, "The Nation's Schools Learn a 4th R: Resegregation," *New York Times,* January 19, 1992, E5.

23. Jonathan Kozol, *Savage Inequalities: Children in America's Schools* (New York: Harper Perennial, 1992), 4.

24. For a good evaluation of the Boston incident, see Gary Orfield, *Must We Bus?* (Washington, D.C.: Brookings Institution, 1978), 144–46.

25. Mary Jordan, "On Track toward Two-Tier Schools," *Washington Post National Weekly Editions* (May 31–June 6, 1993): 31.

26. See, for example, Charles S. Bullock III and Joseph Stewart, "Incidence and Correlates of Second-Generation Discrimination," in *Race, Sex, and Policy Problems,* ed. Marian Palley and Michael Preston (Lexington: Lexington Books, 1979); Robert England and Kenneth Meier, "From Desegregation to Integration: Second Generation School Discrimination as an Institutional Impediment," *American Politics Quarterly* 13 (1985): 227–47; Stephen Wainscott and J. David Woodard, "Second Thoughts on Second Generation Discrimination," *American Politics Quarterly* 16 (1988): 171–92; Kenneth Meier, *The Politics of Second-Generation Discrimination* (Madison: University of Wisconsin Press, 1989).

27. To achieve some degree of school integration the U.S. Supreme Court held in *Swann v. Charlotte-Mecklenburg County Board of Education,* 402 U.S. 1, 91 S. Ct. 1267 (1971), that cross-district busing is an appropriate remedy if it can be demonstrated that school district lines have been drawn in a discriminatory fashion.

28. *Milliken v. Bradley,* 418 U.S. 717, 94 S. Ct. 3112 (1974).

29. Hacker, *Two Nations,* 31–49.

30. Detroit News Wire Services, "'Rights' Backers Hail Denny's Settlement," *Detroit News,* May 25, 1994, 4.

31. Hacker, *Two Nations,* 35.

32. Gregory Gordon, "Feds: Area Is Biased in Renting," *Detroit Free Press,* June 20, 1993, 1.

33. Jerry Knight, "Coloring the Chances of Getting a Mortgage," *Washington Post National Weekly Edition* (October 28–November 3, 1991): 26. Also see Federal Reserve Bank data, 1991.

34. For a good treatment of discriminatory practices in housing, see Charles Lamb, "Equal Housing Opportunity," in *Implementation of Civil Rights Policy,* ed. Charles S. Bullock III and Charles M. Lamb (Monterey: Brooks/Cole, 1984), chap. 3.

35. Ibid., 162.

36. "Deciphering a Racist Business Code," *Time,* October 19, 1992, 21–22.

37. *New York Times,* "Texaco to Make Record Payout in Bias Lawsuit" (November 16, 1996), 1, 23.

38. Harrell R. Rodgers Jr., "Fair Employment Laws for Minorities: An Evaluation of Federal Implementation," in Bullock and Lamb, *Implementation of Civil Rights Policy.*

39. *Griggs v. Duke Power,* 401 U.S. 424 (1971).

40. *Ward Cove Packing v. Atonio,* 490 U.S. 642 (1989).

41. The Civil Rights Act of 1964 is one of the more unique bills ever passed by Congress. There were numerous amendments offered in the House, most of which came from southern representatives who were oposed to the bill. Overall the House turned down 122 amendments applying to all the bill's titles during the debate, which lasted several months. Along with the diversity of civil rights legislation, a longitudinal analysis on the topic is not practical. For background information on the debates in Congress, see *Congressional Quarterly Almanac* (1964): 344–48.

42. Jack Bass and Walter Devries, *The Transformation of Southern Politics* (New York: Basic Books, 1976); Barbara Sinclair, *Congressional Realignment* (Austin: University of Texas Press, 1982); Petrocik, "Realignment"; Whitby and Gilliam, "Longitudinal Analysis."

43. Whitby and Gilliam, "Longitudinal Analysis," 504–18.

44. Key, *Southern Politics.*

45. Carmines and Stimson, *Issue Evolution,* chap. 3.

46. The amendments were combined and converted to an interval level variable. The reliability test yielded values of .82 for fair housing and .92 for civil rights.

47. The percentage of members in the modal category for civil rights legislation was 94 percent, and for fair housing legislation the modal value was 91 percent. The failure of the two logistic models in tables 7 and 8 to produce a reduction in error appears to be due to the high percentage of final passage votes for each bill. Even so the models perform well despite this troubling aspect of the data.

48. The Civil Rights Restoration Act is intended to restore broad coverage of civil rights laws that were restricted by the Supreme Court in *Grove City College v. Bell* (1984). The act provides broader coverage of the provisions in the law that

prohibits institutions receiving federal assistance from discriminating on the basis of race, gender, age, and disability.

49. Sheldon Goldman, "Judicial Selection under Clinton: A Midterm Examination," *Judicature* 78 (1995): 281, 287.

Chapter 4

1. For a discussion, see Benjamin Ginsberg, *The Consequences of Consent* (New York: Random House, 1982), chap. 1.

2. Pitkin, *Concept of Representation.*

3. Eulau and Karps, *Politics of Representation,* chap. 3.

4. David J. Vogler, *The Politics of Congress* (Boston: Allyn and Bacon, 1988), 57.

5. Richard L. Hall and Colleen Heflin, "The Importance of Color in Congress: Minority Members, Minority Constituencies, and the Representation of Race in the U.S. House." Paper presented at the Annual Meeting of the Midwest Political Science Association, Chicago, April 14–16, 1994.

6. Hall and Heflin, "The Importance of Color in Congress." For works on group consciousness, see Marvin E. Olsen, "Social and Political Participation of Blacks," *American Sociological Review* 35 (1970): 682–97; Sidney Verba and Norman H. Nie, *Participation in America* (New York: Harper and Row, 1972); George Antunes and Charles M. Gaitz, "Ethnicity and Participation: A Study of Mexican-Americans, Blacks, and Whites," *American Journal of Sociology* 80 (1975): 1192–1211; Patricia Gurin, Arthur H. Miller, and Gerald Gurin, "Stratum Identification and Consciouness," *Social Psychology Quarterly* 43 (1980): 30–47; Arthur H. Miller, Patricia Gurin, Gerald Gurin, and Oksana Malanchuk, "Group Consciouness and Political Participation," *American Journal of Political Science* 25 (1981): 494–511; Richard D. Shingles, "Black Consciousness and Political Participation: The Missing Link," *American Political Science Review* 75 (1981): 76–91; Pamela Johnston Conover, "The Influence of Group Identification on Political Perception and Evaluation," *Journal of Politics* 46 (1984): 760–85; Pamela Johnston Conover, "The Role of Social Groups in Political Thinking," *British Journal of Political Science* 18 (1988): 51–76.

7. For a more in-depth discussion of the social psychology of race, see Dawson, *Behind the Mule.*

8. William L. Clay Sr., *Just Permanent Interests: Black Americans in Congress, 1870–1992* (New York: Amistad, 1993), 121.

9. Fenno, *Home Style.*

10. Swain, *Black Faces, Black Interests.*

11. For a brief, but excellent, biographical discussion of black members of Congress over time, see Bruce A. Ragdale and Joel D. Treese, *Black Americans in Congress, 1870–1989* (Washington, D.C.: Government Printing Office, 1990); Congressional Black Caucus Office, Washington, D.C. For a more in-depth discussion of members of Congress through 103d Congress, see David Bositis, *The Congressional Black Caucus in the 103rd Congress* (Washington, D.C.: Joint Center for Political and Economic Studies, 1994). For a qualitative assessment of black and white representatives, see Swain, *Black Faces, Black Interests.*

12. Of the African Americans serving in recent congresses, only seven come from districts with a white majority populations, The members are: (1) Alan Wheat from Missouri, (2) Gary Franks from Connecticut, (3) J. C. Watts from Oklahoma, (4) Sanford Bishop Jr. from Georgia, (5) Cynthia McKinney from Georgia, (6) Corrine Brown from Florida, and (7) Julia Carson from Indiana.

13. For a discussion on electoral strategies African Americans might use to win congressional office, see Swain, *Black Faces, Black Interest.*

14. William R. Keech, *The Impact of Negro Voting: The Role of the Vote in the Quest for Equality* (Chicago: Rand McNally, 1968); Feagin, "Civil Rights Voting"; M. Black, "Racial Composition of Congressional Districts"; Bullock "Congressional Voting"; and "Congressional Roll-Call Voting"; Combs, Hibbing, and Welch, "Black Constituents"; Whitby, "Voting Behavior"; Whitby and Gilliam, "Longitudinal Analysis"; Richard Fleisher, "Explaining the Change in Roll-Call Voting Behavior of Southern Democrats," *Journal of Politics* 55 (1993): 327–41.

15. See Whitby and Gilliam, "Longitudinal Analysis."

16. See Combs, Hibbing, and Welch, "Black Constituents"; Whitby, "Voting Behavior."

17. For a discussion of party voting along the dimensions of socioeconomic issues, see Sinclair, *Congressional Realignment;* Sidney Verba and Gary R. Orren, *Equality in America: The View from the Top* (Cambridge: Harvard University Press, 1985).

18. Studies showing the effects of partisanship on legislation beneficial to African Americans include Bullock, "Congressional Roll-Call Voting"; Whitby, "Voting Behavior"; and "Measuring Congressional Responsiveness"; Swain, *Black Faces, Black Interests.*

19. For studies showing the predictive power of partisanship over time, see Bullock, "Congressional Voting"; and "Congressional Roll-Call Voting"; Whitby, "Voting Behavior." For a discussion of the decline in regional differences between southern and nonsouthern Democrats, see David Rohde, "Something's Happening Here; What It Is Ain't Exactly Clear: Southern Democrats in the House of Representatives," in *Home Style and Washington Work: Studies in Congressional Politics,* ed. Morris Fiorina and David Rohde (Ann Arbor: University of Michigan Press, 1989), 137–63.

20. Hall and Heflin, "The Importance of Color in Congress"; Verba and Orren, *Equality in America,* 139–47.

21. The number of amendments (LCCR index) used during the amending process in time period 1 is 16, time period 2 is 22, time period 3 is 19, and time period 4 is 26. The number of bills for final decision bills was 6 in time period 1, 8 in time period 2, 6 in time period 3, and 18 in time period 4.

22. A representative's support score is lowered in the LCCR index for missed votes. In each individual Congress missed votes are rather excessive for a few members, distorting their true voting behavior. For example, in the 103d Congress black congressman Craig Washington of Texas missed six out of fourteen votes in the LCCR index, giving him a rating of 57 out of 100. If his score was based on his eight votes, his score would have been 100. Consequently, for representatives who missed three votes or more on the index compiled by the LCCR, they were deleted

from the analysis. On average this represents about 3 percent of the members in each Congress.

23. The bivariate correlation between the proportion of blacks in the district and the representation of the district by a black member of the House is virtually identical for the amendment and the final passage models in each time period. The bivariate correlation in time period 1 is .60, time period 2 is .63, time period 3 is .58, and time period 4 is .70.

24. Michael S. Lewis-Beck, *Applied Regression: An Introduction* (Beverly Hills, Calif.: Sage Publications, 1980), 58–66.

25. For a similar model, see Swain, *Black Faces, Black Interests,* 215.

26. The South represents the old eleven confederate states of Alabama, Arkansas, Florida, Georgia, Louisiana, Mississippi, North Carolina, South Carolina, Tennessee, Texas, and Virginia.

27. It might be argued that there is an interaction between race and party—that is, the impact of race may depend on the party affiliation of the House member. An interaction term between race and party would thus allow us to determine whether black Democrats are significantly more supportive of black policy preferences than are other combinations of race and party (e.g., white nonsouthern Democrats). An analysis of interaction effects does not show any improvement over the additive model used in this investigation. The most likely reason for the similarity in the two models is that all but one black representative serving during the time periods under investigation were Democrats. Thus, the inclusion of House Republican Gary Franks does not alter the results in any significant way.

28. An analysis was conducted using only white representatives and another using nonblack members (white, Asian, and Hispanic House members). The findings are virtually the same for race. After each congressional election *Congressional Quarterly* gives a list of the representatives from ethnic minority groups. That list is the source for identifying the race of the member. In a single Congress there were less than eighteen members of the House who were identified as being either Hispanic, Asian, or a Pacific Islander. See relevant editions of *Congressional Quarterly Weekly Report,* for the names of racial minorities.

29. David W. Rohde, "The Reports of My Death Are Greatly Exaggerated: Parties and Party Voting in the House of Representatives," in *Changing Perspectives on Congress,* ed. Glenn R. Parker (Knoxvile: University of Tennessee Press, 1990); Whitby and Gilliam, "Longitudinal Analysis."

30. HR 442, "Lungren Amendment to Japanese-American Reparations Act," *Congressional Quarterly Almanac* (1987): 98-H.

31. HR 442, "Adoption of the Conference Report to the Japanese-American Reparations Act," *Congressional Quarterly Almanac* (1988): 84-H.

32. See HR 1278, "Saving and Loan Restructuring/Redlining," *Congressional Quarterly Almanac* (1989): 34-H.

33. See HR 5269, "Crime Bill/Death Row Appeals," *Congressional Quarterly Almanac* (1990): 134-H.

34. See HR 3371, "Omnibus Crime Bill/Race-Based Sentencing," *Congressional Quarterly Almanac* (1991): 32-H.

35. See HR 1, "Civil Rights Act of 1991/Unlimited Punitive Damages," *Congressional Quarterly Almanac* (1991): 32-H.

36. See HR 51, District of Columbia Statehood," *Congressional Quarterly Almanac* (1993): 146-H.

37. Hall and Heflin, "The Importance of Color in Congress."

38. The bivariate correlations between the two sets of race variables are identical for both models. The bivariate correlation for the 100th Congress is .70, 101st Congress is .65, 102d Congress is .70, and 103d Congress is .58.

39. *Congressional Quarterly Weekly Report* (April 13, 1985): 677.

40. Hall and Heflin, "The Importance of Color in Congress," 13–14. For a good recent discussion of voting and floor strategies, see Richard L. Hall, *Participation in Congress* (New Haven: Yale University Press, 1995).

Chapter 5

1. Since passage of the Voting Rights Act of 1965, Hispanics, Asian Americans, American Indians, and native Alaskans have been brought under the protection of the law. Also, the number of states now having to preclear redistricting plans continues to grow as various groups in society as well as political parties file lawsuits claiming unfair treatment.

2. For a good discussion of the different techniques of negative racial gerrymandering, see Frank Parker, "Racial Gerrymandering and Legislative Reapportionment," in *Minority Vote Dilution,* ed. Chandler Davidson (Washington, D.C.: Howard University Press, 1984).

3. For two good discussions on minority vote dilution, see Davidson, *Minority Vote Dilution;* Chandler Davidson and Bernard Grofman, eds., *Quiet Revolution in the South* (Princeton: Princeton University Press, 1995).

4. *Georgia v. United States,* 411 U.S. 526 (1973).

5. *White v. Regester,* 412 U.S. 755 (1973).

6. *United Jewish Organizations v. Carey,* 430 U.S. 144 (1977).

7. *City of Mobile v. Bolden,* 446 U.S. 55 (1980).

8. *Thornburg v. Gingles,* 478 U.S. 30 (1986).

9. They included: Sanford Bishop Jr. and Cynthia McKinney of Georgia; Corrine Brown, Alcee L. Hastings, and Carrie Meek of Florida; Eddie Bernice-Johnson of Texas; Eva Clayton and Melvin Watts of North Carolina; James E. Clyburn of South Carolina; Cleo Fields of Louisiana; Earl F. Hilliard of Alabama; Robert C. Scott of Virginia; and, Albert R. Wynn of Maryland.

10. For some analysis on the relationship between white voters and the electoral success of black congressional candidates, see Bernard Grofman and Lisa Handley, "Minority Population Proportion and Black and Hispanic Congressional Success in the 1970s and 1980s," *American Politics Quarterly* 17 (October 1989): 436–45; Linda Williams, "White-Black Perception of the Electability of Black Political Candidates," *National Political Science Review* 2 (1990): 45–64.

11. *Shaw v. Reno,* 125 L. Ed. 2d 511; 113 S. Ct. 2816 (1993).

12. *Miller v. Johnson,* 132 L.Ed 2d 762; S. Ct. 2475 (1995).

13. *Bush v. Vera,* 64 USLW. 4452 (1996).

14. See Swain, *Black Faces, Black Interests,* 210.

15. Timothy O'Rourke, "The 1982 Amendments and the Voting Rights Paradox," in *Controversies in Minority Voting: The Voting Rights Act in Perspective,* ed. Bernard Grofman and Chandler Davidson (Washington, D.C.: Brookings Institution, 1992), 109.

16. Abigail Thernstrom, *Whose Votes Count?* (Cambridge: Harvard University Press, 1987), 215–16.

17. Grofman and Handley, "Minority Population Proportion," 439–40; Lisa Handley and Bernard Grofman, "The Impact of the Voting Rights Act on Minority Representation: Black Officeholding in Southern State Legislatures and Congressional Delegations," *Quiet Revolution in the South* (Princeton: Princeton University Press, 1995), 335–50.

18. David Ian Lublin, *Gerrymandering for Justice: Racial Redistricting and Black and Latino Representation* (Princeton: Princeton University Press, 1997).

19. *Kirsey v. Board of Supervisors of Hinds County, Mississippi,* 544 F. 2d 139 (1977).

20. David Butler and Bruce Cain, *Congressional Redistricting: Comparative and Theoretical Perspective* (New York: Macmillan, 1992), 15. Also see Swain, *Black Faces, Black Interests,* 197–205; Lublin, *Gerrymandering for Justice.*

21. See, for example, Grofman and Handley, "Minority Population Proportion," 443.

22. Butler and Cain, *Congressional Redistricting,* 134–35.

23. Kevin Sack, "Court Draws Georgia Map of Congressional Districts," *New York Times,* December 14, 1995, A22.

24. Congressional Quarterly Weekly Report, "Special Report: Georgia," *Congressional Quarterly Almanac* (February 24, 1996): 456.

25. Charles S. Bullock III, "The Impact of Changing the Racial Composition of Congressional Districts on Legislators' Roll Call Behavior," *American Political Quarterly* 23 (April 1995): 141–58.

26. Due to the timing of Bullock's research (1990–93), he was only able to use LCCR scores for the pre-redistricting period. As a measure of black policy preferences in the post-redistricting year (1993), Bullock used a surrogate measure of black interests identified by the Joint Center for Political and Economic Studies. While different indices were used, Bullock found both indexes to be highly indicative of black policy preferences. For the investigation here the full range of LCCR scores is used to measure behavioral change and is calculated differently from Bullock's dependent variable.

27. Regressing 1993–94 LCCR scores on 1991–92 LCCR courts statistical danger in that the two sets of variables may be highly collinear. To determine if this collinearity was a problem, a correlation analysis was conducted yielding a value of .52. Based on this result, using raw LCCR scores does not appear to pose a major problem for the analysis.

28. Bullock, "Congressional Voting"; Whitby, "Voting Behavior"; Whitby and Gilliam, "Longitudinal Analysis"; Bullock, "Impact of Changing the Racial Composition."

29. A separate analysis was conducted for southern Republicans to determine if

the racial composition of the district affected their behavior. Not surprisingly, the results revealed that black constituency size has little impact on inducing southern Republicans to cast their roll call votes in a liberal direction.

30. Aage Clausen, *How Congressmen Decide* (New York: St. Martin's Press, 1973), 70–77;

31. Bass and Devries, *Transformation of Southern Politics;* Sinclair, *Congressional Realignment;* Petrocik, "Realignment."

32. John R. Petrocik and Scott W. Desposato, "The Partisan Consequences of Majority-Minority Redistricting in the South, 1992 and 1994" (paper presented at the Annual Meeting of the American Political Science Association, Chicago, August 31–September 3, 1995).

33. Kevin A. Hill, "Does the Creation of Majority Black Districts Aid Republicans? An Analysis of the 1992 Congressional Elections in Eight Southern States." *Journal of Politics* 57 (May 1995): 384–401.

34. For more recent research demonstrating that blacks undermine their own substantive political interests through race-conscious redistricting, see Charles Cameron, David Epstein, and Sharyn O'Halloran, "Do Majority-Minority Districts Maximize Substantive Black Representation in Congress?" *American Political Science Review* 90 (December 1996): 794–812.

Chapter 6

1. James Alt, "The Impact of the Voting Rights Act on Black and White Voter Registration in the South," in *Quiet Revolution in the South,* ed. Chandler Davidson and Bernard Grofman (Princeton: Princeton University Press, 1994), 51–377.

2. Harold W. Stanley and Ricard G. Niemi, *Vital Statistics on American Politics,* 4th ed. (Washington, D.C.: Congressional Quarterly Press, 1994), 399.

3. Davidson and Grofman, *Quiet Revolution,* 399.

4. Ibid., 386.

5. "Growing Black Cause May Have New Voice," *Congressional Quarterly Almanac* (January 2, 1993): 5.

6. Swain, *Black Faces, Black Interests,* 199, 207.

7. "Major Party Black Congressional Candidates," Joint Center for Political Studies, 1994, 1.

8. Lani Guinier, *The Tyranny of the Majority* (New York: Free Press, 1994), 41–70.

9. Cass R. Sunstein, "Voting Rites," *New Republican* (April 25, 1994), 1.

10. Bruce E. Cain, "Voting Rights and Democratic Theory: Toward a Color-Blind Society?" in Grofman and Davidson, *Controversies in Minority Voting,* 273.

References

Adams, John. "Thoughts on Government." In *American Political Writing during the Founding Era, 1769–1805,* ed. Charles S. Hyneman and Donald S. Lutz. Indianapolis: Liberty Press, 1983.

Aldrich, John H., and Forrest D. Nelson. *Linear Probability, Logit, and Probit Models.* Beverly Hills, Calif.: Sage Publications, 1984.

Almond, Gabriel A., and Sidney Verba. *The Civic Culture: Political Atittudes and Democracy in Five Nations.* Princeton: Princeton University Press, 1963.

Alt, James. "The Impact of the Voting Rights Act on Black and White Voter Registration in the South." In *Quiet Revolution in the South,* ed. Chandler Davidson and Bernard Grofman. Princeton: Princeton University Press, 1994.

American Negro Reference Book. Englewood Cliffs: Prentice-Hall, 1966.

Antunes, George, and Charles M. Gaitz. "Ethnicity and Participation: A Study of Mexican-Americans, Blacks, and Whites." *American Journal of Sociology* 80 (1975): 1192–1211.

Aptheker, Herbert. *The History of the American People.* Pt. 2: *The American Revolution.* New York: International Publishers, 1960.

Asher, Herbert, and Herbert Weisberg. "Voting Change in Congress: Some Dynamic Perspectives on an Evolutionary Process." *American Journal of Political Science* (1978): 391–425.

Barker, Lucius J., and Jesse J. McCrory Jr. *Black Americans and the Political System.* Cambridge: Winthrop, 1976.

Barker, Twiley W., Jr., and Lucius J. Barker. "The Courts, Section 5 of the Voting Rights Act, and the Future of Black Politics." In *The New Black Politics,* ed. Michael B. Preston, Lenneal J. Henderson Jr., and Paul Puryear. New York: Longman Press, 1982.

Bass, Jack, and Walter Devries. *The Transformation of Southern Politics.* New York: Basic Books, 1976.

Becker, Carl L. *The Declaration of Independence.* New York: Vintage Books, 1958.

Binion, Gayle. "The Implementation of Section 5 of the 1965 Voting Rights Act." *Western Political Quarterly* (1979): 155–73.

Black, Earl, and Merle Black. *Politics and Society in the South.* Cambridge: Harvard University Press, 1987.

Black, Merle. "Racial Composition of Congressional Districts and Support for Federal Voting Rights in the American South." *Social Science Quarterly* 59 (1978): 435–50.

Bloom, Jack M. *Class, Race, and the Civil Rights Movement.* Bloomington: Indiana University Press, 1987.

Blumberg, Rhoda Lois. *Civil Rights: The 1960s Freedom Struggle.* Boston: Twayne, 1984.

Bobo, Lawrence, and Franklin D. Gilliam Jr. "Race, Sociopolitical Participation, and Black Empowerment." *American Political Science Review* 84 (1990): 377–93.

Bositis, David. *The Congressional Black Caucus in the 103rd Congress.* Washington, D.C.: Joint Center for Political and Economic Studies, 1994.

Bowman, Karlyn. "What We Call Ourselves." *Public Perspective* 5 (1994): 29–31.

Branch, Taylor. *Parting the Waters: America in the King Years, 1954–63.* New York: Simon and Schuster, 1988.

Brauner, Carl. *John F. Kennedy and the Second Reconstruction.* New York: Columbia University Press, 1977.

Brooks, Thomas R. *Walls Come Tumbling Down: A History of the Civil Rights Movement, 1940–1970.* Englewood Cliffs: Prentice-Hall, 1974.

Bullock, Charles S., III. "Congressional Voting and the Mobilization of a Black Electorate in the South." *Journal of Politics* 43 (1981): 662–82.

———. "Congressional Roll-Call Voting in a Two-Party South." *Social Science Quarterly* 66 (1985): 789–804.

———. "Redistricting and Changes in the Partisan and Racial Composition of Southern Legislatures." *State and Local Government Review* (1987): 62–67.

———. "The Impact of Changing the Racial Composition of Congressional Districts on Legislators' Roll Call Behavior." *American Political Quarterly* 23 (1995): 141–58.

Bullock, Charles S., III, and Joseph Stewart. "Incidence and Correlates of Second-Generation Discrimination." In *Race, Sex, and Policy Problems,* ed. Marian Palley and Michael Preston. Lexington: Lexington Books, 1979.

Bureau of the Census. *County and City Data Book, 1994,* U.S. Department of Commerce, Economic and Statistics Administration. Washington, D.C.: Government Printing Office, 1994.

———. *Current Population Reports.* Ser. P-60, no. 180. Washington, D.C.: Government Printing Office, 1992.

———. *Population and Housing Characteristics for Congressional Districts of the 103rd Congress, Georgia.* Washington, D.C.: Government Printing Office, 1990.

———. *Statistical Abstract of the United States.* Washington, D.C.: Government Printing Office, 1995.

Butler, David, and Bruce Cain. *Congressional Redistricting: Comparative and Theoretical Perspectives.* New York: Macmillan, 1992.

Cain, Bruce. "Voting Rights and Democratic Theory: Toward a Color-Blind Society?" In *Controversies in Minority Voting: The Voting Rights Act in Perspective,* ed. Bernard Grofman and Chandler Davidson. Washington, D.C.: Brookings Institution, 1992.

Cameron, Charles, David Epstein, and Sharyn O'Halloran. "Do Majority-Minority Districts Maximize Substantive Black Representationn in Congress?" *American Politcal Science Review* 90 (1996): 794–812.

Carmines, Edward G., and Robert Huckfeldt. "Party Politics in the Wake of the Voting Rights Act." In *Controversies in Minority Voting: The Voting Rights Act in Perspective,* ed. Bernard Grofman and Chandler Davidson. Washington, D.C.: Brookings Institution, 1992.

Carmines, Edward G., and James A. Stimson. *Issue Evolution: Race and the Transformation of American Politics.* Princeton: Princeton University Press, 1989.

Clausen, Aage. *How Congressmen Decide.* New York: St. Martin's Press, 1973.

Clay, William L., Sr. *Just Permanent Interests: Black Americans in Congress, 1870–1992.* New York: Amistad, 1993.

Combs, Michael, John R. Hibbing, and Susan Welch. "Black Constituents and Congressional Roll Call Votes." *Western Political Quarterly* 37 (1984): 424–34.

Congressional Quarterly 1957, 1960, 1964, 1965, 1970, 1975, 1981, 1987, 1988, 1989, 1990, 1991, 1993. *Congressional Quarterly Almanac* Washington, D.C.: Government Printing Office.

Congressional Quarterly Weekly Report 1985, 1991, 1992, 1996. *Congressional Quarterly Almanac.* Washington, D.C.: Government Printing Office.

Conover, Pamela Johnston. "The Influence of Group Identification on Political Perception and Evaluation." *Journal of Politics* 46 (1984): 760–85.

Conover, Pamela Johnston. "The Role of Social Groups in Political Thinking." *British Journal of Political Science* 18 (1988): 51–76.

Davidson, Chandler, ed. *Minority Vote Dilution.* Washington, D.C.: Howard University Press, 1984.

Davidson, Chandler, and Bernard Grofman, eds. *Quiet Revolution in the South.* Princeton: Princeton University Press, 1995.

Dawson, Michael C. *Behind the Mule: Race and Class in African-American Politics.* Princeton: Princeton University Press, 1994.

"Deciphering a Racist Business Code." *Time,* October 19, 1992.

Detroit News Wire Services. "'Rights' Backers Hail Denny's Settlement." *Detroit News,* May 25, 1994.

Du Bois, W. E. B. *The Souls of Black Folks.* 1903. New York: Fawcett Publications, 1968.

Dye, Thomas R. *The Politics of Equality.* New York: Bobbs-Merrill, 1971.

Enelow, James M. "Saving Amendments, Killer Amendments, and Expected Utility Theory of Sophisticated Voting." *Journal of Politics* 43 (1981): 1062–89.

Enelow, James M., and David H. Koehler. "The Amendment in Legislative Strategy: Sophisticated Voting in the U.S. Congress." *Journal of Politics* 42 (1980): 396–413.

England, Robert, and Kenneth Meier. "From Desegregation to Integration: Second Generation School Discrimination as an Institutional Impediment." *American Politics Quarterly* 13 (1985): 227–47.

Erikson, Robert S. "Malapportionment, Gerrymandering, and Party Fortunes in Congressional Elections." *American Political Science Review* 66 (1972): 1234–45.

Eulau, Heinz, and Paul D. Karps. "Puzzle of Representation: Specifying Components of Responsiveness." In The Politics of Representation, ed. Heinz Eulau and John C. Wahlke. Beverly Hills, Calif.: Sage Publications, 1978.

Exec. Order 8802. *Federal Register* 6 (1941): 3109.

Exec. Order 9981. *Federal Register* 12 (1948): 4313.

Eyes On the Prize, PBS Television Documentary, pt. 1.

Fenno, Richard. *Home Style: House Members in Their Districts.* New York: Scott, Foresman and Co., 1978.

Feagin, Joe. "Civil Rights Voting by Southern Congressmen." *Journal of Politics* 34 (1972): 484–99.

Fiorina, Morris. *Representatives, Roll Calls, and Constituencies.* Lexington, Ky.: Lexington Books, 1974.

Fleisher, Richard. "Explaining the Change in Roll-Call Voting Behavior of Southern Democrats." *Journal of Politics* 55 (1993): 327–41.

Foner, Eric. *Reconstruction, 1863–1877: America's Unfinished Revolution.* New York: Harper and Row, 1988.

Foster, Lorn S., ed. *The Voting Rights Act: Consequences and Implications.* New York: Praeger, 1985.

Franklin, John Hope. *From Slavery to Freedom: A History of Negro Americans.* New York: Vintage Books, 1969.

Garrow, David J. *Protest at Selma.* New Haven: Yale University Press, 1974.

Gillette, William, *The Right to Vote: Politics and the Passage of the Fifteenth Amendment.* Baltimore: John Hopkins Press, 1965.

Gilliam, Franklin D., Jr., and Kenny J. Whitby. "Race, Class, and Attitudes toward Social Welfare Spending: An Ethclass Interpretation." *Social Science Quarterly* 70 (1989): 88–100.

Ginsberg, Benjamin. *The Consequence of Consent.* New York: Random House, 1982.

Goldman, Sheldon. "Judicial Selection under Clinton: A Midterm Examination." *Judicature* 78 (1995): 281, 287.

Gordon, Gregory. 1993. "Feds. Areas Is Biased in Renting." *Detroit Free Press,* June 20, 1993.

Grofman, Bernard, and Lisa Handley. "Minority Population Proportion and Black and Hispanic Congressional Success in the 1970s and 1980s." *American Politics Quarterly* 17 (1989): 436–45.

Grofman, Bernard, Lisa Handley, and Richard G. Niemi. *Minority Representation and the Quest for Voting Equality.* Cambridge: Cambridge University Press, 1992.

Grofman, Bernard, and Chandler Davidson, eds. *Controversies in Minority Voting: The Voting Rights Act in Perspective.* Washington, D.C.: Brookings Institution, 1992.

Guinier, Lani. *Tyranny of the Majority.* New York: Free Press, 1994.

Gurin, Patricia, Arthur H. Miller, and Gerald Gurin. "Stratum Identification and Consciouness," *Social Psychology Quarterly* 43 (1980): 30–47.

Hacker, Andrew. *Two Nations: Black and White, Separate, Hostile, Unequal.* New York: Charles Scribner's Sons, 1992.

Hall, Richard. *Participation in Congress.* New Haven: Yale University Press, 1995.

Hall, Richard L., and Colleen Heflin. "The Importance of Color in Congress: Minority Members, Minority Constituencies, and the Representation of Race in the U.S. House." Paper presented at the Annual Meeting of the Midwest Political Science Association, Chicago, April 14–16, 1994.

Handley, Lisa, and Bernard Grofman. "The Impact of the Voting Rights Act on Minority Representation: Black Officeholding in Southern State Legislatures and Congressional Delegations." In *Quiet Revolution in the South,* ed. Chandler Davidson and Bernard Grofman. Princeton: Princeton University Press, 1994.

Hill, Kevin. "Does the Creation of Majority Black Districts Aid Republicans? An Analysis of the 1992 Congressional Elections in Eight Southern States." *Journal of Politics* 57 (1995): 384–401.

Hochschild, Jennifer. *What's Fair? American Beliefs about Distributive Justice.* Cambridge: Harvard University Press, 1981.

Hochschild, Jennifer. *Facing Up to the American Dream: Race, Class, and the Soul of the Nation.* Princeton: Princeton University Press, 1995.

Jaynes, Gerald David, and Robin M. Williams Jr., eds. *A Common Destiny.* Washington, D.C.: National Academy Press, 1989.

Jewell, Malcolm E., and Samuel C. Patterson. *The Legislative Process in the United States.* New York: Random House, 1966.

Joint Center for Political Studies. "Major Party Black Congressional Candidates." Washington, D.C.: Joint Center for Political Studies, 1994.

Jordan, Mary. "On Track toward Two-Tier Schools." *Washington Post National Weekly Editions* (May 31–June 6, 1993).

Keech, William R. *The Impact of Negro Voting: The Role of the Vote in the Quest for Equality.* Chicago: Rand McNally, 1968.

Key, V. O., Jr. *Southern Politics in State and Nation.* New York: Knopf, 1949.

Kingdon, John W. *Congressmen's Voting Decisions.* New York: Harper and Row, 1981, 1989.

Kluger, Richard. *Simple Justice: The History of Brown v. Board of Education and Black America's Struggle for Equality.* New York: Knopf, 1975.

Knight, Jerry. "Coloring the Chances of Getting a Mortgage." *Washington Post National Weekly Edition* (October 28–November 3, 1991).

Knoke, David, and N. Kyriazis. "The Persistence of the Black-Belt Vote: A Test of Key's Hypotheses." *Social Science Quarterly* 57 (1977): 900–906.

Kozol, Jonathan. *Savage Inequalities: Children in America's Schools.* New York: Harper Perennial, 1992.

Kousser, J. Morgan. *The Shaping of Southern Politics: Suffrage Restriction and the Establishment of the One-Party South, 1880–1910.* New Haven: Yale University Press, 1974.

Kousser, J. Morgan. "The Voting Rights Act and the Two Reconstructions." In *Controversies in Minority Voting: The Voting Rights Act in Perspective,* ed. Bernard Grofman and Chandler Davidson. Washington, D.C.: Brookings Institution, 1992.

Krehbiel, Keith. "Deference, Extremism, and Interest Group Ratings." *Legislative Studies Quarterly* 19 (1994): 61–77.

Ladd, Everett Carll, Jr. "Negro Politics in the South: An Overview." In *Negro Politics in America,* ed. Harry A. Bailey Jr. Columbus: Charles E. Merrill, 1967.

Lamb, Charles M. "Equal Housing Opportunity." In *Implementation of Civil Rights Policy,* ed. Charles S. Bullock III and Charles M. Lamb. Monterey: Brooks/Cole, 1984.

Lawson, Steven F. *Black Ballots.* New York: Columbia University Press, 1976.

———. *In Pursuit of Power: Southern Blacks and Electoral Politics, 1965–1982.* New York: Columbia University Press, 1985.

———. *Running for Freedom.* New York: McGraw-Hill, Inc., 1991.

Lewis-Beck, Michael. *Applied Regression.* Beverly Hills, Calif.: Sage Publications, 1980.

Lowenberg, Gerhard. "Comparative Legislative Research." In *Comparative Legislative Behavior: Frontiers of Research,* ed. Samuel C. Patterson and John C. Wahlke. New York: John Wiley, 1972.

Lublin, David Ian. *Gerrymander for Justice? Racial Redistricting and Black and Latino Representation.* Princeton: Princeton University Press, 1997.

Marable, Manning. *Black American Politics: From Washington Marches to Jesse Jackson.* London: Verso, 1985.

Massey, Douglas, and Nancy A. Denton. *American Apartheid.* Cambridge: Harvard University Press, 1993.

Matthews, Donald R., and James W. Prothro. *Negroes and the New Southern Politics.* New York: Harcourt, Brace and World, 1966.

Mayhew, David. *Party Loyalty among Congressmen.* Cambridge: Harvard University Press, 1966.

McAdam, Doug. *Political Process and the Development of Black Insurgency.* Chicago: University of Chicago Press, 1982.

McClain, Paula D., and Joseph Stewart Jr. *Can We All Get Along?* Boulder: Westview Press, 1995.

McPherson, James M. *The Struggle for Equality: Abolitionists and the Negro in the Civil War and Reconstruction.* Princeton: Princeton University Press, 1964.

Meier, August, and Elliot Rudwick. *From Plantation to Ghetto.* New York: Hill and Wang, 1966.

Miller, Arthur H., Patricia Gurin, Gerald Gurin, and Oksana Malanchuk. "Group Consciousness and Political Participation." *American Journal of Political Science* 25 (1981): 494–511.

Miller, John Chester. *Thomas Jefferson and Slavery.* New York: Free Press, 1977.

Miller, Merle. *Lyndon: An Oral Biography.* New York: G. P. Putnam's Sons, 1980.

Morin, Richard. "From Colored to African American." *Washington Post,* January 21, 1994, A17.

Morris, Aldon D. *The Origins of the Civil Rights Movement.* New York: Free Press, 1984.

Myrdal, Gunnar. *An American Dilemma.* New York: Harper and Brothers, 1994.

National Election Studies, Center for Political Studies, University of Michigan, 1992.

Navasky, Victor. *Kennedy Justice.* New York: Atheneum, 1971.

New York Times. "1996 Election Results." (November 7, 1996).

Oleszek, Walter J. *Congressional Procedures and the Policy Process.* Washington, D.C.: Congressional Quarterly Press, 1996.

Olsen, Marvin E. "Social and Political Participation of Blacks." *American Sociological Review* 35 (1970): 682–97.

Orfield, Gary. *Congressional Power: Congress and Social Change.* New York: Harcourt, Brace, Jovanovich, 1975.

———. *Must We Bus?* Washington, D.C.: Brookings Institution, 1978.

Orfield, Gary, and Franklin Monforth. "Status of School Desegregation: The Next Generation." Reprinted in Karen DeWitt, "The Nations' Schools Learn a 4th R: Resegregation." *New York Times,* January 19, 1992, E5.

O'Rourke, Timothy. "The 1982 Amendments and the Voting Rights Paradox." In *Controversies in Minority Voting Behavior,* ed. Bernard Grofman and Chandler Davidson. Washington, D.C.: Brookings Institution, 1992.

Parker, Frank. "Racial Gerrymandering and Legislative Reapportionment." In *Minority Vote Dilution,* ed. Chandler Davidson. Washington, D.C.: Howard University Press, 1984.

Petrocik, John R. "Realignment: New Party Coalition and the Nationalization of the South." *Journal of Politics* 49 (1987): 347–75.

Petrocik, John R., and Scott W. Desposato. "The Partisan Consequences of Majority-Minority Redistricting in the South, 1992 and 1994." Paper presented at the Annual Meeting of the American Political Science Association, Chicago, August 31–September 3, 1995.

Pitkin, Hanna F. *The Concept of Representation.* Berkeley: University of California Press, 1967.

Pouissant, Alvin F. "The Price of Success," *Ebony* 10 (1987): 76–80.

Prothro, James W. *Negroes and the New Southern Politics.* New York: Harcourt, Brace and World, 1966.

Ragsdale, Bruce A., and Joel D. Treese. *Black Americans in Congress, 1870–1989.* Washington, D.C.: U.S. Government Printing Office, 1990.Rieselbach, Leroy. *Congressional Politics: The Evolving Legislative System.* Boulder: Westview Press, 1995.

Rodgers, Harrell R., Jr. "Fair Employment Laws for Minorities: An Evaluation of Federal Implementation." In *Implementation of Civil Rights Policy,* ed. Charles S. Bullock III and Charles M. Lamb. Monterey: Brooks/Cole, 1984.

Rodgers, Harrell R., Jr., and Charles S. Bullock III. *Law and Social Change: Civil Rights Laws and Their Consequences.* New York: McGraw-Hill, 1972.

Rohde, David. "The Reports of My Death Are Greatly Exaggerated: Parties and Party Voting in the House of Representatives." In *Changing Perspectives on Congress,* ed. Glenn R. Parker. Knoxville: University of Tennessee Press, 1990.

———. "Something's Happening Here; What It Is Ain't Exactly Clear: Southern Democrats in the House of Representatives." In *Home Style and Washington Work: Studies in Congressional Politics,* ed. Morris P. Fiorina and David Rohde. Ann Arbor: University of Michigan Press, 1989.

Sack, Kevin. "Court Draws Georgia Map of Congressional Districts." *New York Times,* December 14, 1995, A22.

Salamon, Lester M., and Steven Van Evera. "Fear, Apathy, and Discrimination: A Test of Three Explanations of Political Participation." *American Political Science Review* 67 (1973): 1288–1306.

Scher, Richard, and James Button. "Voting Rights Act: Implementation and Impact." In *Implementation of Civil Rights Policies,* ed. Charles Bullock III and Charles M. Lamb. Monterey: Brooks/Cole, 1984.

Schneider, Jerrold. "Analyzing Votes in Congress." In *Congress and Public Policy,* ed. David C. Kozak and John D. Macartney. Homewood, Ill.: Dorsey Press, 1982.

Schuman, Howard, Charlotte Steeh, and Lawrence Bobo. *Racial Attitudes in America.* Cambridge: Harvard University Press, 1989.

Shannon, W. Wayne. *Party, Constituency and Congressional Voting.* Baton Rouge: Louisiana State University Press, 1968.

Shingles, Richard D. "Black Consciousness and Political Participation: The Missing Link." *American Political Science Review* 75 (1981): 76–91.

Sinclair, Barbara. *Congressional Realignment.* Austin: University of Texas Press, 1982.

Sitkoff, Harvard. *The Struggle for Black Equality, 1954–1980.* New York: Hill and Wang, 1981.

Smith, Steven S. *The American Congress.* Boston: Houghton Mifflin, 1995.

Stanley, Harold W. *Voter Mobilization and the Politics of Race: The South and Universal Suffrage, 1952–1984.* New York: Praeger, 1987.

Stanley, Harold W., and Richard G. Niemi. *Vital Statistics on American Politics.* 4th ed. Washington, D.C.: Congressional Quarterly Press, 1994.

Statistical Abstract of the United States. Washington, D.C.: Government Printing Office, 1972, 1993, 1996.

Strong, Donald S. *Negroes, Ballots and Judges: National Voting Rights Legislation in the Federal Courts.* Tuscaloosa: University of Alabama Press, 1968.

Sunstein, Cass R. "Voting Rites." *New Republican,* April 25, 1994.

Swain, Carol. *Black Faces, Black Interests: The Representation of African Americans in Congress.* Cambridge: Harvard University, 1993.

Swinney, Everette. "Enforcing the Fifteenth Amendment, 1870–1877." *Journal of Southern History* 27 (1962): 202–18.

Tate, Katherine. *From Protest to Politics: The New Black Voters in American Elections.* Cambridge: Harvard University Press, 1993.

Thernstrom, Abigail. *Whose Votes Count?* Cambridge: Harvard University Press, 1987.

Timpone, Richard J. "Mass Mobilization or Government Intervention? The Growth of Black Registration in the South." *Journal of Politics* 57 (1995): 425–42.

Turner, Julius. *Party and Constituency: Pressures on Congress.* Baltimore: Johns Hopkins Press, 1951.

U.S. Department of Commerce, Economic and Statistics Administration. "Population and Housing Characteristics for Congressional Districts of the 103rd Congress, Georgia." *Bureau of the Census* (1992): G-2 Georgia.

Vaughn, P. H. "The Truman Administration's Fair Deal for Black America." *Missouri Historical Review* 70 (1976): 291–305.

Verba, Sidney, and Norman H. Nie. *Participation in America.* New York: Harper and Row, 1972.

Verba, Sidney, and Garry Orren. *Equality in America: The View from the Top.* Cambridge: Harvard University Press, 1985.

Vogler, David J. *The Politics of Congress.* Boston: Allyn and Bacon, 1988.

Wahlke, John, Heinz Eulau, William Buchanan, and Leroy Ferguson. *The Legislative System: Explorations in Legislative Behavior.* New York: John Wiley, 1962.

Wainscott, Stephen, and J. David Woodard. "Second Thoughts on Second Generation Discrimination." *American Politics Quarterly* 16 (1988): 171–92.

Walton, Hanes, Jr. *Invisible Politics: Black Political Behavior.* Albany: SUNY Press, 1985.

Watters, Pat, and Reese Cleghorn. *Climbing Jacob's Ladder: The Arrival of Negroes in Southern Politics.* New York: Harcourt, Brace and World, 1967.

Weissberg, Robert. "Collective vs. Dyadic and Collective Representation in Congress." *American Political Science Review* 72 (1978): 535–47.

Whalen, Charles, and Barbara Whalen. *The Longest Debate: A Legislative History of the 1964 Civil Rights Act.* New York: New American Library, 1986.

Whitby, Kenny J. "Voting Behavior of Southern Congressmen: The Interaction of Race and Urbanization." *Legislative Studies Quarterly* 10 (1985): 505–17.

———. "Measuring Congressional Responsiveness to the Policy Interests of Black Constituents." *Social Science Quarterly* 68 (1987): 367–77.

Whitby, Kenny J., and Franklin D. Gilliam Jr. "A Longitudinal Analysis of Competing Explanations for the Transformation of Southern Congressional Politics." *Journal of Politics* 53 (1991): 504–18.

Williams, Linda. "White-Black Perception of the Electability of Black Political Candidates." *National Political Science Review* 2 (1990): 45–64.

Wilson, William J. *The Declining Significance of Race.* Chicago: University of Chicago, 1980.

Wofford, Harris. *Of Kennedys and Kings: Making Sense of the Sixties.* New York: Farrar, Straus and Giroux, 1980.

Wood, Floris W., ed. *An American Profile—Opinions and Behavior, 1972–1989.* New York: Gale Research, 1990.

Woodward, C. Vann. *The Strange Career of Jim Crow.* New York: Oxford University Press, 1966.

Court Cases

Brown v. Board of Education, 349 U.S. 294 (1954).
Bush v. Vera, 64 USLW. 4452 (1996).
City of Mobile v. Bolden, 446 U.S. 55 (1980).
Civil Rights Cases, 109 U.S. 3 (1883).
Georgia v. United States, 411 U.S. 526 (1973).
Gideon v. Wainwright, 372 U.S. 335 (1963)
Gitlow v. New York, 268 U.S. 652 (1925).
Griggs v. Duke Power, 401 U.S. 424 (1971).
Grove City College v. Bell, 465 U.S. 555 (1984).
Guinn v. United States, 238 U.S. 347 (1915).
Harper v. Virginia Bd. of Elections, 383 U.S. 663 (1966).
Hurtado v. California, 110 U.S. 516 (1884).
Kirsey v. Board of Supervisors of Hinds County, Mississippi, 544 F. 2d
    139 (1977).
Miller v. Johnson, 132 L. Ed. 2d 762; S. Ct. 2475 (1995).
Milliken v. Bradley, 418 U.S. 717, 94 S. Ct. 3112 (1974).
Oregon v. Mitchell, 400 U.S. 112 (1970).
Plessy v. Ferguson, 163 U.S. 537 (1896).
Powell v. Alabama, 278 U.S. 45 (1932).
Shaw v. Reno, 125 L. Ed. 2d 511; 113 S. Ct. 2816 (1993).
Slaughterhouse Cases, 16 Wallace 36 (1873).
Smith v. Allwright, 321 U.S. 649 (1944).
Swann v. Charlotte-Mecklenburg County Board of Education, 402 U.S.
    1, 91 S. Ct. 1267 (1971).
Thornburg v. Gingles, 478 U.S. 30 (1986).
United States v. Cruikshank, 92 U.S. 542 (1876).
United Jewish Organizations v. Carey, 430 U.S. 144 (1977).
United States v. Reese, 92 U.S. 214 (1876).
Wards Cove Packing v. Atonio, 490 U.S. 642 (1989).
White v. Regester, 412 U.S. 755 (1973).

Index

References to figures and tables are indicated by italic page numbers.

Adams, John, 6
Alaskans, native, 170n. 1
Amendment vs. final stage voting, *31,
36, 37,* 40, *41,* 42, 43–45, 46–47,
66, 73–77, *74, 76, 105, 106,* 107,
108, 109. See also Civil rights leg-
islation voting
An American Dilemma (Myrdal), 1
Americans with Disabilities Act, 100
Asian Americans, 170n. 1
Atlanta, Ga., 60
At-large elections, 138

Balanced Budget Amendment, 101
*Behind the Mule: Race and Class in
African-American Politics* (Daw-
son), 83
Bernice-Johnson, Eddie, 170n. 9
Biracial campaign strategy, 142
Birmingham, Ala., 57
Bishop, Sanford, Jr., 117, 126, 142,
168n. 12, 170n. 9
Black, Merle, 12, 26–27, 38, 161n. 22
Black Codes, 50
*Black Faces, Black Interests: The Rep-
resentation of African Americans
in Congress* (Swain), 85–86
Black majority districts
consequences of, 131–33, 141–44
numbers of, 38, 117–18, 131
pros and cons of, 119–20, 121
Blacks
effects of at-large-elections, 138

migration to North, 53–54
policy preferences, 8–9
poverty level, 9
service in Congress, 86–87, *88–90*
status of voting rights, 137–39
strategies for election, 141–44
views of upper-class, 158n. 17
voter registration of, 22, 23–24
Black vs. *African-American* terms, 8
Boston, Mass., 60
Brady Bill, 101
Brooke, Edward W., 84–85
Brown, Corrine, 117, 142, 168n. 12,
170n. 9
Budget Resolution for the poor, 98
Bullock, Charles, 127, 171n. 26
Bush, George, 59, 75, 78
Bush v. Vera (1996), 112, 118–19
Butler, Caldwell, 33, 122
Butler, David, 120

Cain, Bruce, 120, 122
Carmines, Edward, 30
Carson, Julia, 142, 168n. 12
City of Mobile v. Bolden (1980), 25,
115–16
Civil rights, account of, through 1960,
50–56
Civil Rights Acts
1866, 50
1875, 2, 50–52
1957, 22, 136
1960, 22–23

Civil Rights Acts (*continued*)
　　1964, 23, 58, 60, 61, 63–65, 75, 77,
　　　136, 166n. 41
　　1968, 59, 61–62
　　1990, 100
　　1991, 59, 64, 66, *68, 69, 72*
Civil Rights Cases (1883), 51–52
Civil rights legislation voting
　　account of, 135–37
　　analysis of voting, 65–67, 69–70
　　impact of district racial change,
　　　127–31, *130*
　　discussion of voting on, 75–77
　　impact of issues, 97–98, *99,* 100–103
　　impact of party, 87, *105, 106, 108,
　　　109,* 110–11
　　impact of race, 87, 90, 97–98,
　　　100–102, 103–4, *105, 106,* 107,
　　　108, 109, 110, 111, 139–41
　　impact of redistricting, 120–27
　　impact of region, *105, 106, 108, 109*
　　impact of urbanization, *105, 106,
　　　108, 109*
　　race and nature of proposal, 97
　　role of party, 97
　　since 1964 act, 77–79
　　See also Amendment vs. final stage
　　　voting; Voting behavior; Voting
　　　rights legislation
Civil rights movement, 22, 56–60
Civil Rights Restoration Act, 1988, 78,
　　98
Clausen, Aage, 132
Clay, William L., 140
Clayton, Eva, 170n. 9
Clinton, Bill, 78
Clyburn, James E., 170n. 9
Commission on Civil Rights, 22, 58
Committee on Fair Employment Prac-
　　tices, 55
Compromise of 1877, 21
The Concept of Representation (Pitkin),
　　4–5
Congressional Black Caucus, 84, 139,
　　140
Congressional Redistricting: Compara-

tive and Theoretical Perspectives
　　(Cain), 120
Connor, Eugene "Bull," 57
Conyers, John, Jr., 140
Cracking, 114–15
Cumulative voting, 142–43

Dawson, Michael, 83
Dawson, William L., 84–85
Deal, Nathan, 124
Dellums, Ronald V., 140
Democrats, nonsouthern, 30, 39,
　　66–70, 73–74, 102
Democrats, southern, 32, 35, 39,
　　42, 43, 66–70, 73–74, 102, 124,
　　132
Denny's restaurant chain, 61
DePriest, Oscar, 54, 84–85
Desegregation, 55, 60
Desposato, Scott, 133
Diggs, Charles C., Jr., 84–85
District of Columbia statehood, 101
Dixiecrat Party, 55
Dred Scott decision, 1857, 19
DuBois, W. E. B., 3
Due process clause, 52

Elementary and Secondary Education
　　Reauthorization Act, 101
Enelow, James, 12
Enforcement Act, 1870, 19–20
Enforcement Act, 1871, 20
Equal Employment Opportunity Com-
　　mission (EEOC), 58, 59, 63–65
Equal opportunity, 58
　　education, 60–61
　　employment, 63–65
　　housing, 61–63
　　public accommodations, 61
Espy, Mike, 115
Eulau, Heinz, 5, 82
Evers, Medgar, 57

Fair Employment Practices Commis-
　　sion, 54
Fair Housing Act, 1968, 59

Fair Housing Act, 1988, 59, 66, *67, 68, 71,* 136
Fair Housing Bill, 98
Fair Housing legislation, 166n. 47
Family and Medical Leave Act, 100, 101
Fenno, Richard, 38, 84
Fields, Cleo, 170n. 9
Fifteenth Amendment, 2, 19, 20
Florida, 117
Foglietta, Thomas M., 116
Fourteenth Amendment, 2, 50–52
Franchise, struggle for, 18–22
Franks, Gary, 84–85, 100, 101, 142, 168n. 12

Gays in the Military Act, 101
Georgia, 117, 118
    district maps of, *125, 127*
    redistricting, 122–27, *123*
Gerrymandering. *See* Redistricting
Gilliam, Franklin D., Jr., 43, 87
Gingrich, Newt, 124
Goldwater, Barry, 24
Grandfather clause, 55
Griggs v. Duke Power (1971), 64
Grofman, Bernard, 119
Group consciousness, 82–85, 110
Guinier, Lani, 143
Guinn v. United States (1915), 21

Handley, Lisa, 119
Harper v. Virginia State Board of Elections (1966), 22
Hastings, Alcee L., 170n. 9
Hate Crime Statistics Act, 98, 100
Hawkins, Augustus, 77
Hayes, Rutherford B., 20
Hill, Kevin, 133
Hilliard, Earl F., 170n. 9
Hispanics, 170n. 1
Home Style (Fenno), 38, 84
Hughes, William J., 100
Hurtado v. California (1884), 52
Hyde, Henry J., 100

Indians, American, 170n. 1

Japanese-American Redress Act, 98
Jefferson, Thomas, 1
Jewell, Malcolm, 11
Jim Crow laws, 21
Johnson, Andrew, 135
Johnson, Lyndon B., 24, 57, 75
Joint Center for Political and Economic Studies, 171n. 26
Jordan, Barbara, 84–85

Karps, Paul, 5, 82
Kennedy, Edward, 76–77, 100
Kennedy, John F., 57, 136
Kersey v. Board of Supervisors of Hinds County, Mississippi (1977), 119–20
Key, V. O., Jr., 21, 69
King, Martin Luther, Jr., 24, 57
Kingdon, John, 12, 132
Koehler, David, 12
Kousser, J. Morgan, 47–48
Ku Klux Act, 1871, 20

Leadership Conference on Civil Rights (LCCR) scores, 11, 98, 100, 102, 122, 124, 162n. 27
Lewis, John R., 140
Literacy tests, 22, 26
Louisiana, 117
Lowenberg, Gerhard, 4
Lublin, David, 119

Majority-minority districts. *See* Black majority districts
Martin Luther King Jr. Holiday, 136
McKinney, Cynthia, 117, 124, 126, 142, 168n. 12, 170n. 9
Meek, Carrie, 170n. 9
Mfume, Kweisi, 140
Miller v. Johnson (1995), 112, 118, 126
Minimum Wage Increase Act, 100
Mississippi, 114–15
Mitchell, Arthur W., 84–85
Mobile, Alabama, 115
Mosely-Braun, Carol, 84–85

Mount Clemens, Mich., 62
Myrdal, Gunnar, 1

National Association for the Advancement of Colored People (NAACP), 53
National Motor Voter Registration Act, 101
National Voter Registration Bill (1993), 136
Nixon, Richard, 32
North Carolina, 116, 126

O'Connor, Sandra Day, 118
O'Rourke, Timothy, 119
Orren, Gary, 90

Packing, 115
Patterson, Samuel, 11
Pay Equity bill, 98
Petrocik, John, 133
Pitkin, Hanna, 4–5, 82
Plessy v. Ferguson, 52
Poll tax, 21, 26
Powell, Adam C., Jr., 84–85
Privileges and immunities clause, 51

Quiet Revolution in the South, 138

Randolph, A. Phillip, 54
Reagan, Ronald, 32, 75, 78
Reconstruction, 20
Redistricting, 131
    account of, 114–20
    the case of Georgia, 122–26
    consequences of, 131, 141–44
    impact on white majority districts, 121–22
    map of districts in Georgia, *125, 127*
Representation
    model for, 6–7
    race and quality of, 82–86
    substantive, 5–6, 81, 110–12
    types of, 4–5
    and view of constituency, 84–85

Republicans, nonsouthern, 30, 39, 66–70, 73–74, 102
Republicans, southern, 32, 39, 60–66, 73–74, 102, 172n. 29
Roll call votes
    amendment vs. final stage, 11–12
    LCCR index, 11
    usefulness of, 9–10
    See also Amendment vs. final stage voting
Roosevelt, Franklin D., 54

Savings and Loan Restructuring/Redlining, 100
Schneider, Jerrold, 12
Scott, Robert, C., 170n. 9
Segregation, 52–53
Shaw v. Reno (1995), 112, 118, 121
65 percent rule, 119–20, 144
Slaughterhouse Cases (1873), 51
Slavery, 19
Smith, Steven, 13
Smith v. Allwright (1944), 21
South Africa Sanctions, 136
South Carolina v. Katzenbach (1966), 25
Stevens, Jonn Paul, 118
Stimson, James, 30
Swain, Carol, 85–86, 90, 119, 142
Swann v. Charlotte-Mecklenburg County Board of Education, 165n. 27

Taney, Roger B., 19
Texaco, 63–64
Texas, 117, 118
Thernstrom, Abigail, 119, 138
Thirteenth Amendment, 2, 50
Thornburg v. Gingles (1986), 116, 131, 141
Three-fifths compromise, 18
Thurmond, Strom, 55
Towns, Edolphus, 101
Truman, Harry S., 55
Twenty-fourth Amendment, 21–22

United Jewish Organizations v. Carey (1977), 115
United States Supreme Court, 20
  erodes civil rights, 50–52
  opposition to black majority districts, 141
  and redistricting, 115, 116, 117–19
  rules on employment practices, 64–65
  supports segregation, 53
United States v. Cruikshank (1876), 20
United States v. Reese (1876), 20
Urbanization, 34, 35, 39

Verba, Sidney, 90
Vogler, David, 82
Voter Education Project (VEP), 23–24
Voting behavior, 166n. 47
  and district racial makeup, 26–27
  influence of black constituents, 43–45, 71, 75
  influence of party, *31,* 35, 71
  influence of region, 29, 35, 71, 75
  influence of urbanization, 73
  influences on, 70–73
  longitudinal analysis, *31,* 161n. 22
  method of analysis, 33–34, 91–93
  model for, 13–15
  and race, *94, 95,* 96–97
  variations in, 42
Voting district constituencies, 38
Voting patterns, 12–13
Voting Rights Act, 1965, 2, 18, 22
  and black congressional representation, 84–85

explanation of, 24–26
  impact of, 46, 136, 137, 141
  and redistricting, 114, 115, 116
  renewal of, 38, 39
Voting Rights Act, 1970, 22
Voting rights complaints, 25, 32–33
Voting Rights Language Assistance Act, 101
Voting rights legislation
  analysis of voting, 28–29, *30, 31, 32–33, 36, 37*
  attempts to dilute, 47
  Democratic support, 29, 33
  influence of party, 46
  influence of race, 33–35, 38–39, 46
  influences on votes, *45*
  Republican support, 29
  See also Amendment vs. final stage voting; Civil rights legislation voting

Wards Cove Packing Co. v. Atonio (1989), 64
Watts, J. C., 84–85, 117, 140, 142, 168n. 12
Watts, Melvin, 170n. 9
Wheat, Alan, 168n. 12
Whitby, Kenny, 43, 87
White majority districts, 121–22, *122*
White primary, 21, 55
Woodward, C. Vann, 21
Wynn, Albert R., 170n. 9

Young, Andrew, 84–85